THE SCOT... wEDDING PLANNER

A Complete Guide to Getting Married in Scotland including Legal Requirements and a Directory of Venues

Nicola Taylor

Unbound Press Ltd
The Scottish Wedding Planner
An Unbound Press Book: ISBN 978-0-9558360-2-2

Originally published in Great Britain
by Unbound Press Ltd 2009

Unbound Press Books are published by
Unbound Press Ltd,
Apartment 3/1, 54 Hughenden Lane, Glasgow, G12 9XJ
www.unboundpress.com

CONTENTS

ABOUT THE AUTHOR

Nicola Taylor has worked with Highland Country Weddings and its fore-runner since 1998. Over that period she has attended many weddings throughout the Highlands and the central belt in various capacities, including agency representative, witness and 'photographer's moll'.

ACKNOWLEDGEMENTS

The author would like to thank all those people who helped in the writing of this book by the provision of information, advice or encouragement. I am especially indebted to Janis Maclean and Natasha Honan, whose advice based on their vast experience of organising and attending weddings throughout Scotland has been invaluable. Thanks to them also for putting me in touch with Peter Mok and Graham Smith, Kerry and Steve Pantony, and Joanne and Craig Dickson. They, as well as Julie and Graham White, Emma and Mark Goodjohn, Ellie and David Thomson and Fiona & Graham McGirr kindly shared their wedding stories. I wish them all the best for their married lives!

In addition my gratitude is due to the numerous personnel at venues and public bodies who responded to my queries with alacrity and good humour.

And finally, a big thank you to all those couples whose weddings I have attended over the years, every one of them an occasion to remember. Without that personal experience of so many and varied weddings this book would not have been nearly so easy, nor so much fun, to write!

Telephone Numbers
International Telephone Codes. Throughout this book, UK telephone codes have been used. For those calling UK numbers from abroad, the international code is 0044 (or +44) and the initial 0 is dropped. So 0131-222 5555 is 0044 131-222 5555 when calling from outside the UK.

INTRODUCTION

I dreamed of a wedding of elaborate elegance; a church filled with flowers and friends. I asked him what kind of wedding he wished for; he said one that would make me his wife. (Anonymous)

Whatever type of wedding you dream of, the large or the small, the elaborate or the simple, the traditional or the unconventional, it should be an extraordinary occasion; one which you will both remember forever. Scotland is an extraordinary country, undoubtedly one of the most beautiful in the world. Its untamed landscape has an elemental, uplifting quality which gives a fitting backdrop to the deeply serious, profoundly happy emotions of a wedding. In addition, it has some of the most fabulous venues in the world. From castles to ancient chapels to grandly elegant country hotels, the choice is unsurpassed.

On top of all that, the marriage laws in Scotland make it possible for residents of anywhere in the world to marry there and to choose whether they want a religious, non-religious or civil ceremony. Furthermore, the recent Civil Partnership legislation has allowed same-sex couples for the first time to make a public, and legally-approved, commitment to each other. With different regulations from elsewhere in the United Kingdom, and most importantly no residential requirement, it is easy to combine your wedding with a holiday in one of the world's most romantic countries.

Whether you and your partner are Scottish born and bred, or whether you are travelling across the world to marry in this most beautiful of countries, this book explains everything you need to know to help you arrange your wedding in Scotland and has tips and advice from other couples who tied the knot there.

As Wilfred Arlan Peterson wrote: *Happiness in marriage is not something that just happens. A good marriage must be created.*

Marrying in Scotland can't fail to be a perfect first step towards creating that happy marriage!

Regions & Major Towns

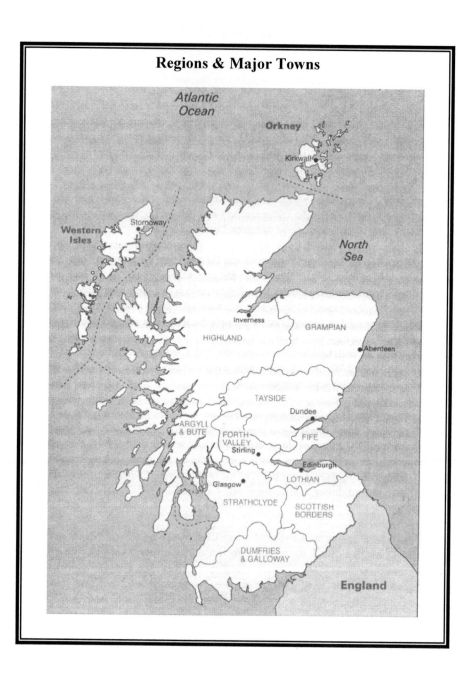

A MARRIAGE MADE IN HEAVEN

Why Scotland?

Looking for a stunning venue for your wedding? One which combines romance, beautiful scenery and splendid historic surroundings? Well, Scotland is probably the most romantic country in the world. Unique venues, including fairytale castles and imposing estate houses; a breathtaking and beautiful landscape, with misty glens, tranquil lochs, uplifting mountains; a sense of permanence and spectacle with its stirring music, history and tradition: Scotland has it all.

Add to this the ease of getting married in Scotland, whatever your nationality, it is hardly surprising that although in recent years there has been an overall drop in the numbers of weddings taking place in Scotland, there has been a significant increase in the numbers of weddings where either one or both partners were not resident in Scotland. In fact, Scotland is fast becoming one of the most popular worldwide venues for weddings.

Locality

Traditionally, it was expected that a couple would get married in the local church or registry office of the bride or the groom – more often than not, the bride, as conventionally it is her 'special day' more than his. However, it is becoming increasingly popular for couples to plight their troth in a place chosen for other reasons than locality. To make their wedding day truly special, they want to marry and stay in a unique and beautiful location. This may not even be in their home country.

Although many couples still want a traditional wedding, with their whole extended family and friends around them to witness their vows, contemporary weddings are tending to become smaller. This is partly because of the general trend towards smaller families and partly, with the far greater mobility of people today, because families are very often widely spread, relatives living a long distance from each other, often in different countries.

Where once a local venue was generally most convenient, because families tended to live reasonably close, now this is far less likely to be the case. Getting married in a different country may involve the guests in no extra travel than if they were to travel to the bride's or groom's home town.

Frequently, couples wish to make the ceremony itself a very intimate and personal affair, with only themselves involved, or perhaps with just their closest friends or relatives with them. By having their wedding in a different country, this makes it easier to explain to the wider family and friends why they are not invited to the ceremony – the cost, time and logistics would make it impractical to invite everybody.

If your budget is limited, of course, it makes sense to restrict it to just you and maybe a couple of guests. This way, you can spend what money you can spare on paying for just what you want, rather than having to spread the money too thinly and end up with a wedding which is unsatisfactory for both you and your guests.

If you prefer to have an intimate ceremony with just the two of you, yet don't want to upset your friends and family, there is always the option to throw a big party on your return home, and invite everybody and his dog!

Where money is not an issue, you may decide to marry abroad and still invite a large number of guests. The falling cost and increasing ease and speed of travel mean that this is more achievable than it ever was. You can combine the most important day of your life with an unforgettable holiday for your friends and family.

Once you have decided you wish to marry away from your home town, or even country, the next question is, where to go? Scotland is a favourite destination for weddings for a number of different reasons.

Romance

In the first place, romance is high on the agenda. What couple doesn't want their wedding to be as romantic as possible?

Scotland has been synonymous with romantic marriage for hundreds of years, thanks to Gretna Green. Once the law in England was changed in 1754, preventing anybody under the age of 21 marrying without parental consent, there began a flood of eloping couples heading for Scotland, where they could marry from the age of 16 without the need for their parents to agree. As Gretna Green was the first village over the border from England, it soon became the place for eloping couples to make for, with local blacksmiths ready and willing to marry them 'over the anvil' in exchange for money. There are many tales of couples making a dash for Gretna with angry fathers in hot pursuit!

Since the first recorded marriage at Gretna in 1772, its popularity continues today, and there are now over 4,000 weddings a year at Gretna Green, about 17% of the total marriages in Scotland.

But there's much more to the romance of Scotland than eloping couples. The history of the country is full of colourful, sometimes tragic, heroes and heroines, from Bonnie Prince Charlie to Rob Roy, Robert the Bruce to William Wallace(Braveheart), Mary Queen of Scots to Flora MacDonald. The works of Scotland's most famous writers, Sir Walter Scott and Robert Burns, are full of stories and poems of romantic love and daring deeds.

And then there's the most romantic aspect of all, the country itself. As you travel through the country, it seems that around every corner is another breathtaking scene. Dramatic mountains surrounded by heather-clad glens, all reflected in the mirror-clear water of isolated lochs; an unspoiled landscape full of wildlife including stags and hosts of birds; lonely seashores, with islands appearing from the mists in the distance; tranquil meadows lining the banks of rushing salmon rivers.

And finally, if you needed more, sitting amongst the gorgeous landscape, highlighting it like jewels in a stunning setting, are literally thousands of castles, stately homes and picturesque ruins, any one of which would make an unforgettable wedding venue. Just think of those gorgeous wedding photographs to show to the folks back home!

History, Myth & Legend

If you want historic surroundings for your wedding, you can't do much better than Scotland. It has been inhabited for around 8,000 years, with evidence of ancient lives still to be seen in the form of dwellings, cairns and burial mounds throughout the country. Among the most striking of these archaeological remains are the stone circles to be found at Callanish in Lewis and Brodgar in Orkney. Imagine getting married beside these standing stones as the sun sets in high summer...

Over many centuries Scotland has attracted settlers from all over Europe. First came the Picts from Ireland, followed by the Romans, and later, the Vikings from Scandinavia – not forgetting the regular cross-border attempts by the English to subjugate the fiercely independent Scots.

These settlers laid claim to different areas of the country, which has given different regions their distinctive characters. In fact, it wasn't until the 15th Century that Scotland as we know it today came into being. The modern name for the country derives from the Scoti, a Celtic tribe originally from Ireland. Prior to the adoption of the name 'Scotland' the land was divided into many smaller kingdoms. The Highlands was called Caledonia by the Romans, a name which continues in used to the present day, particularly poetically.

The universal love of a good story has led to much of Scotland's war-filled, harsh and violent history becoming inextricably linked with a more romantic version of its past. For example, the picture that we have of the dashing and dramatic Rob Roy, alleged hero of the 1715 Jacobite uprising, owes far more to the romantic versions of his life painted by Daniel Defoe in his 1723 fictionalised biography, *Highland Rogue,* followed by *Rob Roy* by Sir Walter Scott and the 1995 Hollywood film. These depictions romanticise and glorify the deeds of a man who was in fact little more than a cattle rustler, thief and bandit.

CALEDONIA!

There are many songs and poems which celebrate Scotland under its more romantic name. Sir Walter Scott, in *The Lay of the Last Minstrel,* wrote:

O Caledonia! stern and wild,
Meet nurse for a poetic child!
Land of brown heath and shaggy wood,
Land of the mountains and the flood,
Land of my sires! What mortal hand
Can e'er untie the filial band,
That knits me to they rugged strand!

Scott's friend, James Hogg, known as the Ettrick shepherd, wrote a poem entitled *Caledonia.*

Caledonia! thou land of the mountain and rock,
Of the ocean, the mist, and the wind-
Thou land of the torrent, the pine, and the oak,
Of the roebuck, the hart, and the hind;

Far more recently, in the 1980s, Dougie Maclean wrote his own take on the theme, in a haunting song which has become something of a Scottish anthem.

Oh, but let me tell you that I love you
That I think about you all the time
Caledonia you're calling me
And now I'm going home
If I should become a stranger
You know that it would make me more than sad
Caledonia's been everything
I've ever had.

A supreme example of the way fiction has overtaken fact is the delicious story of how the statue of William Wallace erected outside the visitor centre at the Wallace Memorial in Stirling has been beheaded on a number of occasions by people upset that the statue looks far too much like Mel Gibson in his portrayal of Braveheart!

Perhaps the best-known 'fact' about Scotland is that there is a monster living in Loch Ness. This myth has a most illustrious history, with the first documented sighting of the beast being by no less a personage than St Columba himself, the man responsible for bringing Christianity to Scottish shores.

Nessie isn't the only mythical being alive and well in Scotland. Tales and legends of ghosts and kelpies, fairies and giants are common.

CHARLIE & FLORA

The meeting of Bonnie Prince Charlie and Flora Macdonald is one of the great romantic tales of Scotland. After the Young Pretender's devastating defeat at Culloden in 1746, he went on the run to escape the English government troops who were after his blood, and lived as a fugitive for five months.

Flora Macdonald met him on the island of Uist when she was 23 and she helped him escape to Skye, disguised as a serving maid. After his escape from there back to Europe, Flora Macdonald was arrested and imprisoned for a year before being pardoned.

She went on to marry and have seven children, while the prince ended his days in exile, a disillusioned drunkard, no longer 'Bonnie' or even regal. As a final romantic flourish to the tale, it is said that Flora's funeral shroud was made from the sheet on which Bonnie Prince Charlie slept while on Skye.

The incident is commemorated in *the Skye Boat Song*, which was actually written well over 100 years later. The massive death and suffering caused by the terrible battle at Culloden is evident in the words.

Speed bonnie boat like a bird on the wing
Onward the sailors cry
Carry the lad that's born to be king
Over the sea to Skye
Loud the wind howls, loud the waves roar,
Thunderclaps rend the air
Baffled our foes, stand by the shore
Follow they will not dare

Many's the lad fought on that day
Well the claymore did wield
When the night came, silently lain
Dead on Culloden field
(Chorus)

Though the waves heave, soft will ye sleep
Ocean's a royal bed
Rocked in the deep, Flora will keep
Watch by your weary head
(Chorus)

Burned are our homes, exile and death
Scatter the loyal men
Yet e'er the sword cool in the sheath
Charlie will come again.
(Chorus)

Wherever you look, Scotland's history, myth and legend intermingle – and when you see the hundreds of castles, gothic-style stately homes and historic monuments, the moody and mysterious lochs and glens, read the poems and stories and see the artwork produced by artists over the centuries, it is small wonder that fact and fiction mingle in such an inspiring fashion.

SCOTLAND'S MOST HAUNTED

Glamis Castle in Angus, childhood home of the late Queen Mother, is claimed to be the most haunted building in Scotland, with an impressive total of at least nine ghosts and one monster. This was reputed to be a hideous and sub-human child born into the Strathmore family some 200 years ago which lived to an immense age, dying in the 1920s.

Ancestry

Throughout history, the Scots have been renowned for travelling the world, both by choice, in search of adventure or a better life, and sadly through coercion, notoriously during the Highland Clearances of the late 18th and early 19th centuries. Many of those with Scots blood love to come back and trace, or at least visit, their roots. A wedding is a great time for reflecting on family history, so it is not surprising that many brides or grooms with Scottish ancestry decide to marry in Scotland, often in the area where their original clan hailed from. They may even find long-lost relatives living in the area.

And while on the subject of clans, a marriage in Scotland gives even grooms without Scottish roots the excuse to wear Highland Dress, which has to be the most dashing form of wedding suit in the world – a kilt outfit including sporran and skean dhu! While it is traditional for the bride to wear a stunning fairytale gown, all too often the poor groom is condemned to a boring grey suit. Not so in Scotland – here both bride and groom dress to impress!

Here's to it!
The fighting sheen of it,
The yellow, the green of it,
The white, the blue of it,
The swing, the hue of it,
The dark, the red of it,
Every thread of it!

The fair have sighed for it,
The brave have died for it,
Foemen sought for it,
Heroes fought for it,
Honour the name of it,
Drink to the fame of it –
THE TARTAN!
Murdoch Maclean

GETTING BACK TO YOUR ROOTS

The place where the Clan Chief lives is known as the Clan Seat, normally a castle. As a member of the clan you may be able to marry there. The various Clan society websites, of which there are branches worldwide, will tell you where the historical seat of your clan is.

Clan Societies

Rampant Scotland's excellent website has an exhaustive index of clans with links to clan society websites, family histories, tartans and much more. www.rampantscotland.com/clans.htm

Ancestral Weddings

This is just a very small selection of the clan seats where you could arrange your wedding.

- Clan Brodie: Brodie Castle, Forres
  www.scotland-inverness.co.uk/Chatelaine/BRODIE.HTM
- Clan Chisholm: Erchless Castle, Beauly
  www.georgegoldsmith.com/houses/detail.html?id=234
- Clan Cumming: Inverlochy Castle, foothills of Ben Nevis
  www.inverlochycastlehotel.com
- Clan Macleod: Dunvegan Castle, Skye
  www.scotland-inverness.co.uk/Chatelaine/DUNVEGAN.HTM

Genealogy

If you want to find about more about how to research your Scottish family history, these two websites are invaluable:

Scotland's People: The official government source of genealogy data for Scotland. www.scotlandspeople.gov.uk

Scottish Genealogy Society: www.scotsgenealogy.com

Food, Drink & Music

Once the ceremony is over, the celebrations begin – and the Scots just love a good party!

If you want a stunning wedding breakfast, you'll be spoiled for choice. Scotland is renowned for its superb quality luxury foods, including game: wild venison, grouse, pheasant and partridge; meat: superb Aberdeen Angus beef and Scotch Lamb; fish and seafood: wild salmon, lobsters and prawns; many varieties of soft fruits which thrive on Scotland's southern farmlands: including strawberries, raspberries, gooseberries, blackcurrants, redcurrants and brambles (blackberries).

And of course you can always go for the more unusual Scottish delicacies – haggis, Arbroath smokies, black and white puddings, with crannachan (made with raspberries, oatmeal, cream and, of course, whisky) to follow.

To wash it all down in real Scottish style, alongside the essential wines and champagne, go for Scottish ales, whisky, Drambuie or even Atholl Brose.

WELL WELL WELL...

The unusual liqueur Atholl Brose has a suitably romantic tale to explain its origins. It is claimed to date from 1475 when, under sentence of death for raising a rebellion against the king, Iain MacDonald, the last Lord of the Isles, fled to the hills. Discovering where MacDonald was drawing water, the Earl of Atholl ordered that the well be filled with a mixture of whisky, honey, herbs and oatmeal. MacDonald was tempted to sample the delightful mixture, and the fugitive was captured.

Recipe for Atholl Brose

4 bottles whisky
1 bottle cream
1 lb oatmeal
1 lb honey
1 tablespoonful brandy

- Pour the whisky over the oatmeal and leave it in a cool place, covered with a cloth, for 72 hours.
- Strain off the whisky through a cloth into the container from which it will be finally served. The oatmeal now becomes a by-product and can be used to make porridge the following day.
- Place the cream in a separate jug and add the tablespoonful of brandy. (This prevents the cream from curdling when it hits the whisky). Pour the cream very slowly into the whisky, stirring continuously with a wooden spoon.
- Add the slightly warmed honey, pouring very slowly and stirring continuously.

Good Atholl Brose requires:
Long soaking
Slow and careful mixing
Plenty of tasting!

To save all that trouble, it is possible to buy it ready-made! For details see www.gordonandmacphail.com/op_brandsDunkeld.html

If you and your guests can still move after all that, you can either have a standard musical group playing whatever music you want, or a genuine Scottish ceilidh, with Scottish country dancing to traditional instruments including fiddles, bagpipes, tin whistles, accordions and the haunting sound of the clarsach (Celtic harp.)

A CEILIDH

The Gaelic word ceilidh (pronounced *kay-lee*) originally meant 'social visit'. As these visits often developed into a party where story-telling and singing took place, the word came to mean any organised gathering where music, and later Scottish country dancing, took place.

In towns and villages across Scotland, the ceilidh is a regular feature of the social gathering, and traditional wedding ceremonies are always followed by a ceilidh, where much drinking as well as music and dancing take place.

Although the dances require a knowledge of the steps, this does not mean that novices cannot join in. Prior to each dance, the dancers will be taken through the steps, which are generally fairly simple. And don't worry about going wrong during the dance – the more experienced dancers will put you right – no great finesse is required, all that is asked is that you join in whole-heartedly and enjoy yourself!

There are ceilidh bands available to hire for your wedding throughout Scotland. Contact details for many of them can be found in *Organise It Yourself.*

Legalities

For practical reasons too, Scotland is an ideal place for your wedding. It is a fairly simple and easy process. There is no residential requirement for bride or groom prior to the wedding date, you can choose from a religious, non-religious or civil ceremony, and the marriage is valid and legal in every country.

This means that, whether you or your partner are from the UK, the USA, or beyond, even if each of you is a national of a different country, there are few formalities required other than the production of various personal documents and the completion of a small number of official forms. This legal paperwork must be submitted to the Registrar in the area where the wedding will take place between three months and 15 days prior to your wedding. If everything is in order, you can then go ahead and enjoy your marriage made in heaven – in the most heavenly country in the world!

For detailed advice on the legal requirements for your wedding in Scotland, see *Marriage Legislation.*

Type of ceremony

- Religious: In Scotland, priests and ministers of religion, are licensed to perform wedding ceremonies anywhere, indoors or outdoors. So you can have a religious wedding ceremony in churches and chapels, in your own home, in the largest castle or the smallest ruin, at the top of a mountain or by the side of a loch. As long as the minister and the land or building owner agrees, the choice is practically limitless.
- Non-religious: Celebrants of certain non-religious and non-denominational spiritual organisations are also authorised to marry couples in a similarly wide range of places. For example, the Findhorn Foundation in Moray, a spiritual community, has licensed celebrants who will perform a non-religious marriage ceremony in your chosen location. In 2005, humanist weddings

were legalised in the UK and the Humanist Society now has licensed celebrants throughout Scotland.

- Civil: Civil ceremonies may only be performed by a registrar authorised by the Registrar General, and before 2002 these could only be performed in official register offices. Now, however, civil ceremonies may be carried out by registrars in certain places which have been approved and licensed by local authorities. The number of approved premises is growing by the day, so there is now a very wide range of locations if you prefer a civil ceremony outside a registry office.

HUMANISM AT THE ZOO

Scotland's first humanist wedding, between Karen Watts from Ireland, and Martin Reijns from the Netherlands, took place in June 2005 at Edinburgh Zoo. Prior to this, couples choosing a humanist wedding ceremony had to have a civil ceremony beforehand to legalise the marriage. After claims that this was discriminatory, the rules were relaxed to allow humanist celebrants to carry out legal ceremonies in their own right.

Humanists believe that people can live ethical lives without religious beliefs. The bride said, 'Neither of us are religious and it would have felt hypocritical to get married in a church. But at the same time we wanted something more meaningful than the legal civil ceremony.'

At the time of writing, humanist weddings are not legal in England and Wales. The Humanist Society is pushing for the same change to take place as in Scotland, but because the marriages laws are different from those in Scotland, new legislation will be needed to bring this about, so it will be neither quick nor easy to do.

Civil Partnership

21st December 2005 was a highly significant date in the UK, as far as making a commitment to the one you love is concerned. This was the first date on which same-sex couples could seal their mutual love and long-term commitment in a legal ceremony, which aside from allowing them to make a public statement about their relationship, also affords them similar legal rights to heterosexual married couples in relation to social security benefits, inheritance rights and the like. Now gay couples can enjoy similar rights, if they go through a civil partnership ceremony.

Despite the headlines and articles which appeared in the media at the time, proclaiming 'Gay Marriages' were now legal, a civil partnership is not a marriage, even though similar benefits accrue from both.

Peter Mok & Graham Smith were delighted with their registrar in Dornoch, Sutherland
We rose early on the day of the ceremony to meet with the Registrar, Angie, to go through the details. She was extremely efficient, fun and obviously as happy as we were about our civil partnership.

Although Civil Partnerships should normally be performed at any approved venue, a high profile row broke out in December 2005, when it emerged that registrars in the Western Isles (in the Comhairle nan Eilean Siar council area) were refusing to take part in civil partnership ceremonies on the islands, on moral grounds. They would register civil partnerships, as the law obliged them to, but would not provide a ceremony outwith registrars' offices. This fully complied with the letter of the new legislation, but it was certainly not in the sprit of the law.

The Western Isles were the only council area to take this stance, although in August 2005 Highland, Shetland and Dundee City Councils were all of a mind to perform only a basic registration, the absolute minimum which was required by the legislation when it came into force. However, in the face of an outcry from gay rights campaigners and others, they all backed down.

The advice from the General Register Office in Scotland is that no individual registrar should be made to perform a ceremony if their personal beliefs prevent them from doing so. It is wise, therefore, to check with the registrar before deciding on your venue for a civil partnership.

SCOTLAND'S FIRST GAY 'WEDDINGS'

The first civil partnership on mainland Britain took place on 20th December 2005 (one day early, due to a bureaucratic slip-up) at Edinburgh's India Buildings register office, followed by a wedding breakfast at Edinburgh Castle and a blessing at St Margaret's Chapel within the grounds of the castle.

The happy couple, John Maguire and Laurence Scott-Mackay travelled from their home in Washington DC for the ceremony.

Over 140 same-sex couples had booked their 'weddings' in Scotland by the time civil partnerships became legal on 21st December 2005. Edinburgh was the most popular destination for these couples, followed by Glasgow and Fife.

Renewal of Vows

The romance of Scotland's castles, mountains and glens is not the sole preserve of the new bride and groom. Couples who are already married – for one year or fifty! – can publicly reaffirm their love and commitment for each other in a vow renewal ceremony. Renewal of your wedding vows has no legal obligation attached to it. It does not involve registering the marriage again with the state, nor is there a specific form of ceremony that you must follow.

You can design your own form of ceremony and speak your own words, jointly and together, in front of witnesses and guests. The ceremony you choose can be religious in tone, and performed by a minister, or it can have no reference to any religion and be performed by a non-religious celebrant or official representative of the Humanist Society.

Commitment Ceremony

There are some couples for wom the traditional wedding service, civil or religious, is simply not appropriate and yet you have just as strong and loving a commitment to each other as any man and wife. It is possible to celebrate your commitment to each other, publicly and without legal complication, at a venue of your choice in any part of Scotland – an unforgettable way to say 'I am yours, forever.'

A commitment ceremony can be:

- Religious in tone and performed by a minister.
- Performed by a non-religious celebrant or official representative of the Humanist Society.
- You can design your own form of ceremony and speak your own words, jointly and together, in front of witnesses and guests or without anybody else present.

Blessing

This is an additional ceremony which takes place after the official marriage ritual. Usually it take place very soon after the wedding ceremony, often on the same day. It may be religious or secular in nature and may be performed by a minister or a non-religious celebrant.

A couple may choose to have a blessing for a variety of reasons:

- Interdenominational or inter-faith couples may choose to be married in one religious tradition and have a blessing in the other.
- Catholics are not allowed to re-marry in church, so divorcees often opt for a blessing after a civil marriage.
- They may have a small wedding ceremony and then have a larger celebration at which all their family and friends attend and a blessing is performed.

Choice of Words

Whatever sort of ceremony you choose to have, there is a degree of choice in the form of words used. The minister, celebrant or registrar should always discuss this with you in advance so you have a ceremony which you are happy with. Even where you choose a traditional religious ceremony, or are restricted by the legal requirements of a civil ceremony, you can usually introduce certain elements – poems or songs, for example – which make your ceremony totally unique to you and your partner.

You can write your own words for commitment and renewal of vows ceremonies, because they have no legal standing. However, if you are not confident about writing your own words, don't worry – your celebrant will help you and make suggestions, and there are also books and websites which can help. You may even like to hire a wedding planner to help you with all the arrangements including the form of the ceremony. There is further guidance and advice below in *Typical Ceremonies*.

A ROMANTIC BLESSING

Tanya & Mark Sears chose to marry at home in the United States, then travelled to Scotland for their honeymoon, during which they had a religious blessing at Urquhart Castle beside Loch Ness.

Choice of Venues

There are thousands of places in Scotland where you can marry, indoors and outdoors. As explained above, if you choose a civil ceremony over a religious ceremony, you are more restricted in the venues where you can legally marry. However, since the rules were changed in 2002, the number of venues approved and licensed for civil weddings is growing all the time. At the time of writing in 2008, around 750 venues had been licensed. Alongside the many hotels, there are more unusual places where you can have your civil ceremony including castles, sports stadia, golf clubs, tourist attractions, museums – even an old jail and a boat!

A full listing of 'Approved Places for Civil Marriage', by place or council area, can be found on the General Register Office for Scotland website: www.gro-scotland.gov.uk/regscot/getting-married-in-scotland/civil-marriages-in-approved-places.html

For an extensive listing of the best venues in Scotland for religious and civil weddings, including the most romantic, the most luxurious, the most unusual and the small but perfectly formed, see *Directory of Wedding Venues.*

Large or Small?

There is no requirement for wedding couples to have any guests at their wedding if they choose not to. Although two witnesses are required, these can be any adults, and it is not uncommon for staff at your chosen venue to act as your witnesses. If you employ a wedding planner to make arrangements for you, they should ensure there are two witnesses available on the day. So if you want the simplest and quietest of 'get away from it all' marriages, with just you and your partner and no guests at all, this is no problem.

If you want to invite all your family and friends and have all the trimmings, including pipers and horse drawn carriages or luxury limos, a multi-tier wedding cake and oceans of flowers, that too can be arranged. There are many venues to choose from which can cater for large weddings, and where they cannot accommodate all your guests, there will always be places nearby where they can stay.

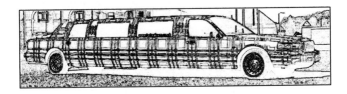

CELEBRITY WEDDINGS

Getting married in Scotland has become a very fashionable thing to do, after a rash of celebrity weddings in exclusive venues. Every time these weddings hit the headlines, they are inevitably accompanied in the newspapers and on TV with ravishing shots of magnificent Scottish castles and stunning scenery. This, together with the almost *de riguer* pipers – and often the bridegroom and guests – in full Highland dress, not to mention the beautiful bride photographed against even more beautiful backdrops, ensures that many other couples choose to marry in such surroundings.

Madonna is undoubtedly the most famous celebrity bride of recent years. Her marriage to film director Guy Ritchie, at Skibo Castle in the Highlands, in December 2000, resulted in a boom in Scottish weddings with couples travelling from around the world to tie the knot in the Highlands and elsewhere. When asked why she chose to marry in the Highlands, Madonna said, 'Scotland is dripping in atmosphere. It is so beautiful…And my husband and I are both obsessed with history, and we wanted to go to a place that had history.'

Skibo Castle is a favourite venue for high profile couples, because the management and staff ensure that absolute privacy is observed for the couple and their often equally famous guests. Scottish film star Robert Carlyle chose Skibo Castle for his 1997 wedding to Anastasia Shirley.

Actress Ashley Judd followed in their footsteps when she married her racing car driver husband, Dario Franchitti, at Skibo a year after Madonna.

Dress designer Stella McCartney, daughter of Beatle Paul and also designer of Madonna's wedding dress, chose Scotland for her 2003 wedding to publisher Alasdhair Willis. The ceremony took place at Mount Stuart on the island of Bute amid strict security as coachloads of celebrity guests arrived.

Facts & Figures

For many years marriage rates have been declining throughout the UK: in the early 1970s there were over 40,000 weddings per year, but the annual total has declined over the intervening decades to around 30,000 per year. Thanks to the growing trend in 'tourist' weddings, the numbers are on the increase in Scotland. In 2004 there were more weddings than in any year since 1994. The increase was mainly accounted for by weddings where neither bride nor groom was a Scottish resident. But there has also been a slight increase in the number of Scottish couples marrying, which may be partly accounted for by the 2002 change in the law, which allowed civil marriages in other venues than registry offices.

In 2007, there were over 30,000 marriage and civil partnership ceremonies in Scotland. In over a quarter of these, neither of the partners was a Scots resident.

Gretna Green is the single most popular place for so-called 'tourist' weddings, and there has been a rapid growth in their numbers over the last 25 years, from fewer than 100 a year in the 1970s to around 4000 in 2007. Although the original reason for Gretna becoming popular for weddings in the 18th and 19th centuries was so that people under the age of consent (in England) could be married, this pattern has changed. Today, very few Gretna weddings involve someone aged under 21, even fewer under the age of 18. The average age of brides and grooms is, in fact, higher than the Scottish average age, at 33 and 36 respectively.

The most popular months for weddings in Scotland, not surprisingly, are June to September, with numbers trailing off in the winter months. However, it is interesting that February 14th is the most popular date for weddings at Gretna, although it is not especially popular elsewhere in Scotland.

The popularity of civil weddings compared with religious ceremonies has risen steadily since the 1970s. In 2007 over half of the weddings in Scotland were civil ceremonies, compared with around one third in 1971. The law change in 2002 gave a boost to the popularity of civil weddings, once couples could choose to have a civil ceremony in a venue of their choice rather than in a register office. During 2007 there were nearly 8,000 civil ceremonies in approved venues, compared with 2003 when there were less than 3,500. There has been a corresponding decrease in the numbers of religious marriages since 2002.

If we bring gay weddings into the picture, it is inevitable that there will be a continuing increase in tourist weddings. In 2007 there were 688 Civil Partnerships in Scotland, 339 male and 349 female couples.

The General Register Office for Scotland (GROS) produces an annual report with a detailed breakdown of these figures. The report can be read in full on their website http://www.gro-scotland.gov.uk

How Much Will It Cost?

As the figures above indicate, Scotland is growing in popularity as a place to get married. Over the past few years, as venues from hotels to castles to stately homes to national monuments have realised that so many people from around the world love the thought of marrying in Scotland, there has been a great increase in the number of places for couples to choose from.

Many venues have their own wedding planners, who will help you arrange your special day. However, although that may be all the assistance you need if the ceremony, reception and accommodation are all in the same venue, you may wish to marry in one location, have your reception elsewhere, and find accommodation for yourselves and your guests in one or more other places. In such a case, you will either need to arrange all these things yourself or call in a professional wedding planner, who will make sure you have everything you desire to make your day perfect, from the wedding cake, flowers, music and transport down to the wacky extras you might want to make your wedding day truly unique – a hundred white doves or a fly-past by the Red Arrows, maybe!

Of course, all this costs money. One of the first things you need to decide, before you even begin to draw up the guest list, is what your budget will be. A recent survey came up with the disquieting news that couples seriously underestimate the cost of getting married. Of the couples surveyed, on average they thought their wedding would cost them about £6,500, whereas it is estimated the average cost of a UK wedding is around £15,000 - £17,000.

The boom in weddings in Scotland in recent years has both advantages and disadvantages for couples. The disadvantage is that now that venues and service providers have recognised the potential income they can make, some are getting greedy and pushing prices up. On the plus side, there is far more competition for your money and if you shop around you may be able to get a good deal. You should always aim to get three or more quotes for the services you require. And tell the service providers you're doing this – it might encourage them to give you a better rate to beat the competition!

This applies whether you wish to hire a wedding planner to arrange everything for you, or if you wish to organise it and hire all the individual service providers yourself. If you choose to use a wedding planner, you should compare what is being offered by different companies as well as the price they charge.

Of course, to look at bald figures and go for the cheapest may be a false economy. It is very important to investigate what is and isn't included in the price, whether you are hiring a wedding planner, a castle or a kilt.

Getting to Scotland

By Air
The main airports are situated at Edinburgh, Glasgow, Glasgow (Prestwick), Aberdeen and Inverness. There are also small airports at Barra, Benbecula, Campbeltown, Islay, Kirkwall, Stornoway, Sumbrugh, Tiree and Wick. There are frequent flights between the mainland and the islands, and regular inter-island services.

British Airways fly to the longest list of destinations, but you will pay higher prices. It is worth checking out the low-cost airlines such as Ryanair and easyJet. Many routes will involve travel via London, with onward flights to Scotland.

By Rail
It is possible to reach the UK by train via the Channel Tunnel, either as a foot passenger or with your vehicle.

All the major Scottish cities can be reached by train from the south, but connections to smaller areas are not always available, or where they are may not be very frequent. In the north west Highlands there are no train services. As bus services are also limited in this area, a car is pretty much essential.

Trains between Glasgow, Edinburgh, Aberdeen and Inverness and London run from either Kings Cross or Euston. Depending on the route, Scottish rail services are run by First ScotRail, Great North Eastern Railway and Virgin Trains.

First ScotRail run the Caledonian Sleeper service between London Euston and Glasgow, Edinburgh, Fort William, Aberdeen and Inverness.

By Road
There are just eight motorways in Scotland, all in the southern half of the country. The main trunk road in the Highlands is the A9 which runs from Falkirk to Thurso. This is the quickest route to take to the north west Highlands, as the west coast route, although beautifully scenic, is indirect and much of it is on minor roads. Turn left at Inverness to reach the north west coastal regions.

By Sea

Of the many passenger ferry operators sailing to Great Britain from continental Europe and Ireland, very few sail into Scottish ports, on a small number of routes. These include Stena Line, Smyril Line, Superfast Ferries and P&O Irish Sea. There is a far wider choice of destinations if you sail to England or Wales then travel on to Scotland by other means of transport.

FERRY ROUTES FROM SCOTLAND

From	To
Stranraer	Belfast
	Larne
Troon	Belfast
	Larne
Lerwick	Bergen
	Seysdisfjordur
Aberdeen	Bergen
Cairnryan	Larne
Rosyth	Zeebrugge

Transport Information & Booking

General:
The UK Public Transport Information website gives links to all forms of public transport available throughout Scotland. www.pti.org.uk

Air:
easyJet: www.easyjet.com
Ryanair: www.ryanair.com
British Airways: www.britishairways.com
Skyscanner: Search for and compare cheap flights throughout Europe. www.skyscanner.net
Cheap Flights: www.cheapflights.co.uk/Scotland

Rail:
For information about train times and fares telephone the national rail enquiries service on 08457-484950 or see www.firstgroup.com/scotrail. Train tickets for all UK services can be bought on-line at www.thetrainline.com. Tickets may also be booked by telephone with rail companies, or by telephone or in person from railway stations.
National Rail Enquiries: tel 08457-484950
National Express East Coast: www.nationalexpresseastcoast.com
First ScotRail: www.scotrail.co.uk
Virgin Trains: www.virgintrains.co.uk
Eurostar: tel 08705-186186; www.eurostar.com

Eurotunnel: tel 08705-353535 (UK); 0810-630304(France); 070-223210
(Belgium); 0900-5040540 (Netherlands); 01805-000248 (Germany);
www.eurotunnel.com.

Ferries:

Comprehensive details of routes and operators, plus links to ferry operators'
websites:
www.seaview.co.uk
www.ferry-to-scotland.com

HISTORY & TRADITIONS

Secular & Christian Marriage

It was not until Christianity became widely established in Scotland that marriage as we recognise it today began to be adopted. Historians are divided on the detail of pre-Christian marriage rites and customs, but there is a consensus that there were various forms of 'Celtic secular marriages' in Scotland, similar to those which have been documented in ancient Irish law tracts. As these old Celtic laws appeared to sanction concubinage, polygamy and divorce, it is not surprising that there was great conflict with the Christian idea of marriage, a conflict which must have caused problems for many centuries.

Although Christianity was first introduced to Scotland as early as the third century AD, the Celtic influence didn't appreciably decline in the Lowlands until the 12th century, while in the Highlands, Celtic secular marriage was still common among the clans as late as the 17th century.

Marriage within the Christian Church in Scotland followed canon law, based on the laws of Ancient Rome. These stated that anybody could marry as long as they were not in holy orders, were not already married and did not marry anyone related too closely to them (within the so-called prohibited degrees of kinship). In addition, women had to be at least 12 years of age, men at least 14. These remained the legal ages for marriage in Scotland until as late as 1929.

Handfasting

It is generally agreed that early marriages often involved a rite called 'handfasting'. What is not agreed is exactly what form this took. It seems most likely that it purely related to pre-marriage betrothals, during which the couple joined hands, sometimes through a hole in a stone, and agreed to marry at a later date.

It is commonly claimed, however, that handfasting signified a trial marriage. It seems that the apparent evidence for this comes from Walter Scott's depiction of a handfasting ceremony in his book *The Monastery*, where the ceremony binds the couple in a trial marriage lasting a year and a day, after which they could chose to continue as man and wife or to go their separate ways. However, as the novel was written by Scott in 1820 as a medieval romance, it can hardly be regarded as necessarily historically accurate.

The most compelling historical evidence is that couples were betrothed by using a form of words which expressed their intention to marry at some time in the future. Marriage ceremonies used a similar form of words where they used the present tense to state that they agreed to be man and wife from that moment forward. Although it appears there was no set form of words to be used, unlike in the modern Christian ceremony, at a betrothal they would exchange consents saying, in essence 'I will take you to be my husband/wife in six months time' (or whatever time they chose). After the agreed betrothal period, they would again exchange consents, this time saying 'I take you to be my husband/wife from this day forth.' The only exception to this was if, during the betrothal period, sexual intercourse took place between the couple. If this occurred (and was admitted, presumably!) they would be deemed to be married from that moment, sex being taken to imply present tense consent.

It has become quite a fashion now for couples marrying in Scotland to wish to go through a form of a handfasting ceremony. The rise in popularity of the rite stems from the movie, Braveheart, in which Mel Gibson, in the role of William Wallace, was handfasted with his girlfriend Murron. In the scene, their wrists are bound together with rope in the time-honoured fashion, a symbol of their lasting union and the origin of the phrase 'tying the knot'. If you wish to include some version of this rite in your ceremony, you mast discuss it with the person performing the ceremony in advance to ensure that they agree.

It is interesting to note that in these early days, there was no requirement for any witnesses to be present when the couple exchanged their consents to be married. It was a matter purely between themselves. However, it was perhaps not surprising that many couples chose to have their friends or family present, both to celebrate their union and to ensure that either party could not later deny having married the woman (or man) in question.

Church Weddings

As the Church increasingly exerted its influence over society, religious weddings became the norm, but they continued to include certain aspects of the older, secular, ceremony. Weddings were initially performed outside the church, at the church door or, where there was one, under the 'marriage porch'. It may be that the reasoning behind this was to advertise the fact to the local people that the couple was henceforth united, a form of witnessing a marriage. One suspects in the early days that it was also a subtle form of advertising by the church, to persuade passers-by that this was the 'proper' way to get married in the eyes of God, and that they should therefore convert to the new religion.

At these church door weddings the bride would wear her hair long and loose as a symbol of her virginity, a custom that was described as 'being married in her hair'. She was given away, usually by her father, and then the priest joined the couple's right hands, just as at a handfasting. The vows exchanged by the couple were also very similar to those used during a handfasting ceremony. After they were pronounced man and wife, the husband presented his wife with her dowry, usually in the form of money. Although there was then a prayer and benediction, only afterwards, or sometimes the following day, would the couple and their guests enter the church to take part in a bridal mass. The mass was not deemed to be part of the wedding ceremony itself.

Even at this stage in the development of the wedding ceremony, there was no actual requirement for a priest to be present. The simple exchange of consent, followed by sexual intercourse between the couple, was deemed in 1236 by no less a personage than Pope Gregory IX to constitute a valid union.

However, the Church was concerned that this casual attitude was the cause of many incestuous unions. In response to their disquiet, Pope Innocent III introduced the practice of the calling of banns. This required that the coming marriage should be announced on three Sundays prior to the ceremony, so that any questions of forbidden kinship between the couple could be brought to light. The calling of banns continued in Scotland until 1977, after which time couples were required to send advance notice of their marriages to the local Registrar, who would ensure that there were no prohibitions against their union.

There were, over succeeding centuries, certain changes in the legal and canonical requirements for church weddings, including a reduction in the list of forbidden degrees of kinship and an increase in the days on which weddings could take place. Originally this had been Sunday only, but as this caused problems for the church as guests were so busy carousing to celebrate the marriage that they had a tendency to miss the afternoon service. Eventually, weddings were permitted on any day of the week – except, in a complete reversal of the original ruling, on Sundays. The ceremonies were moved inside the church, although the modern practice of posing for photographs outside the church, with passers-by free to stand and watch from outside the church gate, is a relic of the days when exchanging marriage vows took place at the church door, in sight of the local people.

However, apart from these technical changes, in essence religious wedding ceremonies have remained much the same until the present day.

Civil Weddings

One of the biggest changes to weddings in Scotland came about in 1939, when civil marriages were introduced. Scotland was apparently very late in making it possible to marry without the benefit of clergy – civil marriages had been performed in France since 1792 and in England since 1836. However, as it had continued to be acceptable in Scotland (although frowned upon) for people to contract marriages simply by exchanging private vows and consummating their union, in fact civil marriages in all but name had been contracted for centuries.

'Irregular marriages' which did not follow the letter of church law, had been punished by the imposition of a fine for some time, and when the first Registrars were introduced in 1856, their role was to issue a registration certificate which effectively simply waived the fine.

Some magistrates would, for a fee, register a so-called 'Rutherglen marriage' and issue a certificate. This strictly speaking did not constitute a regular marriage, but many couples believed it did, and it was a lucrative source of income for many magistrates. But in the various ad hoc forms of registration to be found, the certificate was never anything more than a receipt for the fine they would otherwise have had to pay.

In 1939 an official marriage act put the relationship between husband and wife on a legal footing, finally outlawing marriage by declaration between the couple, and by the promise of marriage followed by sexual relations, the two planks of the traditional handfasting ceremony.

Gretna Green

Scottish law has always followed a different system from English law, and the laws relating to marriage are no exception. Even today, because there is no requirement for couples to have resided in Scotland before their marriage, it is far easier for couples from outside Scotland to marry in the country than is the case in England.

The most notorious instance of differences north and south of the border led to the strongest connection in the popular consciousness between weddings of Scotland. The tiny village of Gretna Green, just over the border from England, came to unexpected prominence in 1754 when the marriage laws in England and

Wales were tightened. After this date, couples had to be married by a clergyman, and this required the knowledge, if not the consent, of their parents. In Scotland, however, couples could still marry without the involvement of clergy, and in any event, the legal age of consent was 16 in Scotland, but had been raised to 21 in England and Wales. This led to an influx of eloping couples heading for Scotland in search of someone to marry them – so-called 'runaway weddings'. Local people in towns and villages just north of the border proved happy to oblige.

It is not clear why Gretna Green became the favoured place for such marriages, but it rapidly became a lucrative pastime for the villagers, no doubt bringing welcome income to those who could provide services – feeding, watering and accommodating them, in addition to performing wedding ceremonies in a number of venues, including the blacksmith's shop.

The popularity of being married by the blacksmith led to the tradition of 'marrying over the anvil', when the marriage vows were sealed by the hammering of the anvil. The thinking behind the custom was that, like the metals which were forged by hammering, couples were joined together in the heat of their vows and were thus bound tighter for eternity.

Although it was never the case that *only* a blacksmith could perform the ceremony, one Joseph Paisley turned this common belief to his advantage, and between 1791 and 1814 he had a virtual monopoly of presiding over wedding ceremonies at Gretna Green. He was certainly a colourful character: an enormous man of prodigious strength and renowned for his stentorian voice as well as his huge appetite for alcohol, it was said he could 'straighten horseshoes in their cold state'.

The first recorded marriage at Gretna Green was in 1772, and it has become increasingly popular ever since, despite the fact that there are no reasons other than romantic ones for marrying there rather than elsewhere in Scotland. Today there are over 4,000 weddings a year at Gretna Green, amounting to around 17% of all marriages in Scotland.

The Irish Connection

It is not commonly known that Portpatrick in Dumfries once played a similar role to Gretna Green. The town was once the main port for travellers from Ireland to Scotland, and thus was the marriage venue for many under-age lovers from Ireland, which had the same marriage laws as England.

Recent Developments

Of far more recent date are two changes in the law which made Scotland an even more attractive destination for couples wishing to express their love formally. he Marriage (Scotland) Act 2002 for the first time allowed civil marriage ceremonies to take place at a venue other than a register office. Local authorities are now able to approve and license a wide variety of other venues for the purpose, including castles, other historic monuments, hotels and tourist attractions.

LOVE & LITERATURE

It is perhaps not surprising that Gretna Green should have become synonymous with romance. Literature and history abounds with tales of couples who were so in love that they would go to the lengths of a difficult and hazardous journey to the uncivilised north, sometimes with furious parents, intent on stopping the marriage, in hot pursuit.

One of the most famous instances in literature occurs in *Pride and Prejudice* when Lydia Bennet elopes with the disreputable George Wickham, leaving this note for her friend:

My dear Harriet,

You will laugh when you know where I am gone, and I cannot help laughing myself at your surprise to-morrow morning, as soon as I am missed. I am going to Gretna Green, and if you cannot guess with who, I shall think you a simpleton, for there is but one man in the world I love, and he is an angel. I should never be happy without him, so think it no harm to be off. You need not send them word at Longbourn of my going, if you do not like it, for it will make the surprise the greater when I write to them and sign my name Lydia Wickham. What a good joke it will be! I can hardly write for laughing. Pray make my excuses to Pratt, for not keeping my engagement and dancing with him to night. Tell him I hope he will excuse me when he knows all, and tell him I will dance with him at the next ball we meet, with great pleasure. I shall send for my clothes when I get to Longbourn; but I wish you would tell Sally to mend a great slit in my worked muslin gown before they are packed up. Good bye. Give my love to Colonel Forster. I hope you will drink to our good journey.

Your affectionate friend,

Lydia Bennet

One of Jane Austen's earliest works, *Love & Friendship,* written when she was just 14, shows she had already recognised the literary, and satirical,mileage afforded by couples eloping to Scotland:

The amiable M'Kenzie, whose modesty, as he afterwards assured us, had been the only reason of his having so long concealed the violence of his affection for Janetta, on receiving this Billet flew on the wings of Love to Macdonald Hall, and so powerfully pleaded his Attachment to her who inspired it, that after a few more private interviews, Sophia and I experienced the satisfaction of seeing them depart for Gretna-Green, which they chose for the celebration of their Nuptials, in preference to any other place, although it was at a considerable distance from Macdonald-Hall.

In Mansfield Park too, Austen has Julia Bertram eloping to Scotland with Yates, from all of which we can assume that the practice was fairly common, certainly among the comfortable middle classes – those, presumably, who could afford such a journey, which can't have been cheap – normally depicted by Jane Austen as indulging in questionable affairs of the heart.

The only restriction on potential venues is that they must be indoors, and must not have any religious connection or connotation. In practice, this does not greatly limit a couple who wish to marry in a religious building, as all ministers in Scotland are licensed to perform religious ceremonies in any venue.

A second piece of legislation was far more controversial. This was the Civil Partnership Act, which came into force in December 2005. It allowed same-sex partners to go through a registration ceremony which gave them many of the legal protections of a heterosexual marriage ceremony.

Although the Civil Partnership Act applies throughout the United Kingdom, only in Scotland may registration ceremonies take place outside a register office, as long as they are in approved venues.

For more detailed information on the current legislation regarding marriage and civil partnerships in Scotland, see *Marriage Legislation* and *Civil Partnerships*.

Customs & Traditions

However modern or unusual a wedding you choose, there are certain customs and traditions which are almost bound to be included in the preparations, in the ceremony or in the celebration afterwards. At the very minimum, for example, the bride is almost certain to have a wedding ring. In fact, the standard Christian or civil wedding ceremony includes the placing of the ring on the bride's finger as an integral part. In almost all cases, the customs are concerned with bringing luck or warding off bad spirits, to help ensure the couple have a long and happy married life. Most such traditions are very old, and it is often unclear how and when exactly they began. These are the most common customs which brides and grooms in Scotland include in their weddings.

Betrothal presents: Today, where the couple choose to have a period of engagement before their wedding, an engagement ring, bought by the man for his future wife, is seen as an essential item. The custom goes back many centuries, when lovers would exchange rings as a token of love, and to mark their betrothal. The earliest betrothal rings tended to be plainer that today's jewelled rings, and were usually made from silver or copper and ornamented with two clasped hands.

However, often the bride-to-be would not be given a ring for her betrothal gift: other gifts were more common before the late 19th century. Snuff boxes engraved with symbols signifying love and constancy were popular, or the man would present his sweetheart with a hand-carved wooden quaich (a drinking vessel). Perhaps the most romantic gift, however, is the Luckenbooth brooch, versions of which go back as far as the 16th century. This is a small heart-shaped brooch, made from silver or, more rarely, gold and often adorned with garnets. Traditionally, the brooch was later used to fasten the shawl of the couple's first baby at its Christening.

Feet washing: On the night before the wedding, the ceremony of feet washing was universal throughout Scotland for centuries, not dying out until the late 19th cntury. Friends and relations would visit the homes of prospective bride and groom and wash their feet in a tub of water – in wealthier homes, sometimes wine was used. Every visitor had to take their turn at washing the feet, and the whole occasion was generally an excuse for a party, being accompanied by eating, drinking and singing. When the bride's feet were being washed, it was customary for her mother to drop a ring into the tub. Whichever of the visiting girls was the first to retrieve the ring from the tub would be the next to marry.

Often the feet washing of the groom was an even more raucous affair, with some smearing soot, deemed to be lucky, on his feet, legs and face as others tried to wash it off. Less frequently, the bride was subjected to the same treatment by her female friends.

Stag and Hen Parties: It can be seen how the mischievous behaviour and the drinking connected with the marriage-eve feet-washing may have developed into the custom of the bride and groom having separate pre-wedding parties, with their female and male friends respectively. At the men's stag night, the imbibing of a great deal of alcohol, culminating in the blackening of the groom, plus other less harmless practical jokes such as removing his clothes, and/or leaving him chained to a lamppost, is par for the course.

The women's hen-night was once a more restrained affair, with the bride getting together with her girlfriends to enjoy a night out, but nowadays some brides-to-be seem to be determined to outdo the men at their own game, and drink as much or more alcohol than them!

A rapidly growing modern tradition is for brides and grooms to head abroad with their friends for their stag and hen parties, sometimes having a short break of two or more days where they really live it up.

Travel Companies Specialising in Stag and Hen Parties
ReleaseTravel: www.releasetravel.co.uk
Travel Quest: www.travel-quest.co.uk/tqstag.htm

Jumping the chanty: In the towns and cities of central Scotland, the last day at work before the wedding often had its own ritual. The bride's friends would dress her up in a parody of her wedding dress, using lace curtains, paper flowers and sometimes a vegetable bouquet. A 'chanty' (chamberpot) was filled with salt in which were hidden various lucky charms. The bride had to carry this as she and her friends walked – or sometimes they pushed her in a barrow – around the workplace and the streets while people wished her good luck and pushed silver coins into the salt. During the celebrations the bride would 'jump the chanty' three times for luck.

Window Shower: In a variation of this tradition, as the bride passed along streets of tenements (tall apartment buildings) occupants of the tenements would open their windows and throw down coins.

The Date: Traditionally in Scotland May is deemed the unluckiest month for a wedding, June the best month. This is a belief that is losing its hold, perhaps due to the increasing numbers of foreign couples marrying in Scotland. Monthly wedding statistics show that the 'wedding season' starts in April rising smoothly to a peak in August and September, then tailing off again.

Wedding dresses: The romantic long white wedding dress with train and veil is, perhaps surprisingly, a relatively recent tradition. It was Queen Victoria who started the trend, by marrying in white in 1840, and many classic wedding dresses do have a distinctly Victorian style. Prior to this time, the colour of the bride's wedding costume was not an issue. She would generally wear the most fashionable and attractive outfit in the style of the day she could afford.

There are several other traditions connected with the bride's wedding costume. The most well-known of these is the old rhyme which describes certain items she should include:

> *Something old*
> *Something new*
> *Something borrowed*
> *Something blue.*
> *And a lucky sixpence for your shoe.*

- The 'something old' symbolises a link with the past, and usually takes the form of a piece of jewellery belonging it the bride's mother or grandmother.
- The 'something new' represents good fortune in her future life.
- The 'something borrowed' should be loaned by a happily married friend, to bring good luck to the new marriage.
- The 'something blue' nowadays often takes the form of a single blue garter. Blue was traditionally a colour symbolising purity and fidelity.
- Placing a silver coin in the bride's left shoe is an old Scottish custom, intended to avert evil. In some places the bridegroom too wore silver in his shoe.
- Finally, it is deemed to be bad luck for the groom to see the bride in her wedding dress before they meet at the church altar or place of marriage.

Kilts: The history of tartan and the wearing of the kilt is worthy of a chapter in itself. For a detailed account see www.users.zetnet.co.uk/tartan/history.htm. Suffice it to say here that nowadays, although generally a kilt outfit is termed 'Highland dress', at the vast majority of Scots weddings, whether in the Lowlands or the Highlands, the groom, his best man and a fair number of the guests, will wear the kilt.

Bagpipes: It is traditional for a piper to play – or 'pipe in' the bride – as she arrives at the wedding venue and makes her way to join her husband to be. The pipes play again as the bride and groom leave after the ceremony, as man and wife.

Gun Salute: Once it was the custom in the Highlands for the young men to fire off guns during the procession to and from the church, in order to scare off evil spirits. Needless to say, this is a custom that would not be acceptable – or lawful – today.

Wedding rings: The moment of the wedding ceremony, whether religious or civil, which actually marks the uniting of the partners, is the putting of the wedding ring on the woman's finger. This only became an essential part of the UK wedding ceremony in the 19th century. Traditionally the wedding band should be of plain gold, although it is now becoming more common for wedding rings to be engraved. Celtic designs are appropriate for a Scottish weddings.

The practice of the husband also having a wedding band is of far more recent date, and it is not an essential part of the ceremony. It is normal to place the ring on the third finger of the left hand, some say because it directly linked by a vein to the heart. But other fingers, and even the thumb, have been used in the past.

Confetti: The practice of showering confetti on the happy couple as they leave the church dates back to the ancient fertility practice of scattering rice on the couple as a sign that their union should be fruitful.

Tossing the bouquet: After the ceremony it customary for the bride to throw her bouquet, and all the unmarried females scramble to catch it. The one who catches it is supposed to be the next to be married.

Tossing the garter: The bride is also expected to toss her garter for the young men to catch. This is a far more decorous remnant of the old custom of 'bedding'. Here the bride's attendant would accompany her to the bedroom, undress her and put her to bed to await the groom. The rest of the guests would nosily rush in when the groom joined her and indulge in mock fighting and attempting to carry off the bride's clothing.

Wedding cake: The modern tiered wedding cake stems from an Ancient Roman fertility rite, where a cake made from wheat or barley was broken over the bride's head as a sign of fertility. Over time it became customary to pile up several cakes and the bride and groom would try to kiss over it without knocking it down. The fairly plain original cakes became more elaborate, filled with fruit and alcohol and decorated with white icing, the tiers separated by pillars. It is traditional to save the top tier of the cake for the first baby's Christening.

Just Married: In order to prevent the bride and groom slipping away quietly while the wedding reception is in full flow, leaving the guests to continue drinking and dancing, it is customary for some of the younger guests to slip outside first and decorate their car, with a banner saying 'Just Married' and tying tin cans, old shoes and the like to the back bumper, so if they should try to escape unnoticed, the racket would alert the other guests.

Carrying the bride over the threshold: The husband should carry his new wife over the threshold of the home they will share. This is to prevent the bad luck which would be caused if the bride were to stumble as she went into the house.

Honeymoon: The derivation of the word honeymoon is open to much debate. Among other theories, some say it refers to an ancient custom of the man's father-in-law supplying him with free mead (a wine made from honey) for a month after the marriage; others say, rather sardonically, that it refers to the fact that the first month of the marriage is the sweetest. But whatever the derivation, it has now come to mean a holiday that the married couple take together immediately after their wedding.

THE QUAICH

One peculiarly Scottish custom you might like to include in your wedding celebrations is
to share a drink from a quaich with your guests. The quaich (pronounced 'quake') is a wide, shallow two-handled drinking vessel unique to Scotland. Traditionally made of wood, they are now more often found in pewter or silver, often beautifully engraved.

A dram of whisky or brandy (sometimes ale, when larger quaichs were used) were shared as a cup of welcome or farewell, and symbolised friendship.

It is appropriate to use a traditional Scottish toast to accompany the drinking:

> *May the best ye've ever seen*
> *Be the worst ye'll ever see*
> *May a moose ne'er leave yer girnal*
> *Wi' a tear drap in his e'e*
> *May ye aye keep hale an' he'rty*
> *Till ye're auld eneuch tae dee*
> *May ye aye be jist as happy*
> *As we wish ye aye tae be.*

Translated into modern English, this means:

> *May the best you have ever seen*
> *Be the worst you will ever see*
> *May a mouse never leave your girnal**
> *With a tear drop in his eye*
> *May you always keep hale and hearty*
> *Till you are old enough to die*
> *May you always be just as happy*
> *As we wish you always to be.*

A 'girnal' was a household chest for storing grain.
Quaichs in various designs may be bought online from www.scotweb.co.uk

A TRADITIONAL SCOTTISH WEDDING

There are few components of a wedding which are absolutely mandatory – as long as the statutory notice period is observed, the vows are exchanged and the marriage schedule signed in the presence of two witnesses, anything else is down to the agreement of the bride and groom and whoever is performing the ceremony.

However, weddings are a time for tradition and in Scotland there are many traditions which can shape one's wedding day. There are also traditional roles which you may invite your friends and close relations to carry out for you on the day. So, to help you decide which aspects of a conventional Scottish wedding day you want to include in your own wedding, here is a description of the sort of wedding which you can find taking place in towns and villages throughout Scotland every day of the year.

If the conventional is not for you, later in the book are some suggestions for 'alternative' weddings!

Invitation to a Wedding

Mary Whittier & James Ferguson
Request the pleasure of your company at their marriage
at Strathdarrach Chapel at 2pm on 1ˢᵗ June.
Followed by a reception at
Strathdarrach Castle.

The Arrival

The first people the guests meet as they arrive at the ancient stone chapel in the grounds of the castle are Craig and Hugh, the bride's and groom's eldest brothers. Today they are acting as ushers, carrying out their role of meeting, greeting and seating the guests. Once Craig has directed them where to park their cars, they walk to the chapel where heather and Scottish thistle corsages and buttonholes are provided to attach to their wedding outfits. Hugh then shows them to their seats for the ceremony. As is traditional, the bride's family and friends are seated on the left side of the chapel, the groom's on the right, behind their respective positions when they stand at the altar to exchange their vows.

James the bridegroom and his best man (and best friend) Tom arrive in good time, resplendent in their kilts. The minister has also arrived, from the local town. James hands over the wedding schedule which he collected from the register office a few hours earlier, and stands nervously chatting to the minister, running through the order of events so everything goes according to plan. Tom makes a last minute check of his sporran to make sure he has the wedding ring to hand to James at the crucial moment.

James's parents are among the last of the guests to arrive, and are seated in the front pew behind their son. The left hand front pew is still empty, reserved for the bride's parents. In the pews behind, on their respective sides are the bride and groom's grandparents and uncles and aunts, with more distant relatives and friends seated further back.

There is a low murmur of anticipation as people check their watches. Nearly 2pm – will the bride be late? That's her prerogative – in fact, many of the guests will be disappointed if she arrives on time! Outside they can hear the piper warming up with a selection of his favourite traditional tunes.

The ushers await the arrival of the bridal convoy and Tom, the best man, keeps a lookout at the door of the chapel. James is on strict instructions to stay inside the chapel, as it is deemed to be bad luck for him to see his bride in her finery before she begins her walk up the aisle. In fact, he has not been allowed to see even a picture of her dress – this will be his first sight of her in her wedding clothes.

At 2:05, Craig indicates to the best man that the first car is drawing into sight. Word goes round the church that soon the blushing bride will be there. The piper falls silent and makes his way to stand beside the cars.

The bridal convoy consists of two vintage limousines. First comes the grandest, a beautiful ivory Rolls Royce, decorated with the traditional two white ribbons tied across the bonnet (hood), from the windscreen to the centre-front. Following closely behind is a silver grey Bentley, from which emerge the bride's mother and attendants. Hugh escorts Mrs Whittier to the chapel and shows her to her seat in the front pew.

The bride's attendants are Mary's married sister Janis, and her two young children Connor and Morgan, who are respectively the Matron of honour, page boy and bridesmaid. Janis, dressed in a dark blue silk dress, fusses about tidying their outfits, Connor wearing his first kilt, and Morgan in a pretty dress of pale blue taffeta with white flowers in her hair.

Meanwhile, the photographer, who has been taking photographs of the bride and her attendants getting ready at home, drives up in his own car and prepares to take pictures of the bride as she steps down from the Rolls. First to emerge is her father, who has travelled with her. He, of course, is dressed in his kilt, the same tartan as his young grandson Connor. While this is the first time Connor has worn the kilt, his grandfather's has seen many many weddings over the years, including his own, and that of his first daughter, Janis, when he gave her away to her husband five years previously. He is now about to do the same for his younger daughter.

He walks round the car and opens the door, and Janis helps Mary to alight from the car in her gorgeous ivory gown, holding her bouquet of white roses – the Rolls has been specially chosen to match the all-important dress. Janis arranges the train of the dress carefully so the photographer can get some stunning shots. Mary has followed the stipulations of the old rhyme, the dress being the 'something new', while she is wearing her grandmother's gold cross and chain around her neck as the 'something old', her best friend has lent her some tiny gold earrings for the 'something borrowed' and she is wearing a blue garter under her dress for the 'something blue'. Finally, she wears a silver sixpence in her left shoe for luck.

Once the photographer has taken several photographs of the bridal party and the car, Janis settles the veil over her sister's face and gathers up the train of her dress, showing Connor and Morgan how to stand either side of her and help carry the train to ensure it does not drag on the ground. The piper begins to play the old favourite tune *Come to Mairi's Wedding* and leads the bride, on her father's arm and followed by her attendants, slowly towards the chapel. At the door, the piper steps to one side and the bridal party pause on the threshold. The photographer has been clicking away every step of the way, and will continue to do so during the ceremony. He has, as a matter of courtesy, spoken with the bride and groom and the Minister to ensure that none of them have objections to him taking candid shots during the service and all have agreed they would like this, as long as he is discreet and not too disruptive!

The Service
As the small chapel does not have an organ, Mary has asked her close friend Maggie, an accomplished musician, to play some traditional tunes on the clarsach (the Gaelic small harp) as she walks up the aisle. She takes her father's arm and walks beside him, her bridesmaid and page boy following behind. At the altar, the minister asks, 'Who gives this woman to be married to this man?' Mr Whittier replies, 'Her mother and I,' kisses Mary on the cheek and relinquishes his daughter to his soon to be son-in-law. He takes his seat next to his wife, while Mary hands her bouquet to her matron of honour, who also sits down, with Connor and Morgan beside her as it has been agreed the two children are unlikely to be able to stand still throughout the service! Tom, the best man, stands to the right of the groom, ready to hand the ring to James when the Minister directs him.

The minister begins the ceremony by inviting everyone present to share in the service. (See below for examples of typical wedding ceremonies.)

After the vows are exchanged and the minister proclaims James and Mary husband and wife, James lifts the veil from his new wife's face and they kiss, the photographer ensuring he gets a picture of that poignant moment.

The marriage schedule is then signed by James and Mary, the minister, and Tom and Janis who have been asked to act as witnesses. While the schedule is being signed, Maggie plays again on the clarsach. After the legal formalities have been completed, the piper prepares to pipe the newly-weds from the chapel, leading them up the aisle arm in arm, with the bridesmaid and page boy following behind The guests stand while the procession passes, and then follow them out of the chapel.

Outside, the ushers help the photographer to organise the bride and groom and their guests for a series of formal posed photographs. Some of the guests take this opportunity to throw confetti over the newly-married couple.

The Reception
As the weather is fine, and it is just a short walk across to the castle where the reception will be held, the piper plays again as he leads the entire bridal party and guests in a walking procession to the grand entrance.

Before they enter the castle, there is a call for the bouquet to be tossed, so all the unmarried women cluster together, to try to catch Mary's bouquet when she throws it into the throng. There's a huge cheer when James's sister Fiona catches it and much joking with her boyfriend David – tradition has it that whoever catches the bouquet will be the next to marry. Then Tom removes Mary's garter and tosses that to the unmarried men who all vie to catch it. When the catcher proves to be none other than David, there is delighted agreement by everybody that he will soon be walking up the aisle with Fiona!

The castle owner then comes forward and welcomes the bride and groom. He fills a silver quaich with whisky and it is passed from hand to hand, everybody taking a small sip and exchanging the Gaelic toast, *Slainte Mhath!* (Meaning *Good Health* and pronounced s*lange avah.*)

Inside, the grand hall of the castle has been decked out with flowers and tartan ribbons. The tables are beautifully laid, with a long top table at the far end of the room, and round tables for the other guests. The bride and groom stand by the door and welcome their guests who offer their congratulations as they pass into the hall. Some of the guests have brought wedding gifts with them for the happy couple. These are placed on the table set up in the hall on which are displayed the gifts previously received.

The Wedding Breakfast

Waiters are on hand to offer glasses of champagne to the arriving guests as they find their seats, indicated by heather-decorated name cards, for the wedding breakfast – so-called at whatever time of the day the meal is taken.

The bridal party take their seats at the top table, following the traditional pattern:

Matron of Honour	Groom's Father	Bride's Mother	Groom	Bride	Bride's Father	Groom's Mother	Best Man

In front of the top table is a smaller table, decorated with white roses and tartan ribbons, on which the three tier wedding cake is displayed.

The meal is served, a carefully chosen menu of superb Scottish produce.

Starter
Venison Pate with Oatcakes
or
Leek & Potato Soup

Main Course
Scotch Roast Beef
or
Fillet of Wild Salmon
served with a selection of seasonal vegetables

Dessert
Cranachan with Raspberries & Whisky
or
Selection of Scottish Cheeses

The Speeches & Toasts

After the meal, champagne is served, ready for the toasts. Tom, the best man, who is acting as the toastmaster and MC, stands and asks Mary's father to propose a toast to the bride and bridegroom. He takes his seat and Mary's father stands, to make a short speech in which he welcomes the groom's parents, relatives of both families and other guests. He finishes by welcoming the groom to his family and saying some complimentary and moving words about his daughter. He then asks the guest to raise their glasses to the happy couple, wishing them every happiness for their future life together. The guests stand and raise their glasses, then drink.

James next gives a speech in which he thanks his new father-in-law, followed by thanks to all the guests for attending and for their gifts and best wishes. He also thanks his parents-in-law for the gift of their daughter and his own parents for their love and care. Finally he thanks Janis, Connor and Morgan for acting as Mary's attendants, and proposes a toast to them. They are each presented with a small gift as a memento of the day.

Tom replies on behalf of the attendants, and proceeds to amuse all present with a wickedly funny speech he has been preparing for weeks, in which he punctures any sense of dignity his old friend James might have remaining. He proposes a toast to all four parents, and then goes on to read the cards, messages and greetings which have been received.

Tom then invites the bride and groom to cut the cake. They move to the small table James picks up the silver knife which has been provided and hands it to Mary. James places his right hand over his new wife's right hand, and they cut the wedding cake together. The wedding cake is then taken away by a waiter to be cut into portions. The bridal party and guests move out to the lawn, where coffee and wedding cake are served. Portions of cake have been placed in small boxes to be sent to various invitees who were unable to attend on the day. The photographer takes the opportunity for some outdoor shots of the bride and groom.

The Ceilidh

While the guests chat and enjoy the sunshine, the castle staff are busy clearing tables and rearranging the hall in readiness for the evening ceilidh. Mary's friend Maggie is providing the music with her ceilidh band. In addition to the small harp she played during the ceremony, she also plays fiddle and tin whistle, more suitable for lively Scottish country dance tunes. The other members of the band arrive – another fiddler, an accordionist and a mandolin player. The pay bar is opened, and guests begin to wander in to buy drinks.

Additional guests who have been invited for the evening ceilidh are now arriving, and they are greeted by Mary and Tom, who accept further gifts from those who have brought them.

Gradually the guests drift back into the hall and purchase drinks from the bar. Tom rounds up the rest of the guests with the announcement that the bride and groom will take the floor for the first dance which, as is traditional, is a waltz. They take a few turns round the floor, and are then joined by the matron of honour dancing with the best man, followed by the bride's mother dancing with the groom's father and the groom's mother with the bride's father. Thereafter, other couples join them on the floor.

After these formalities are over, the band strikes up a lively tune and announce the first dance, the old-favourite *The Gay Gordons*. Nobody is left out of the Scottish dances, as one or other of the band members always 'calls' the dances before they start, walking the dancers through the steps, and those who know the dances help those who don't to get through them with as few hitches as possible. But as with any ceilidh, the inevitable errors and mix-ups just add to the fun and hilarity of the occasion!

As the evening wears on, much drink is taken, dances are danced and laughter is shared. The bride slips away during the evening and changes into her 'going away' outfit. She and the groom are to spend the night in a hotel at a secret destination before flying to their holiday abroad the following day. Mary's mother has been charged with the responsibility of getting her dress safely back home.

At a pre-arranged moment some of the younger guests sneak outside and decorate the back bumper of the wedding limousine with a variety of old shoes and tin cans, and tie a banner proclaiming 'Just Married' across the back window. When the bride and groom are ready to leave, the wedding guests accompany them outside and wave them off as they are driven to their hotel for the night.

Some of the guests then make their own excuses and leave, while the hard core continue to celebrate until the band plays the last dance and everybody goes home tired but happy.

CEREMONIES

Whatever kind of ceremony you choose, the words used and vows exchanged can vary. You should discuss with the person solemnising your marriage or any other ceremony of commitment exactly what you and they wish to include. In most cases the minister or the celebrant will wish to meet with you both beforehand to discuss both the importance of the commitment you are making and the order of events.

These are examples of the form ceremonies may take, but you can amend certain aspects of them to suit the sentiments you wish to express as a couple on your special day.

Church of Scotland Wedding Service
Taken from the Book of Common Order, Saint Andrew Press (1994).

- The groom and best man take up their positions for the ceremony.
- The bride makes her entrance, accompanied by the person who is to give her away if appropriate.
- The minister welcomes everybody present and invites them to share in the service.
- A hymn of the couple's choice may be sung.
- The minister speaks a few words about the binding nature of marriage and its religious significance, after which the bride and groom confirm their intention to marry.
- A prayer is said.
- A reading may be given, which could be a passage from the bible, or may be something secular such as a love poem or something specially written for the occasion.
- The couple join hands and exchange their vows, the groom first, followed by the bride. The minister will break the vows down into 'bite-sized' pieces which the couple repeat after him – there's no need to memorise them. There are two versions of the vows. The couple choose which they prefer prior to the ceremony.

Version A
Groom: In the presence of God and before these witnesses I, James, give myself to you, Mary, to be your husband, and take you now to be my wife. I promise to love you, to be faithful and loyal to you for as long as we live.
Bride: In the presence of God and before these witnesses I, Mary, give myself to you, James, to be your wife, and take you now to be my husband. I promise to love you, to be faithful and loyal to you for as long as we live.

Version B
Groom: I, Henry, take you, Helen, to be my wife. In the presence of God, and before this congregation, I promise and covenant to be a loving, faithful and loyal husband to you as long as we both shall live.

Bride: I, Helen, take you, Henry, to be my husband. In the presence of God, and before this congregation, I promise and covenant to be a loving, faithful and loyal wife to you as long as we both shall live.

- The bride and groom may also wish to exchange their own personal vows, in the form of a favourite poem or passage, or something written especially for the occasion.
- The best man passes the ring or rings and says a few words about their symbolic significance.
- The groom places the ring on the third finger of his bride's left hand and says: [name] I give you this ring in God's name, as a symbol of all that we have promised and all that we share. If the groom also has a ring, the bride places it on his ring finger and repeats the same words.
- The minister joins the couple's hands and pronounces them married. They kneel and a blessing on their marriage is spoken and a hymn may be sung.
- The marriage schedule is signed by the minister, the couple and two witnesses.
- Either the minister or a friend of the couple reads a passage from the bible.
- The minister addresses the congregation and a prayer is said for the new marriage.
- A final hymn is sung and the minister blesses the newly-weds and congregation.
- The couple leave the church, followed by the bridal party and guests.

Civil Wedding Ceremony

- The bride and groom and two witnesses must be present. Other guests may be present if wished – the registrar will advise you of the number of guests that can be accommodated in the register office marriage room.
- The registrar will stand, and say: 'My name is...... In my capacity as registrar for the district of...... I have been appointed by the Registrar General for Scotland as a person authorised to solemnise civil marriages in accordance with the provisions of the Marriage (Scotland) Act 1977. Before I proceed with this civil marriage ceremony, it is necessary that you should identify yourselves by answering the following questions:
- (To man): 'Are you John Henderson whose usual residence appears on this Marriage Schedule as......?'
- (To woman): 'Are you Ann Smith whose usual residence appears on this Marriage Schedule as......?'
- The registrar will then say: 'We are now assembled here in order that I may solemnise your marriage in the presence of these witnesses in accordance with the law of Scotland. I confirm that the requirements of that law preliminary to your marriage have been satisfied. Before you, John, and you, Ann, are joined in marriage it is my duty to remind you of the binding character of the vows you are about to make. Marriage

according to the law of this country is a union of one man with one woman, voluntarily entered into for life, to the exclusion of all others.'

- Everyone present will then be asked to stand.
- Registrar (to the man): 'The legal impediments to marriage have already been explained to you. Please repeat the following declaration after me: I, John, solemnly and sincerely declare that I know of no legal impediment to my marrying Ann.'
- Registrar (to the woman): 'The legal impediments to marriage have already been explained to you. Please repeat the following declaration after me: I, Ann, solemnly and sincerely declare that I know of no legal impediment to my marrying John.'
- Registrar (to the man): 'Please repeat after me: I solemnly and sincerely declare that I, John, accept you, Ann, as my lawful wife, to the exclusion of all others.'
- Registrar (to the woman): 'Please repeat after me: I solemnly and sincerely declare that I, Ann, accept you, John, as my lawful husband, to the exclusion of all others.'
- If there is a wedding ring, the registrar will ask the bridegroom to place the ring on the bride's finger (normally the third finger of the bride's left hand, but not necessarily so). If the bride is giving a ring in exchange she may wish to place it on the bridegroom's finger at this stage also. Thereafter the registrar will say: 'As a seal to the contract into which you are both entering, this ring is / these rings are given and received.'
- Registrar: 'Following the binding declaration which you have made before me in the presence of these witnesses, I hereby declare that you John and you Ann are now husband and wife.'
- The Registrar will then ask the company to sit down while the Marriage Schedule is signed. The bridegroom will sign it first, followed by the bride (signing her pre-marriage surname) then by the registrar and the two witnesses. The witnesses' addresses, if not already appearing on the Schedule, will be entered.

Humanist Wedding Ceremony

Taken from 'Sharing the Future' by Jane Wynne Willson, British Humanist Association (2005).

There is no set form of words for a Humanist ceremony: the bride and groom often write their own ceremony, choosing vows which have most meaning for them as a couple. The clebrant will always be happy to assist and make suggestions about the form of the cermeoy during the weeks prior to the marriage. However, whatever the form of words used, most ceremonies will follow a similar basic framework.

- Entry of bride and groom, to music if desired.
- Introductory words from the celebrant who welcomes everyone and talks briefly about the couple and the commitment they are about to make.
- Celebrant's remarks about what a Humanist view of marriage entails.
- The marriage, including exchange of these vows, which are obligatory to make the ceremony legal:

- 'I call upon these persons here present to witness that I, Craig Robinson, take thee, Elizabeth Browne, to be my lawful wedded wife.'
- 'I call upon these persons here present to witness that I, Elizabeth Browne, take thee, Craig Robinson, to be my lawful wedded husband.'
- Celebrant pronounces them husband and wife.
- Celebrant's closing words and good wishes for the future.
- The marriage schedule is signed by the celebrant, the couple and their two witnesses.
- Exit of bride and groom, again accompanied by music if desired.

Civil Partnership Ceremony

There is no requirement in law for words to be exchanged by the proposed civil partners. All that is required is the signing of the civil partnership document. Registrars will, however, have their own suggestions for words to use if you wish to mark the occasion with a ceremony. This is one possibility:

- Non-religious music may be played as guests assemble.
- The Registrar will introduce him or herself and give a personal welcome to you and your guests.
- Registrar: We are gathered here to formally witness the celebration of John Hunter and Peter Burns in their civil partnership ceremony.
- This place in which you are now met has been duly sanctioned according to the law for the registratin of civil partnerships and we are gathered here to witness the formation of the civil partnership by John and Peter. If any person present knows of any lawful impediment to this civil partnership, you should declare it now.
- John and Peter have invited you here to share in their special day, and in return, you are here to show your support and encouragement to them.
- Non-religious reading by one of the persons present.
- John and Peter have found in each other's company great happiness, fulfilment and love, and they now wish to affirm publicly their relationship and to offer to each other the security which comes from vows sincerely made and faithfully kept. Your ceremony today declares your love, care and support for each other. May this love sustain you through all of your life in a relationship of permanence and continuing commitment.
- Registrar: John and Peter, please turn towards each other and join hands as you each in turn repeat after me:
- I, John, take you, Peter, to be my beloved partner. To love and cherish you, to honour and comfort you, to stand by you in sorrow or in joy, in hardship or in ease and to be your closest friend.
- I, Peter, take you, John, to be my beloved partner. To love and cherish you, to honour and comfort you, to stand by you in sorrow or in joy, in hardship or in ease and to be your closest friend.
- A ring is a sign of the special bond between two people – an unbroken circle symbolising unending and everlasting love, and is the outward sign of the lifelong promises you have made to each other.

- John, please place the ring on Peter's finger and repeat after me: 'I give you this ring as a token of our commitment and as a symbol of all that we share.'
- John and Peter, you have made your promises to each other in the presence of myself and your witnesses here assembled. May today form a milestone in your lives which you will look upon with much love and joy in your life together. It now gives me great pleasure to declare that you are partners for life.
- The registrar, the partners and their two witnesses sign the register.
- The couple and their guests exit.

Renewal of Vows

A renewal of vows has no legal standing, and can take place at any time during a marriage, whether the original wedding service was religious, non-religious or civil. This is an example of a religious vow renewal:

- We have come together in the presence of God to give thanks with Norman and Alison for 10 years of married life, to rejoice together and to ask for God's blessing. I invite you now to recall the vows that you made at your wedding.
- Husband and wife face each other and hold hands.
- The husband says: 'I, Norman, took you, Alison, to be my wife...' The wife says: 'I, Alison, took you, Norman, to be my husband...' The couple say together: '...to have and to hold from that day forward, for better, for worse, for richer, for poorer, in sickness and in health, to love and to cherish, till death us do part, according to God's holy law, and this was our solemn vow. Today, in the presence of our family and friends, we affirm our continuing commitment to this vow.
- The minister says to the congregation: 'Will you, the family and friends of Norman and Alison, continue to support and uphold them in their marriage now and in the years to come? Congregation; 'We will.'
- Husband and wife touch their wedding ring(s), saying: 'I gave you this ring as a sign of our marriage. With my body I honour you, all that I am I give to you, and all that I have I share with you, within the love of God, Father, Son, and Holy Spirit.'
- A souvenir certificate may be signed during the ceremony by the couple and two witnesses.

Blessing

A blessing may involve a reading, hymn, song or prayer. Traditional wedding music may be played or something that has special meaning for the couple. Here's a suggestion for a non-religious blessing ceremony.

- Bride and groom enter together, as husband and wife, to their chosen music.
- Celebrant welcomes the couple and their guests.
- Celebrant: 'We are grateful for the ties of love which bind us together, giving dignity, meaning, worth and joy to all our days; for the peace accorded us this day, and for the hope of a bright future for all gathered here.'
- Reading of a favourite poem of the couple.
- Celebrant: 'Now that you, David, and you, Michelle, have been joined together in marriage, may your life be a shared adventure, may you find in each other companionship as well as love; understanding as well as compassion. May the home you share be an island where the pressures of the world can be sorted out and brought into focus; where tensions can be released and understood; and where you can enjoy the warmth of humour and love.'
- Love song with special meaning for the couple.
- Celebrant: 'As you share your life together, may you find an ever richer joy in loving and learning together.'
- Bride and groom exit followed by guests.

Useful Books & Websites

There are many books and websites with suggested prose and poetry readings and vows for your wedding. This is just a small selection.

Writing your own vows:
www.weddingguide.co.uk/articles/ceremonies/vows.asp
Wedding Readings, Poems & Vows: Available from www.confetti.co.uk.
Words for the Wedding: Creative Ideas for Choosing & Using Hundreds of Quotations to Personalise Your Vows, Toasts, Invitations & More: Wendy Paris & Andrew Chesler, (Perigree Books, 2001).
Cultural Wedding Vows:
www.documentsanddesigns.com/verse/cultural_vows.htm

MARRIAGE LEGISLATION

Marriage in the United Kingdom
Although the law relating to marriage in Scotland is by and large unique, there are some aspects which are common throughout the United Kingdom.

Minimum Age
Throughout the United Kingdom and the British Crown dependencies of Guernsey, Jersey and the Isle of Man, the minimum legal age for getting married is 16 years. In all these places, except Scotland, the consent of parents or legal guardians is required, in writing, if the intended bride and groom are under 18. Provided you are of the legal minimum age, you will not need to obtain parental consent, written or in person, to marry in Scotland.

Prohibited Marriages
Throughout the United Kingdom and the British Crown Dependencies of Guernsey, Jersey and the Isle of Man, there are what is know as 'forbidden degrees of relationship' within which you cannot marry, and which apply to illegitimate and legitimate relationships equally.

A man may not marry his:
- Mother, step-mother or adoptive mother.
- Daughter, step-daughter, or adoptive daughter.
- Sister, half-sister or step-sister.
- Father's mother (grandmother).
- Mother's mother (grandmother).
- Father's father's former wife (step-grandmother).
- Mother's father's former wife (step-grandmother).
- Son's daughter (granddaughter).
- Daughter's daughter (granddaughter).
- Wife's son's daughter (step-granddaughter).
- Wife's daughter's daughter (step-granddaughter).
- Son's son's wife (grandson's wife).
- Daughter's son's wife (grandson's wife).
- Father's sister (aunt).
- Mother's sister (aunt).
- Brother's daughter (niece).
- Sister's daughter (niece).

A woman may not marry her:
- Father, step-father or adoptive father.
- Son, step-son or adoptive son.
- Brother, half-brother or step-brother.
- Father's father (grandfather).
- Mother's father (grandfather).
- Mother's mother's former husband (step-grandfather).
- Father's mother's former husband (step-grandfather).

- Son's son (grandson).
- Daughter's son (grandson).
- Husband's daughter's son (step-grandson).
- Husband's son's son (step-grandson).
- Son's daughter's husband (granddaughter's husband).
- Daughter's daughter's husband (granddaughter's husband).
- Father's brother (uncle).
- Mother's brother (uncle).
- Brother's son (nephew).
- Sister's son (nephew).

Additionally, in Scotland, a man may not marry his great-grandmother or great-grand-daughter and a woman may not marry her great-grandfather or great-grandson.

Other Prohibitions: You must both be free to marry. You must not already be married and you must also be of different sex at birth, even if one or both have undergone gender change surgery. For more on same sex civil partnerships, see below.

Exceptions: In England, Scotland and Wales (not Northern Ireland, Isle of Man, Guernsey and Jersey) the Marriage Act, 1986, allows for certain step-relatives and relatives-in-law to marry.

Step-relatives may marry provided they are at least 21 years of age. The younger of the couple must at no time before the age of 18 have lived in the same household as the older person. Neither must they have been treated as a child of the older person's family.

In May 2006, the law in Scotland was changed to allow marriages between parents-in-law and children-in-law. So, a man may marry his mother-in-law or daughter-in-law, a woman may marry her father-in-law or son-in-law, provided the previous marriage was ended by divorce from or the death of their previous partner. This is another area where the law is different on both sides of the Scottish/English border. Marriage between in-laws is still forbidden in England and Wales and there are no plans to change that situation.

Cousins: In spite of the list of prohibited relationships, you can marry a cousin. However, it is advisable to take medical advice about whether your decision would have implications for the health of any children of the marriage.

Second & Subsequent Marriages

For all civil marriages – that is, those taking place at a Register Office or elsewhere when conducted by a Registrar – second and subsequent marriages are bound by the same rules as those regulating first marriages: the rules relating to age and forbidden degrees of relationship, for example. In addition, at the time of notification of the intended marriage, the registrar will require proof that the first or previous marriage has ended by divorce or death of the former spouse. The decree absolute in the case of divorce, or the death certificate in the case of death of the spouse, will be sufficient documentary proof.

Different churches, however, have different rules. And although the Church of Scotland might be thought of as the main Church you would consider when arranging your marriage in Scotland, all the other major Churches, and many minor ones, are represented and each has its own requirements with regard to second and subsequent marriages.

- **The Church of Scotland.** If yours is to be a second or subsequent marriage, you will encounter few problems with plans to marry within the Church of Scotland. However, its ministers do have considerable discretion in this area so you should check with the minister in question first . Widows and widowers are unlikely to come across any difficulties with Church of Scotland policy when remarrying.
- **The Church of England.** Much depends on individual ministers' personal views about the enduring sanctity of the marriage vows. For many, the phrase 'till death us do part' means just that, and some ministers will simply not marry divorcees. Some will, however, especially where the divorcee is the 'wronged one' in the break-up of the previous marriage, in which case the minister may use his or her discretion. You should speak with the minister of the church where you intend to marry before making any firm plans. In the event of a previous spouse having died, the Church of England is unlikely to raise any objection to the widow or widower remarrying, either to a widower or widow, respectively, or to a first-time bride or groom.
- **The Roman Catholic Church.** If you are a divorcee, and if your former spouse is still alive, and if your previous marriage took place within the Roman Catholic Church, the divorce will not be recognised. The Catholic Church does not accept that the State has any right to dissolve a marriage through divorce under civil law. The only avenue for you, if this is the case, is to seek to have the previous marriage declared null and void after petitioning the church for this purpose.

  It is possible that if your previous marriage ceremony was performed within another Church – and therefore not recognised as valid by the Roman Catholic Church – a priest may be able to marry you on the 'second' occasion. Because civil ceremonies are not recognised by the Roman Catholic Church, a priest can and will marry you if you are a

51

divorcee and your previous marriage was of this type. There are no prohibitions on the marriages of widows or widowers. However, in all cases of second or subsequent marriage, you must meet with the priest beforehand to discuss these matters.

- **Non-Conformist.** Churches such as the Methodist and Baptist Churches generally take a more relaxed approach to second and subsequent marriages than do the traditional Churches. Divorcees and bereaved spouses should not experience any great problem in marrying again within these Churches, although individual ministers should always be approached beforehand for a discussion about these matters.
- **Quaker.** Application to remarry must go before the regular meeting of the Quaker Church's members, where a collective decision will be reached depending on the individual's circumstances.

If you or your partner find it impossible to marry again in the Church of your choice or birth, you should speak with the minister or priest to consider the possibility of a civil ceremony, followed by a religious service of blessing in church. The form of such a service (sometimes known as a service of prayer and dedication) varies according to the Church involved. The details of the service may often be negotiated with the minister.

Marriage in Scotland

Getting married in Scotland is relatively simple from a legal point of view, regardless of your nationality and where you are resident.

Detailed information relating to your particular circumstances can be obtained from *Marriage/Civil Partnership Section*, New Register House, Edinburgh EH1 3YT; tel 0131-334 0380; www.gro-scotland.gov.uk.

Who Can Marry In Scotland?

Any two persons can marry in Scotland, regardless of where they live or their nationalities, provided:

- The conditions regarding minimum age, forbidden degrees of relationship and second or subsequent marriages are adhered to.
- They are of different sex.
- They are capable of understanding the nature of the marriage ceremony and are capable of giving informed consent to marry.
- The marriage would be regarded as valid in their own country should they not be UK nationals.
- They complete the required paperwork and pay the appropriate fees.

Where Can You Marry in Scotland?

The two most recent pieces of legislation which give the Scottish marriage its unique legal flavour are the Marriage (Scotland) Acts of 1977 and 2002. They relate to the places where marriages can legally take place and the form of those marriages, religious or civil.

Marriage (Scotland) Act 1977: A religious ceremony solemnising a marriage can only be performed by a religious celebrant authorised to do so under the Marriage (Scotland) Act 1977. The ceremony may be Christian or non-Christian and may take any form agreed between celebrant and the couple intending to marry.

If you opt for a religious marriage, it is the celebrant (minister or priest, for example) who is 'licensed' to perform the ceremony and he or she can perform that ceremony anywhere in Scotland – in any building, on any land, even half-way up a mountain if that is what you wish and provided the celebrant, and the owner of the land or building, agree!

Marriage (Scotland) Act 2002: A civil ceremony solemnising a marriage may only be performed by a registrar or an assistant registrar duly authorised by the Registrar General. The 2002 legislation extended the places in which such ceremonies could take place. Prior to this date, civil ceremonies could only take place in register offices, but the new Act allowed local authorities to approve and license other venues for the purpose.

If you opt for a civil ceremony, then you can choose to marry either in a register office or an approved venue.

Should you wish to undergo a civil marriage ceremony in a location which is not currently licensed for that purpose, you can apply to the local authority for temporary approval of that location. You should consult the relevant local authority about the application procedure in such cases and also the fee payable.

Details of all register offices and approved venues are available from *Marriage Section of the Registrar General,* General Register Office for Scotland, New Register House, Edinburgh EH1 3YT; tel 0131-334 0380; www.gro-scotland.gov.uk/regscot/groslocate/index.html

The full list of approved places can be viewed at: www.gro-scotland.gov.uk/regscot/getting-married-in-scotland/civil-marriages-in-approved-places.html

Celebrants

All ordained ministers and priests of recognised Churches in Scotland are authorised to solemnise marriages. In addition, certain non-religious celebrants are authorised to perform marriages.

The Findhorn Foundation in Moray has licensed celebrants who will be happy to work with you to devise a form of non-religious marriage ceremony to your taste, and they will attend your chosen location to perform the ceremony. Contact *The Findhorn Foundation,* The Park, Forres IV36 3TZ; tel 01309-690311; www.findhorn.org

Since late 2005, the Humanist Society also has licensed celebrants. A directory of celebrants can be found on their website at www.humanism-scotland.org.uk

Giving Notice of Marriage

You are both required by law to give notice of your intention to marry:

- To the registrar of the relevant district (see list of register offices in appendices).
- On the appropriate Marriage Notice Form M10 which can be obtained from any registrar for births, deaths and marriages in Scotland.
- No earlier than three months and no later than 15 days prior to the date of the marriage.

Form M10 is an essential document, and the guidance notes should be read carefully. If the instructions are not followed to the letter, you may find your wedding unavoidably delayed. In particular, it is stressed how important it is to submit the completed form in good time.

You must submit the forms early enough to enable the registrar to be satisfied that you are free to marry one another. Normally notices should be with the registrar about four weeks before the marriage, but if either of you has been married before, they should be with the registrar six weeks beforehand. The minimum period is 15 days before the date of the proposed marriage, but if you leave things as late as this you could be faced with the need to postpone your marriage. Only in exceptional circumstances will the Registrar General authorise a marriage to take place if 15 days' notice has not been given.

You will need to have made arrangements for the date and time of your marriage prior to submitting Form M10. If you are having a religious ceremony, contact the religious celebrant who is to take the service, before completing the notice of marriage. For a civil marriage make advance arrangements with the registrar.

Either the bride or groom must attend the register office personally before the marriage, to collect the Marriage Schedule, in the case of a religious wedding, or to finalise arrangements with the registrar if you are having a civil ceremony. Personal attendance is imperative because the registrar may need further information before the marriage can proceed. If it is not clear from your marriage notice form, the registrar might ask whether your parents were married. This is to enable registrars to insert your mother's maiden surname appropriately in your marriage schedule.

When you give notice you will be required to sign a declaration to the effect that the information you give on Form M10 is correct. As a safeguard against bigamous marriages the Registrar General makes a subsequent check of the information. Do not delay giving notice simply because you are waiting for any of the required documents to come to hand. If time is getting short it is better to give notice first and then pass the documents to the registrar when they become available; but they must be made available to the registrar before the marriage. Provided the documents are in order the marriage can proceed as arranged.

Residence Outside Scotland: If you reside in England or Wales, and if you intend to marry either a person residing in Scotland or a person residing in England or Wales who has a parent residing in Scotland:

- You may either give notice of your intention to marry to a registrar in Scotland, or alternatively you may give such notice to the superintendent registrar in the district in England or Wales in which you reside.
- You must obtain from the superintendent registrar the 'certificate for marriage' and send it to the relevant Scottish registrar as soon as possible.
- The person you are marrying should still give notice of his or her intention to marry in Scotland in the usual way.

Residence Outside The United Kingdom: If you normally reside and are domiciled outside the United Kingdom, you should:

- Give notice of your intention to marry to the relevant Scottish registrar in the usual manner.
- Provide also a 'certificate of no impediment to marriage', issued by the relevant authority in your home country. Not all countries issue such a certificate although most European countries do. If you are unable to supply this certificate, you should state the reason why you cannot on Form M10.
- If you have lived in the United Kingdom for the last two years, although previously domiciled elsewhere, you will not be required to produce a certificate of no impediment to marriage.

The Marriage Schedule

Before a marriage can proceed a marriage schedule must be prepared by the registrar in the district where the wedding is to take place. This is prepared on the basis of the information and documents provided by the bride and groom, once the registrar is satisfied that there is no legal impediment to the marriage.

The registrar cannot issue the schedule more than seven days before the marriage and will advise you when to call to collect it. It cannot be collected on your behalf by a relative or friend, nor by your wedding planner – the registrar will issue it only to the prospective bride or bridegroom.

If you are having a non-civil wedding, the marriage schedule must be produced before the marriage ceremony to the person solemnising the marriage.

Immediately after the ceremony the schedule must be signed by both spouses, by the person solemnising the marriage and by the two witnesses. As the schedule is a permanent record an appropriate permanent black liquid ink should be used when signing it – a ball-point pen should not be used. You must arrange for the signed schedule to be returned to the registrar within three days so that the marriage can be registered.

If you are having a civil marriage the registrar will not issue the marriage schedule to you in advance, but will have it available at the marriage ceremony for signature, and will subsequently register the marriage.

Documents You Must Provide: Before the marriage schedule can be issued, you must supply the following documents to the registrar along with your notice of intention to marry (Form M10):

- Your original or authorised copy **birth certificate.** An unofficial photocopy is not acceptable. If you cannot produce this document, you must discuss this matter with the registrar and state the reason on Form M10.
- Where appropriate, a **certificate of divorce** or **annulment** or a **certified copy decree.** A decree of divorce granted outside Scotland must be absolute or final – a decree nisi is not acceptable. If you have been married more than once, only the document relating to the termination of the most recent marriage is required. If you are unable to produce the official decree of divorce or annulment you must state the reason for not doing so. The registrar will require proof of the termination of the earlier marriage.
- In addition, there are certain questions to be answered by parties who submit foreign divorce/dissolution documents:
- What is the name, age and present usual residence of the parties to the proposed marriage?
- When were the divorce/dissolution proceedings started?
- What were the habitual residence and domicile of each of the parties to the divorce/dissolution on (a) date proceedings commenced; and (b) completion of divorce/dissolution?
- If habitually resident in UK what was the period of residence prior to (a) commencement of divorce/dissolution; AND (b) completion of divorce/dissolution?
- What was the nationality of the parties to the divorce/dissolution on date shown in (2) above?
- Did the pursuer appear personally in Court? If not, was he/she represented?
- Were reasonable steps taken to notify the defender that proceedings were being taken against him/her?
- Did the defender appear in Court? If not, was he/she represented?
- Where and when were the parties to the divorce/dissolution married/registered as civil partners?
- The **death certificate** of your former spouse if you are a widow or widower seeking to remarry. Once again, if you cannot produce this document, you must state the reason why. The registrar will need proof of the death of the former spouse

Additionally, if you are domiciled in a country outside the United Kingdom, you should supply:

- The **certificate of no impediment to marriage.** (Nationals of the United Kingdom, United States of America, Canada and Australia do not need to provide this certificate to marry in Scotland.)
- Your valid **passport** or other document allowing you to be in the country.
- If you were born outside the United Kingdom but have acquired British Citizenship, you must produce your **naturalisation/registration certificate** or a **full British passport.**

- If you are already in the United Kingdom and you are not a citizen of a country that is a member of the European Economic Union (or Switzerland), you will need a **Home Office Certificate of Approval** to marry in Scotland. For more information, visit the Home Office website at www.ind.homeoffice.gov.uk.
- In addition to the above documents, if you are subject to immigration control, you must hold a valid **marriage visit visa**; or have a **Home Office Certificate of Approval**; or have **settled status** in the United Kingdom. You will need to apply for the visa before you travel and supply it to the registrar along with your notice of marriage. For more information, see www.ukvisas.gov.uk; or contact your nearest British Embassy, Consulate or High Commission for advice; or call the Immigration and Nationality Enquiry Bureau on 0870 606 7766; or write to *Immigration and Nationality Directorate*, Lunar House, 40 Wellesley Road, Croydon, CR9 2BY for advice.
- Applying for a marriage visit visa is a straightforward procedure, and you should receive it within 10 days of application by mail to your nearest British Embassy, Consulate or High Commission, or on the same day if applying in person. The visa lasts 3 months.
- In the case of an application for a Home Office Certificate of Approval, you should allow 3 months for your application to be processed, but 70% of applications are decided within 3 weeks.
- If any of the above documents is in a language other than English, you must also provide a certified translation in English. The local authority for the area in which you intend to marry will be able to give you details of acceptable translators. Alternatively, seek advice from your country's British Embassy.
- You can expect to receive back from the registrar all original documents provided by you, usually within a week (postal services permitting) of the registrar receiving them. They are not retained by the registrar for any purpose other than for checking the facts contained within them.

EUROPEAN ECONOMIC AREA MEMBER STATES

Austria; Belgium; Cyprus; Czech Republic; Denmark; Estonia; Finland; France; Germany; Greece; Hungary; Iceland; Ireland; Italy; Latvia; Liechtenstein; Lithuania; Luxembourg; Malta; Netherlands; Norway; Poland; Portugal; Slovakia; Slovenia; Spain; Sweden; Switzerland; United Kingdom.

Witnesses

You must have two witnesses, aged 16 years or over, at your marriage, whether it is religious, non-religious or civil.

WEDDING FEES

- Civil ceremony at a registry office with two witnesses, £107.
- Individual local councils generally charge extra if you have more than two witnesses attending, require extra facilities, or for carrying out the ceremony outside Monday to Friday office hours or on Public Holidays. These charges vary by council area, but expect to pay between £150 and £200 depending on your requirements.
- Civil ceremony at an approved venue – fees charged vary by council area, but expect to pay between £150 and £400 depending on your requirements.
- Where the ceremony is a religious or non-religious one, the fee payable to the registrar for administering the submission of legal paperwork and preparing the marriage schedule is £60.50.
- The fee payable to a religious or non-religious celebrant is a private matter between the couple and the celebrant, but a reasonable guide-price would be between £130 and £250.
- Humanist wedding celebrants charge £250 plus 50p per mile travel expenses, and £30 for a wedding rehearsal if one is required.
- Registrars will usually accept payment of fees by cheque drawn on a British Bank, or a sterling bank draft. Some registrars will accept payment of fees by credit card but you will need to confirm this by contacting the relevant registrar.
- If you are using a weddings agency to arrange your marriage, they can normally submit payment of fees on your behalf to the registrar.
- The current fee for a marriage visa is £65, payable in local currency.
- The current fee for a Home Office Certificate of Approval is £295 per applicant.

Renewal of Vows & Commitment Ceremonies

Provided you satisfy the normal entry requirements to the United Kingdom as a visitor or tourist, you will not be required to provide any documents in respect of a Renewal of Vows or Commitment Ceremony held in Scotland.

Entry Regulations

Witnesses, guests, and couples visiting Scotland to renew their vows or for a commitment ceremony should satisfy the regulations regarding entering the UK as a visitor or tourist. To check the requirments regarding your personal circumstances, go to www.ukvisas.gov.uk and www.ind.homeoffice.gov.uk or enquire at your local British Consulate or Mission.

CIVIL PARTNERSHIPS

The UK Civil Partnership Act 2004 came into force on 5ᵗʰ December 2005. For the first time, same-sex couples were able to make a public commitment to one another which gave them some legal protection in the event of the breakdown of the relationship or the death of one partner.

A Civil Partnership is not, legally, a marriage; and a Civil Partnership ceremony is not, strictly speaking, a 'wedding'. It is a legally binding contract between two people which accords each of them certain rights and obligations with regard to property, children and conduct towards each other. The legal benefits include rights to a deceased partner's pension; to a capital sum if the relationship, and thus the partnership, breaks down; and to rights of residence in the shared home. The legal responsibilities include those relating to financial maintenance and the sharing of property in the event of the partnership breaking down. These rights and responsibilities are enforceable by a court of law.

A Civil Partnership is only for same sex couples, and is sometimes referred to as a 'same sex union'. You will commonly see the terms, 'gay weddings' and 'lesbian weddings'. Legally speaking, these are wrong. A Civil Partnership is analogous to a traditional heterosexual marriage but there are significant differences – for example, a heterosexual marriage is not a marriage if it is not consummated, and can be annulled. This is not the case with a Civil Partnership where consummation is not a legal requirement.

It is important to stress that the law relating to Civil Partnerships applies throughout the United Kingdom. However, Scottish law permits Civil Partnership ceremonies to take place not only in registry offices – as is the case in the rest of the United Kingdom; they can take place in any venue licensed by the local authority for that purpose. This is the same as for the traditional heterosexual civil marriage ceremony in Scotland.

There can be no religious element to a Civil Partnership ceremony. It is, as the name implies, solely a civil matter and is sanctioned by the State, not by any recognised Church.

There is no legally prescribed form of Civil Partnership registration ceremony. The Registrar General has suggested a form of ceremony to local registrars but they are not bound to adhere to it. If you have particular wishes with regard to the ceremony, including the words to be used, please contact the registrar for the district within which your Civil Partnership is to be registered and discuss your ideas with him or her.

Because the registration of a Civil Partnership is secular in nature, the legal formalities (and any ceremony that the registrar agrees to perform) must not contain any religious element. However, if you would like to have a religious ceremony or blessing, then you may arrange this entirely separately from the legal formalities of registering your Civil Partnership.

Detailed information relating to your particular circumstances can be obtained from *Marriage/Civil Partnership Section*, New Register House, Edinburgh EH1 3YT; tel 0131-334 0380; www.gro-scotland.gov.uk.

Who Can Register a Civil Partnership In Scotland?

Any two persons can register a Civil Partnership in Scotland, regardless of their nationalities or where they live, provided:

- Both persons are 16 years of age or over.
- The conditions relating to forbidden degrees of relationship are adhered to.
- Each is unmarried or not already registered as a Civil Partner, or the conditions regarding previous marriage or Civil Partnerships are adhered to.
- They are of the same sex.
- They are capable of understanding the nature of a Civil Partnership and giving valid consent.
- They complete the required paperwork and pay the appropriate fees.

Prohibitions

There are degrees of relationship, by consanguinity, by affinity, and by adoption which will render a Civil Partnership registration unlawful. A man may not enter into a Civil Partnership agreement with his blood relatives as follows:

- Father.
- Son.
- Grandfather.
- Grandson.
- Brother.
- Uncle.
- Nephew.
- Great-grandfather.
- Great-grandson.

Or his relatives by affinity as follows:

- Former wife's son or grandson.
- Former Civil Partner's son or grandson.
- Mother's or grandmother's former husband.
- Father's or grandfather's former Civil Partner.
- **The above excepting:-** Parties related by affinity must be 21 years of age or over at the time of the Civil Partnership registration and the younger must not, before his or her 18th birthday, have lived in the same household as the other party and been treated by that person as a child of the family.

Or his relatives by adoption as follows:

- Adoptive father.
- Adopted son.

A woman may not enter into a Civil Partnership agreement with her blood relatives as follows:

- Mother.
- Daughter.
- Grandmother.
- Granddaughter.
- Sister.
- Aunt.
- Niece.
- Great-grandmother.
- Great-granddaughter.

Or her relatives by affinity as follows:

- Former husband's daughter or granddaughter.
- Former Civil Partner's daughter or granddaughter.
- Father or grandmother's former wife.
- Mother's or grandmother's former civil partner.
- **The above excepting**:- Parties related by affinity must be 21 years of age or over at the time of the Civil Partnership registration and the younger must not, before his or her 18th birthday, have lived in the same household as the other party and been treated by that person as a child of the family.

Or her relatives by adoption as follows:

- Adoptive mother.
- Adopted daughter.

Giving Notice of a Civil Partnership

Any Scottish registrar can supply you with the Civil Partnership Notice (Form CP10). Registrars and their contact details are listed at
www.gro-scotland.gov.uk/regscot/groslocate/index.html

- Complete Form CP10 and submit it, along with all other necessary documentation and appropriate fees to the registrar for the district within which your Civil Partnership is to be registered.
- The absolute minimum notification period for a Civil Partnership is 15 clear days but, normally, you should aim to get the notices to the registrar four weeks beforehand or, if either of you has been married previously or been a party to a previous Civil Partnership, the notices should be with the registrar six weeks before the intended registration. As with traditional heterosexual marriages, these timings are built into the system to allow the registrar to satisfy himself or herself that you are free and legally entitled to be partners to a Civil Partnership registration.
- You will need to make out a very strong case of exceptional circumstances to the Registrar General before a Civil Partnership registration could be sanctioned with less than 15 day's notice.

- You need not submit the Civil Partnership Notice to the registrar in person. However, one of you might be required to attend prior to the registration should questions be raised about information supplied by either of you on the form or other relevant documents.
- You will both be required to sign a declaration to the effect that the information you supply in connection with your intended Civil Partnership registration is correct. All details will be checked for accuracy by the Registrar General.
- If you are not a United Kingdom national, you will be asked to provide proof of your nationality and your right to be in the country for the purpose of registering a Civil Partnership.

The Civil Partnership Schedule

Once you have fulfilled all the legal requirements, paid the necessary fees and produced the necessary documents, and once the registrar is satisfied that there is no legal impediment to the registration of your Civil Partnership, he or she will prepare the Civil Partnership Schedule, without which no Civil Partnership registration can take place.

The registrar will produce the schedule at the registration ceremony, wherever that is to be held, the details of which must be confirmed as correct by you both.

The schedule must be signed by both parties to the partnership, by the registrar, and by two witnesses.

The registrar will later extract information from the schedule for the Civil Partnership register. Once this has been done, you can obtain copies of your Civil Partnership registration certificate upon payment of the appropriate fee.

Documents You Must Provide: There are a number of documents you must supply to the registrar along with your Civil Partnership Notice (Form CP10). The documents you must produce are very similar to those required for a heterosexual marriage, listed in *Marriage Legislation*. There are two differences, as follows:

- Unlike persons seeking a traditional heterosexual marriage in Scotland, there is no requirement for you to provide a Certificate of No Impediment in respect of a Civil Partnership registration.
- If you are subject to immigration control, and have neither a Home Office Certificate of Approval nor settled status in the United Kingdom, you must hold a valid **civil partnership visit visa.** This in place of the marriage visit visa. Details of how to apply for this are explained in *Marriage Legislation* – the process is exactly the same for a civil partnership visa.

Registration of Civil Partnerships in Approved Places

The only local authority in which it is not yet possible to register a Civil Partnership other than at a register office, is the Western Isles. Registrars there, although legally obliged to carry out registrations, have declined to offer 'wedding-type ceremonies' on moral grounds.

In all other local authority areas, you may register your Civil Partnership at any place, including a register office, licensed by the local authority for this purpose, also known as 'an approved place'. However, the place or venue must not be in religious premises nor have ever been used solely or mainly for religious purposes.

The full list of approved places can be viewed at:
www.gro-scotland.gov.uk/regscot/getting-married-in-scotland/civil-marriages-in-approved-places.html

Witnesses

You will require two witnesses, both aged 16 years or over, at your Civil Partnership registration, wherever it takes place.

HOW TO ORGANISE THE BIG DAY YOURSELF

Budget

The first thing to decide is how much you can afford to spend on your wedding. It is important to be completely realistic from the very beginning, because although you may want a huge wedding with every one of your friends and relatives present, if you or whoever will be paying for the wedding has a limited budget, you will only end up being disappointed.

It is common for prospective wedding couples to greatly underestimate the cost of their wedding, often finding that it will actually cost them at least twice as much as they budgeted for. A recent survey found that couples guessed that their wedding would cost them £6,500 on average, whereas the actual average cost of a wedding in the UK is £16,000. In addition to underestimating the costs of the main items, it is all too easy to forget other things which are essential for the wedding and have to add them on at the end, thus adding to the total. For this reason it is wise to draw up a checklist right at the start, with everything listed alongside the maximum amount you intend to spend on each item.

The difficulty is that, until you start investigating possible venues, and can tell those venues how many people will be attending, you cannot easily begin to set a budget. Depending on the type of venue you want, the number of guests you will have, and whether you want exclusive use of the venue or are happy for your wedding and reception to take place while other guests are using the venue, you can pay anything from a couple of hundred to several thousand pounds for the hire of the venue.

As the hire of the wedding venue is likely to be the single most expensive item in your budget, the first step is to draw up a shortlist of venues which might be suitable for what you have in mind and contact them for details of their fees. Many of the castles and hotels which advertise weddings will send you a 'wedding pack' which should detail all their fees and explain what is included in the cost. It is unlikely that you will be able to access this information online without contacting the venue direct, as they all stress that each wedding is unique, and costs will therefore vary depending on your specific requirements. Some venues with their own website have an online enquiry form which asks you for basic details of your requirements. They will then contact you with further details.

Once you have a firm idea of the cost of your chosen venue, you know how much you can afford to spend on the rest of the the wedding, keeping within your budget by adjusting the amount you spend on each element.

How Much Will It Cost?

Because every wedding is different, and venues charge vastly different prices depending on what they include in their services, in addition to variations depending on their type, status and popularity, it is extremely difficult to give meaningful guidelines as to how much your wedding might cost.

Depending on what is included, estimates of the average cost of a wedding vary between £15,000 and £20,000

A mid-range survey of the average cost of the wedding day and honeymoon came up with the following:

Typical Costs	£
Bride's dress	683
Groom and best man's suit hire	148
Bridesmaids' dresses	303
Page boy suit hire	57
Rings	1910
Photography	729
Video	595
Reception	5968
Cake	268
Car hire	226
Church fees	447
Flowers	163
Stationery	412
Bride's going away outfit	246
Honeymoon	5215
Total	**17370**

Regional Costs	£
London	22906
Scotland	18227
South-West	17971
West Midlands	17899
East Midlands	17483
North	16945
North-East	16944
North-West	16793
South-East	16383
Wales	16293
East Anglia	15302
Northern Ireland	15296

Ancillaries such as the cost of the engagement ring, proposal night trip away and stag and hen nights push the price up even higher.

One wedding planner says:
It's hard to say what percentage of the total budget for a wedding typically goes on the venue, since all weddings and venues are different. There are so many variables, including the number of guests, whether they stay overnight, and for how many nights, how many meals they take at the venue, and so forth. Some venues, for example, prefer to charge less for their hire fee, but charge correspondingly more for the wedding banquet.

Finding a Venue

With literally thousands of venues to choose from in Scotland, all offering different facilities and a different 'feel' for your wedding, this is the biggest decision you will make. This most important of aspects is dealt with in depth in *Choosing a Venue*. Here you will find advice, information and an extensive directory of unique venues, divided by type and geographical area, to help you choose the one which suits you best.

What Type of Ceremony?

For a wedding ceremony, you can choose between a religious service, a non-religious but 'spiritual' service, and a civil ceremony. If you choose to have a civil ceremony, you may opt to have a religious blessing from a minister either immediately afterwards or some time later.

Civil Partnerships are purely civil ceremonies, but the Church of Scotland allows ministers to give a religious blessing after or during civil partnership ceremonies. The decision on this is left to individual ministers – some will not do so if it is against their conscience.

Commitment ceremonies, which have no legal standing but are a way of heterosexual or homosexual couples publicly expressing their love for and commitment to each other, may be secular, religious or spiritual in tone.

Advice is given below on who to contact if you choose to have a religious or non-religious ceremony. Remember that you will also have to contact the Registrar in the area where you will be married, as this is the person who will prepare your marriage schedule. You will have to collect it from the register office, in person, before your wedding.

Religious Weddings

In Scotland, a religious wedding may be held anywhere, as long as you can find a minister to perform the ceremony. If you choose a church wedding, all you need to do is to contact the church to make the arrangements and a minister will be provided.

If, however, you choose a religious ceremony to be performed anywhere other than a church, it may be less easy to find a minister to carry out the ceremony. If your venue is one which regularly holds weddings, they should be able to arrange a minister to perform the ceremony. If you want to marry in a more unusual location – by a lochside, for example, or on the site of an ancient ruin – you may have to source a minister yourself. You may be able to track one down by contacting the Head Office of the religious denomination you choose, or they may be able to put you in contact with one of their, often retired, ministers who are available to hire for weddings.

If you have difficulty finding anybody to perform your ceremony, you could try contacting a wedding agency. Many of them will provide you with contact details of a minister even if they are not organising the rest of the wedding – they may charge you for providing this information.

CHURCHES OF SCOTLAND

Associated Presbyterian Churches of Scotland: APC Manse, Polvinister Road, Oban, PA34 5TN; tel 01631-567076; www.apchurches.org

Baptist Union of Scotland: 14 Aytoun Road, Glasgow G41 5RT; tel 0141-433 4551; www.scottishbaptist.org.uk

The Church of Scotland: Church Office, 121 George Street, Edinburgh EH2 4YN; tel 0131-225 5722; www.churchofscotland.org.uk

The Free Church of Scotland: 15 North Bank Street, The Mound, Edinburgh EH1 2LS; tel 0131-226 5286; www.freechurch.org

The Free Presbyterian Church of Scotland: Free Presbyterian Manse, Laide, Ross-shire, IV22 2NB; www.fpchurch.org.uk

Methodist Church: Methodist Church House, 25 Marylebone Road, London NW1 5JR; 020 7486 5502;
http://scottishchristian.com/churches/methodist/

Reformed Presbyterian Church of Scotland: Linden House, Westermavisbank Avenue, Airdrie, ML6 0HD; 01236-753971; www.rpcscotland.org

The Roman Catholic Church: Secretariat of the Bishops' Conference of Scotland, 64 Aitken Street, Airdrie ML6 6LT; tel 01236-764061; www.bpsconfscot.com

The Scottish Episcopal Church: General Synod, 21 Grosvenor Crescent, Edinburgh EH12 5EE; tel 0131-225 6357; www.scotland.anglican.org

United Free Church of Scotland: General Secretary, 11 Newton Place, Glasgow G3 7PR; tel 0141-332 3435; www.ufcos.org.uk

United Reformed Church: 340 Cathedral Street, Glasgow G1 2BQ; tel: 0141 332 7667 www.urcscotland.org.uk

---

Most Christian denominations in Scotland will be happy to perform ceremonies, even if you do not belong to the same denomination. The largest Christian denominations in Scotland are the Church of Scotland, the Scottish Episcopal Church, the Free Presbyterian Church (also known as the 'wee free'), the Associated Presbyterian Church and the Roman Catholic church. The minister will normally be happy to devise a service which will suit your particular beliefs. The exception to this is if you are a Catholic. Only a Catholic priest may conduct Catholic weddings, and in normal circumstances it would have to be in a Catholic church. If you find you cannot have a Catholic wedding where you choose, an option may be to marry in your own church and have a blessing later in a Scottish venue. You should always speak to your own priest first to discuss the options with him. An option if you wish to have a Catholic ceremony is to arrange your wedding at Traquair House in the Scottish Borders, an old royal hunting lodge which has a private Catholic chapel in the grounds. For full details, see the *Directory of Venues.*

There is generally no charge for a church wedding, but a donation will always be gratefully accepted. When you hire a minister to marry you outside his own church, he will charge you a fee.

Non-religious Weddings

There are two alternatives if you are not religious, but would like a ceremony which expresses your personal ideals and aspirations and shows your commitment to marriage in a more emotionally satisfying way than a civil ceremony may afford. Certain non-religious groups have legally registered celebrants who can, just like ministers of religion, officiate at wedding ceremonies at any venue in Scotland. These do not have to be 'approved' or 'licensed' venues.

- The Humanist Society of Scotland has registered celebrants living in all parts of Scotland, and they will travel to your chosen venue to officiate at the ceremony. Contact a celebrant in the relevant area by telephone. Their names and numbers are listed on the society's website.
- If you have spiritual beliefs which do not fit with mainstream religious beliefs, try contacting the Findhorn Foundation at Forres, near Inverness. They have registered celebrants who will travel anywhere in Scotland to officiate at your wedding.

THE FINDHORN PHILOSOPHY

The Findhorn Foundation is the educational and organisational cornerstone of the Findhorn Community, and its work is based on the values of planetary service, co-creation with nature and attunement to the divinity within all beings. We believe that humanity is engaged in an evolutionary expansion of consciousness, and seek to develop new ways of living infused with spiritual values. We have no formal creed or doctrine. We recognise and honour all the world's major religions as the many paths to knowing our own inner divinity.

Humanist or Findhorn celebrants will work with you to devise a wedding ceremony which suits you perfectly, and encourage you to include music, songs and readings of prose or poetry of your choice. Each ceremony is individually tailored to the couple, so your wedding will be completely unique.

Websites

The Humanist Society of Scotland: www.humanism-scotland.org.uk
The Findhorn Foundation: www.findhorn.org

Civil Ceremonies

If you choose to have a civil ceremony, there are restrictions on the places where you can marry. You may marry in any register office in Scotland, or at an 'Approved' place which is licensed for Civil Weddings or Civil Partnerships. Contact the registrar in the area where you wish to marry.

Since the law was changed to allow civil weddings in places other than register offices, there has been a rapidly growing list of venues which have been licensed as approved places. There are hundreds to choose from, including castles, hotels and other more unusual locations such as sporting stadia, and more are being added all the time. For an up to date list see the website of the General Register Office for Scotland.

A civil wedding or partnership ceremony must be performed by a registrar. However, you may arrange for a minister or other celebrant to attend and perform a blessing immediately after the ceremony if you wish. Contact them as above to discuss the matter. Please note that Church of Scotland ministers will only attend civil partnership ceremonies if it accords with their individual conscience. Not all ministers will agree to this.

Website
General Register Office for Scotland:
www.gro-scotland.gov.uk/regscot/groslocate/index.html

A ONCE-IN-A-MILLENNIUM OCCASION
Elizabeth and David Prais from Minneapolis made sure their wedding was an occasion never to be repeated – at least, not for a thousand years! They married at the Manor House Hotel in Oban on the stroke of midnight on the Millennium (31st December 1999).

Themed Weddings

Before you start contacting suppliers, it is sensible to try to get a vision of what you want your wedding to be like. Many couples choose a theme for the day, which helps to bring all the disparate elements together into a cohesive whole.

A theme can be as simple as a colour scheme, which runs through everything from the wedding outfits to the flowers, table decorations and wedding cake, or as complex as a full-scale dramatic production, where eveybody including the guests are dressed in appropriate costume.

As you have chosen to have your wedding in Scotland, a theme relevant to the country is a popular choice. Or, if you are marrying in a castle, a stately home, an abbey or a ruin, you could choose a historical theme appropriate to the era building dates from.

Alternatively, the theme can be connected with the season: a Valentine's Day or Christmas wedding, for example; or with a pastime you and your partner are passionate about – maybe on top of a Scottish mountain, if you are both keen hillwalkers.

A MEDIEVAL MARRIAGE

Cindy and Frank Rikkers from the Netherlands married at the ruined Castle Tioram, which sits on a tidal island in Loch Moidart and can be reached on foot via a causeway which is uncovered at low tide. The castle dates from the 13th century so they and their guests dressed in colourful medieval costumes, with plenty of velvet and brocade in evidence for the women, ancient style kilts for the men. The entire party walked across the causeway, the ceremony took place on the shore in front of the castle, and informal photos were taken as the wedding party explored the island and the castle. Timing was crucial, as the wedding party has to ensure that they got back across to the mainland before the tide cut them off!

Ideas for Themes

- A Celtic wedding: Include a handfasting ceremony, exchange wedding rings with celtic knot designs which are reproduced on the stationery and name cards, incorporate traditional Gaelic music played on a clarsach (Gaelic harp).
- A Victorian wedding: Choose as the venue a stately home dating from the era, with couple and guests dressed in Victorian costume and the reception a formal banquet served by candlelight.
- A Sporting wedding: If you are both sports fans, you could marry at Hampden Stadium (soccer) or Murrayfield (rugby). Choose a colour scheme which reflects your team's colours and decorate the reception with sporting memorabilia.
- A Garden wedding: If you are keen gardeners, why not choose one of Scotland's many gorgeous gardens for your wedding. e.g. Inverewe Garden in the Highlands, or Edinburgh's Botanic Gardens.
- A Shopaholic's wedding: Edinburgh's up-market Harvey Nichols store was the first retail shop in Scotland to be granted a civil wedding licence. With views across Edinburgh's historic city centre, a luxury food hall, its own restaurant, and floors full of designer clothes and other goods, everything you need for a luxurious wedding is available under one roof.
- A Lochside wedding: Exchange your vows on the shores of a loch followed by a picnic reception and a boat trip on the loch as the sun goes down.
- A Traditional Scottish wedding: Go all out on the Scottish theme, with the men in kilts, a tartan weddign dress and the bridesmaids with tartan sashes; have a bouquet and buttonholes incorporating thistles and heather; hire a bagpiper; serve a menu full of Scottish produce – haggis, salmon and venison followed by whisky cranachan; have a wedding cake decorated with heather and tartan ribbons; end the night with a ceilidh.

Who To Invite?

This can be a thorny problem – unless you have a very small wedding where you restrict the guest list to your very closest friends and relatives, you may be committed to a very large wedding where you can invite absolutely everybody you know, so nobody is upset by being left out.

At the other end of the scale, there is no need for you to invite anybody at all. There is a legal requirement for two witnesses to attend, but if you ask the venue or the registrar if they can provide two people willing to be witnesses, they will in most cases be happy to oblige.

If you choose a very small wedding, just yourselves and maybe a couple of friends or relatives, you can have a big reception for everybody to attend when you get back home. If you would like to include some form of ceremony at the reception you could arrange to have a blessing when everybody is present.

The Invitations

There are many alternatives when it comes to inviting people to your wedding. The conventional approach is to order personalised invitations from a wedding stationery provider. They will be able to suggest different wordings and different styles of card to suit your requirements. When ordering decide whether you want to include a reply card in the envelope, and whether you want separate reception invitations for guests invited only to the recepetion.

Looking ahead, you may also wish to order thank you cards for your own use when writing thank you notes for wedding gifts. You can also order matching name cards to indicate seating positions for the reception. If you order all your stationery together, well in advance of the wedding – at least three months in advance – you should be able to take advantage of any discounts offered.

When deciding on the design of your stationery, take into account any theme you have in mind. It's a nice touch to use the same colour scheme, for example, on the invitations as will be evident on the day.

If your wedding is to be less formal, and/or you wish to save money, you could make your own invitations, producing them on your home computer or writing individual notes to guests. Oral invitations too are also acceptable, although it is perhaps far safer to have something in writing, leaving no room for error with date, time or place. Always ask your guests to let you know if they will be able to attend, so you have precise numbers for catering. Don't forget to include a reply address, or enclose a reply card with a pre-addressed envelope.

It is useful to include with the invitation details of nearby accommodation for those who are travelling from some distance. Make it clear whether you will be paying for the guests' accommodation or not.

If you are travelling from abroad for your Scottish wedding, the whole business of inviting guests from home may be more complex and will have to be carefully budgeted for. Will you be paying for their flights? If not, consider whether they will be able to afford to pay for their own, as this may cause embarrassment. In such a case, a simple card with the details of the wedding on it may not be sufficient. It may need to be accompanied by details of available flights, airlines and so forth. The easiest and most enjoyable thing may be for everybody to fly as a party – and you may be able to arrange a discount on your flights if you book them all together.

Send out your invitations at least six weeks before the wedding to allow people ample time to make plans to attend. If you have fixed your wedding date a very long time in advance, you might want to give your most important guests prior notification of the date as soon as it is fixed so they can keep it clear in their diaries. Then send them an invitation as a reminder when you send out the rest.

STANDARD INVITATION WORDINGS

When, as is traditional, the parents of the bride act as hosts, the invitation is from them, e.g:

Mr and Mrs John Franklyn
request the pleasure of the company of
....
at the marriage of their daughter Emily
to
Mr Peter Barker
at the Balmoral Hotel, Edinburgh
on Saturday 12th August 2007
at two o'clock

When the couple act as hosts, the wording is changed to suit, e.g:

Miss Mary Downey and Mr Henry Llewellyn
would love you to join them at their marriage
at Aberdeen Register Office
on Wednesday 20th June 2008
at 10:00 am
and afterwards for a lunch reception at
Ardoe House, Aberdeen

There are all sorts of conventions concerning the precise wording of invitations and of replies, and the 'correct' way to do things. Nowadays, people are not such sticklers for form and it is pretty much up to you how you word your invitations, and whether you use a formal or informal approach. One way of cutting down on postage costs is to send email invitations, which may be perfectly acceptable by people who commonly correspond electronically. You may wish to give even those you invite by letter the option of responding by email.

However, if you are a traditionalist and you wish to make sure you do everything 'by the book', the website *Hitched* has articles on all aspects of the etiquette of wedding invitations. www.hitched.co.uk/stationery/index.asp.

Civil Partnership Invitations: The foregoing comments apply, of course, just as much to invitations to Civil Partnership ceremonies, with necessary changes to the wording. It is possible to buy stationery where the words *Civil Partnership* or *Ceremony of Commitment* replace the usual *Wedding Invitation*.

Ring the Changes

Rings have been exchanged by couples for many centuries, both as a token of affection and as a mark of a betrothal. It is only since the nineteenth century, however, that the modern practice of the woman wearing a jewelled engagement ring before her marriage, to be joined by a plain gold wedding band on the wedding day itself, has become common. Of more recent date is the practice of the husband too wearing a ring, although this is still less common than the wife doing so.

Despite the fact that the exchange of wedding rings is now an almost universal practice in the UK, there is actually no legal requirement for either bride or groom to wear a wedding ring. Having a period of engagement before the wedding, accompanied by the man giving his fiancee a ring, seems to be less common than it once was, now that many couples habitually live together for some time before they decide to marry.

However, if you choose to go the traditional route, think about choosing your engagement ring and wedding ring(s) together, as you may want a matching engagement/wedding ring suite. Sometimes the jewelled engagement ring and the plainer wedding band are designed to link together when worn.

If both partners are to wear rings, again it is a nice idea to buy a matching 'his 'n' hers' set.

There is a great choice of wedding rings now available, with the plain yellow gold band often being substitued by an engraved ring in other metals, such as platinum, white or rose gold, silver or a mixture of several.

If you wish your ring to be particularly appropriate for your Scottish wedding, there are some beautiful rings available engraved with or woven into celtic knot designs. If you wish to buy your ring in advance, they are available by mail order. Alternatively, allow extra time to choose your ring once you arrive in Scotland.

What to Wear?

The Bride

Whether you choose to dress traditionally in a full-length white wedding dress, or prefer something less conventional, you will almost certainly be buying your dress long before the big day. If you live outside Scotland, therefore, details of Scottish wedding dress suppliers will probably not be relevant. However, a selection will be found in the *Directory of Suppliers* (below).

If your groom is wearing tartan, you may wish to 'get into the sprit' of the Scottish experience yourself by adding a touch of tartan to your outfit. This could take the form of a discreet tartan ribbon in your bouquet, a tartan shawl to wrap around you (which could be very practical if the weather turns cold or wet) to a full tartan wedding dress, which can be a stunning choice if you really want to make a dramatic entrance!

The kilt is traditionally a male garment, and women do not generally wear them. You will find full length 'evening kilts' designed for women, but this wouldn't generally be seen as appropriate as a wedding outfit, although fine for your guests.

Before you decide on your dress and accessories it is important to consider whether the venue you have chosen will put any restrictions on what it is most appropriate to wear. Because castles were built with a view to keeping people out, many of them are difficult to navigate in a full-skirted, full-length gown with veil, train and high heels. You may find that it is not possible for your wedding car to drive you all the way to the place where the ceremony will take place and that you will be required to walk at least part of the way from the arrival point.

In some places – Urquhart Castle by Loch Ness, for example – there is a fairly long walk down to the castle ruin where the ceremony takes place, so it may be a good idea to take some flat shoes to walk down in, and give your high heels to your attendant to carry. The path at Urquhart Castle is paved, but in other places you may have to negotiate a muddy pathway if it has been raining (not unusual in Scotland, of course!) However, not to worry – it is now quite chic to wear flowered wellingtons with your wedding dress if conditions dictate!

Other venues, such as the Wallace Monument at Stirling, require you to climb many stone stairs up a narrow tower. Wearing a full-skirted wedding gown here would be tricky or even dangerous – and certainly not romantic!

If you are having your ceremony out of doors, remember that Scotland may be cold and/or wet at any time of year, so ensure you and the wedding party have umbrellas and warm cover-ups. When you choose to marry outdoors in the Highlands between May and September you should also bear in mind that you are likely to have uninvited guests in the form of the midge – a tiny biting insect which gathers in swarms on warm overcast days and has an effect out of all proportion to its size! The purchase of midge repellant should be an essential part of your wedding preparations.

Where the terrain may affect your choice of wedding costume, do contact the venue before you pick your outfit so they can advise you.

Transporting your Wedding Dress: If you are travelling to Scotland from abroad, the safest way to carry your wedding dress is probably as hand luggage, but always enquire with the airline when you book your ticket as to what they advise.

You may wish to send your wedding dress separately. This can be a good idea if you will be travelling about the UK before your wedding and do not want to have to carry it with you. You can send it on ahead as a package, but make sure that it is clearly marked as a wedding dress for your personal use so that you can avoid any customs duty or import tax. There should be no duty payable if sending a package within Europe. If sending from other countries you should get advice from the airline or ferry company as to what forms you need to fill in. If sending from the USA or Canada, see below for advice.

You may be able to arrange for a friend, relative or maybe even somebody from your wedding venue to collect the dress for you, and have it nicely pressed ready for your big day. Alternatively, you may be able to leave it at the receiving depot for a certain length of time, but do check whether there is a charge made for storage.

TEMPORARY IMPORT FROM USA OR CANADA

If sending your dress or any other personal effects from the USA or Canada, you do need to fill in a customs form to ensure you aren't charged import duty. Ring CUSTOMS 0845-010-9000 (UK tel. number) for advice. You should write the following code onto the customs form when sending a package from USA/Canada: **CPC530050.** This code allows your package to be classed as a 'temporary import' which means you won't be charged import duty. It basically means that you will be bringing into the UK a certain item which will leave the country after a certain period of time.

If for any reason you end up being charged customs duty, you may have to pay it in order to collect your package, then claim your money back later. Make sure you obtain a C285 repayment form to prove the items leave the UK again. Customs will need to sign this form, and you should enclose your airline ticket with it when claiming reimbursement. For further details see *HM Revenue & Customs:* www.hmrc.gov.uk

---

The conventional approach is not for everyone. Some couples want their wedding day to be deliberately informal or unusual, and should choose their outfits to reflect that aspect of their personalities. From the wild and wacky to the understated and comfortable, it should be your choice.

In the past, the idea of buying a dress especially for one's wedding day, never to be worn again, would have been seen as terribly extravagant. Brides wore their 'best' clothes, or bought a day outfit which could be worn again. This approach saves the expense of a wedding dress, leaving you extra money to spend on something more practical, or even wildly impractical – and think how much extra you would have to spend on your honeymoon!

With the retro style in vogue, you could find yourself a unique wedding dress by going for the vintage look – there are many designs which hark back to previous eras. Or to be really authentic, why not find a genuine vintage wedding dress? Specialist suppliers have some gorgeous creations from different decades. So if you fancy a 1920s flapper style dress, or a romantic full-skirted 1950s satin gown, they are available, beautifully cleaned and restored to as good as new. And they are likely to be no more expensive than a modern 'vintage-style' dress.

Economies can be made without compromising on the wow factor: for instance, splash out on a special dress, but make sure it is a dress you could wear again. There are lots of beautiful evening dresses in the shops, any one of which would make a great wedding dress but still be wearable for dances and other special occasions, including other people's weddings. If you are having a wedding dress specially designed and made for you, discuss with the dress-maker how it could be adapted after the wedding to be useful for other occasions. For example, by shortening and dying it, you could end up with a great party dress.

Where your budget is restricted, there are thrifty ways of getting your wedding dress at a fraction of the cost. Most bridal wear shops generally have a few models which are available to hire. And don't overlook the possibility of buying a secondhand dress. As wedding dresses are bought to be worn only once, what you actually buy is a nearly new dress. By adding your own accessories or even, if you or somebody you know are clever with a needle and thread, by re-designing or re-trimming it, you could end up with a unique gown at a bargain price.

HAIR & BEAUTY

When you spend all that time choosing the perfect outfit, you will want to be sure your hair, make-up and nails are perfect on the day. If you are marrying a long way from home, check in advance that there is somebody locally who can ensure you are looking your best.

There is almost certain to be a salon or a travelling hairdresser and beautician local to the venue. To be on the safe side, ask the staff at your venue or accommodation if they can recommend somebody, and maybe book an appointment for you on the day of the wedding.

Some larger hotels have their own hairdressers and beauticians on-site, together with other therapies such as spas, massages and aromatherapy.

It is a good idea to have a 'dry run' at home at your regular salon. Take along your headdress, tiara or veil and choose a style of hair and make-up which suits it and your dress. Take photographs of the finished look, so that when you are in Scotland, the hairdresser and make-up artist can reproduce it.

Bridesmaids

Deciding on suitable bridesmaids' dresses can be tricky, especially if you are having several attendants of different ages. What looks adorable on a six year old, is most unlikely to suit, or please, a twenty-something.

Another difficult question can be, who should pay for them? If you want your bridesmaids to wear a specific design and colour of dress, which they would not have chosen for themselves, they may begrudge paying for it themselves. A solution is to simply choose a colour, preferably fairly neutral, which each bridesmaid can interpret in her own style. This then allows each girl to choose a dress which she will be able to wear again for other occasions, and she should then be more prepared to pay for her own dress. There are many choices in high street shops, or from bridal wear suppliers, who may also have bridesmaids' dresses for hire.

The modern trend is away from the full-skirted satin or chiffon 'meringue' to a more simple and elegant style. However, if you have very young bridesmaids who really want to dress up as fairy-tale princesses for the day, why not indulge them (and their mothers!) A striking alternative to dressing all your bridesmaids in one colour, is to allow them to be really individual and all choose their own favourites. Or why not have seven bridesmaids, one in each colour of the rainbow – makes for some great wedding photos!

Matron of Honour

If your chief bridesmaid is married herself, she is known as the Matron of Honour. It is her role to help the bride prepare for the day, and to organise the younger bridesmaids and page boys, if there are any, throughout the day. Her dress or suit should be chosen to be appropriate to her age group – she may not wish to be dressed the same way as the rest of the bridesmaids.

The Groom

It is traditional in Scotland for grooms and male wedding guests to wear the kilt. Most Scotsmen will own or hire a kilt in their own family tartan, which they will wear for such celebrations. Many grooms travelling to Scotland to marry take the opportunity to dress up in a kilt, even if they have never worn one before.

If you have Scottish family connections, there will be a family or clan tartan which you are entitled to wear. Each clan has several different versions of their tartan, so you are not restrIcted to one particualr pattern. You can still wear tartan if you do not have Scottish ancestry, as there are a number of 'free' tartans which may be worn by anybody. Alternatively, if you fancy a more contemporary take on the kilt, there are now kilts in plain-coloured fabrics, tweeds, or even leather, available to buy or hire.

There is a large kilt-hire industry in Scotland. You should be able to hire kilts for yourself and your best man and any other guests who wish to indulge, from a town near to your wedding. Many of them now will take orders over the internet, and have the kilts ready for you to pick up on the agreed date. Make sure you return them after the ceremony in good condition, and on time, or you may be charged extra.

Unless you intend to wear your kilt regularly, it is advisable to hire rather than buy, as a kilt can cost between £200 and £500 to buy, and if you want to do it properly you need to also buy such accessories as a sporran, waistcoat and jacket, kilt hose (socks), and a traditional *sgian dubh* (black dagger) to wear tucked into your sock. To hire a complete outfit should cost in the range of £50 - £150 depending on quality. If you or your male guests like the idea of wearing the tartan, but are not brave enough to go the lengths of wearing a kilt, an acceptable alternative is tartan trousers (or trews, as they are often known).

A kilt or tartan are not for everybdy, but a normal lounge suit, a morning suit, or even top hat and tails, are all perfectly acceptable alternatives for a Scottish wedding. If the groom wants to be as colourful and glamorous as his bride, there are some great ranges of suits in historical styles available online and in shops – from Regency dandy to Victorian formality, there are all the frock coats, embroidered waistcoats, top hats, boaters or fancy cravats you could want!

The Best Man

Normally, the best man will wear an outfit of the same type as the groom, so both will be in kilts, or in morning suits, or whatever. Some hire shops will give a discount if you hire several suits, or kilt outfits, at one time, so if several of your wedding guests wish to be similarly attired, it is worth hiring them together, even if you are paying for them individually. If a discount isn't automatically offered, it's always worth asking if they can do a deal. They are after your business so may be happy to oblige!

Page Boy

If you have young male relatives who you want to include in the wedding party, you can either designate them the bride's page boys, or groomsmen. Generally the best solution as far as their wedding costume is concerned is for them to wear a scaled-down version of the groom and best man's outfits.

Parents of the Bride & Groom

The parents of the happy couple may not have a specific role during the day, although they will doubtless have been involved in the behind-the-scenes arrangements, if only to put their hands in their pockets! The bride's father may be asked to give his daughter away, and if so will be called upon to propose one of the wedding toasts.

It should not be overlooked, however, that they may feel this is as important a day for them as for the couple themselves, and will want to dress accordingly. The men would normally dress to suit the choice of the bridegroom and best man – suit or kilt or tartan trews, as appropriate, while the mothers will need little bidding to search for a perfect dress or suit, complete with matching hat! There are many women's dress shops which specifically cater for 'mother of the bride' outfits.

Civil Partnerships

As civil partnerships are so new, there is nothing in the way of 'convention' to be guided by in the manner of dress. As same-sex couples may also be naturally attracted to a flamboyant style of dressing anyway, pretty much anything goes!

A range of solutions have been found to the problem of what is appropriate, with both partners in suits, both (in the case of lesbian couples) in dresses, or one in each. But what if both girls have always dreamt of having their white wedding dress when their big day comes? Well, why not make a really big entrance by having two brides, both in full white dress and veil, and each with their own team of bridesmaids. It has been done!

Harman Hay is a UK company which specialises in clothing for civil partnerships. They have a great range of unusual, gothic, gay and lesbian wedding suits and dresses. See *Directory of Suppliers* for contact details.

A BRIEF GUIDE TO THE KILT

The Kilt

Scotland's national costume, the kilt with sporran and jacket or waistcoat is known as 'Highland Dress' because it was originally only in the highlands that clans, with their own distinctive tartans, were found. However, nowadays, you will find the kilt worn for weddings and other celebrations, and occasionally as daily wear, all over the country.

Originally, Highlanders wore the *feileadh mor*, a large tartan blanket woven from wool. This was wrapped round the body, belted at the waist and pinned over the shoulder.

The modern kilt, knee length and with tailored pleats, is known as the *fealeadh beg* (filibeg). The word 'kilt' is not actually Gaelic, probably coming from an old English word meaning 'to hitch up and fold a garment'. The modern kilt is sometimes worn with a plaid, a long piece of tartan wrapped round the upper body, in effect a two-piece version of the old *feileadh mor*.

Highland Dress Styles

A kilt is normally worn with a sporran. This is a leather or animal fur bag or purse which hangs at the centre front of the kilt, attached by a chain or belt which passes through loops at the back of the kilt waistband.

In addition, woollen kilt hose (socks) with 'flashes' (a kind of garter) are worn. The traditional shoes to wear are 'ghillie brogues' – black leather shoes with laces which tie around the lower leg. A small dagger called a *sgian dubh* (skean doo) should be worn tucked into one sock.

Various styles of shirt, waistcoat or jacket may be worn with the kilt. Depending on the style of the shirt and jacket, a tie or bow tie may be worn. There are three basic styles of Highland dress:

- Daywear: the kilt is worn with a leather sporran, a tweed jacket with matching waistcoat, plain collared shirt and a woollen tie.
- Semi-formal: the kilt is worn with a leather or fur sporran, an Argyll jacket with matching waistcoat, plain or dress shirt, and a woollen tie or a bow tie.
- Evening wear: the kilt is worn with a fur and silver-trimmed sporran, a black Prince Charlie jacket and matching waistcoat, dress shirt and bow tie.

It has become popular in recent years for some grooms to go for the more 'romantic' look, as seen in the *Braveheart* film. The kilt is worn with a full-sleeved Jacobite shirt, fastened with leather or fabric laces, and a sleeveless jacket called a 'potaine'.

Important note: Always heed the advice of the kilt hire people as to how to wear your Highland dress outfit – it is not unknown for a groom to turn up at his wedding wearing the kilt the wrong way round. The pleats always go at the back!

The Tartan

Originally, the Scottish Tartan was an indication of status, the number of colours in the material indicating the rank of the wearer, from one colour for a servant, through to seven for a Chief.

Over the years, however, families (clans) designed their own distinctive tartans. There were various different patterns, using the same range of colours, to be worn on specific occasions or by particular members of the clan. These included:

- The Dress Tartan
- The Clan Tartan
- The Hunting Tartan

Originally, tartans were in the muted colours produced by natural dyes, but today much brighter colours can be achieved, so you may choose from 'ancient' and 'modern' shades of a specific tartan.

In addition to clan tartans there are District tartans which can be worn by anyone from a particular region. There are a few tartans which are known as 'free' tartans and may be worn by anybody, even if they have no connection to a Scottish clan. These include:

- Royal Stewart
- Black Watch
- Flower of Scotland

The Clan

Clan is the gaelic word for 'children', but it is more accurate to translate it as 'family'. The word began to be used in the Highlands in around the 13th cenutry, and a clan comprised an extended family group, the core of which was descended from a common ancestor.

Other families became attached to the major clans over the years, either through marriage or because they had sought protection from a stronger neighbouring clan, or in some cases where they had originally been tenants or servants of the clan chief.

Sometimes these subsidiary family groups adopted the clan name, but in many cases they retained their own family name. In this case they are known as 'septs' of the major clan. Some large clans now have dozens of septs. Members of a sept are entitled to wear the main clan tartans.

Useful books and websites

There are many books and websites which explain the history of the clans and their tartans in far more detail. These are just a few which will help you research your own Scottish clan connections.

Lochcarron Tartans: www.lochcarron.com

Burnetts & Struth Scottish Regalia:
www.burnetts-struth.com/dalglieshtartans.html

Scot Clans: www.scotclans.com

Scottish Clans & Family Names, Malcolm Innes (Mainstream Publishing, 1996)

Gathering the Clans: Tracing Scottish Family Ancestry on the Internet, Alan Stewart (Phillimore & Co, 2004)

What to Eat?

The Reception

The form your reception takes depends partly on the venue you have chosen for your ceremony, partly on the time of day, and partly on personal preferences. The traditional way is to have a 'wedding breakfast' after a morning ceremony, where the assembled guests have a sit-down midday meal of three or more courses, served by waiters. The wedding party sit at the top table, with the rest of the guests at long tables running at right angles to the top table, or at round or square tables spread throughout the room.

A popular alternative is to have a buffet which makes the occasion less formal and allows the guests to mingle more easily. As the guests will need to be able to leave and return to their seats easily, bearing plates piled high with good things to eat, it is best to have round tables seating six to twelve rather than long 'refectory' type tables where it can be difficult to get out from your seat while others are still eating.

If you prefer something with more of a 'party' atmosphere, a cocktails and canapes reception, with drinks and 'finger food', means that you don't need to provide formally laid tables with designated places for the guests. However, do make sure you provide enough chairs for your elderly or disabled guests. Make sure that there are plenty of substantial canapes provided so none of your guests go hungry. This sort of reception might be more suitable for an afternoon wedding, when you can assume that the guests have eaten lunch beforehand, otherwise they could be left feeling a little unsatisifed. However, if you have arranged a full meal or buffet for later in the day, drinks and nibbles could be provided to 'keep them going' until later.

When your guests have some distance to travel, or have work commitments, one option is to have an evening wedding, with the ceremony followed by a sitdown meal or a buffet, then a dance which carries on late into the evening. This means those travelling any distance only need to spend one night at a hotel, whereas a midday event might require them to stay both the night before and the night after the wedding. Do check, however, if there is any restriction on how late you can party. Check if the venue has a late drinks licence, and whether there is a cut-off time after which no music may be played. Each venue will be subject to local authority planning and licensing laws which may include certain restrictions designed for the comfort of local residents.

If you have a large guest list, the most suitable place for your reception is likely to be a hotel, a large castle, or a place with large function rooms, such as a conference centre or sports stadium. Any other type of venue is unlikely to be able to accommodate you all.

An alternative to this is to hire a local community hall near to where the ceremony is to take place. Most towns and villages in Scotland have a public hall, and they are keen to attract functions such as wedding receptions, to augment their often limited funds. They usually have all the facilities an outside caterer would require, including a kitchen and space to set up a bar. They may need to apply for a special licence for each event involving alcohol, but as long as you book far enough ahead, this should not be a problem.

If you are having a smaller wedding, you need to ensure that the reception is in a room which is not so big that you and your guests feel you are 'rattling around' in it, as this can lead to an uncomfortable and cold atmosphere. Hotels may have a smaller dining room suitable for your party, or may be able to provide a large table to seat all of you within their main dining room. Community halls too often have a choice of larger or smaller rooms most suited to the size of your wedding party.

Castles often have sumptuous dining halls which provide a magnificent setting for a reception. Bear in mind that many of them will only seat a limited number, maybe no more than 20 or so, but this can allow for an intimate 'dinner party' atmosphere for smaller weddings.

Formal Meal

For a formal wedding breakfast or evening meal, a hotel is the simplest choice because they will be able to cater for your requirements using their own staff. When you book your reception you will undoubtedly be sent details of the wedding catering choices they have available. Usually they will send you a number of set menus at different prices per head, so you can choose one which will suit your budget. They should include vegetarian options on the menu, but will almost certainly want to know in advance how many of your guests are vegetarians. Ask your guests to let you know whether they have any special dietary requirements.

There are a number of venues which do not have their own in-house catering staff who work with outside caterers to provide the wedding food. Some have given exclusive rights for catering their weddings to specific companies, while others allow you to hire outside caterers of your choice, although they may recommend particular local caterers. Historic Scotland and the National Trust for Scotland generally use specific outside caterers for specific venues. Details of the facilities and caterers available can be found on their website or by ringing them.

Glasgow City Council arranges weddings at a number of council-run venues, including museums, historic buildings and country parks. The catering is provided by their own specialised catering company.

If your wedding reception is taking place in a private house, in a marquee, or maybe even a picnic in a park, outside caterers will be able to provide all the food and drink, if you do not want the 'do it yourself' approach. There are many independent caterers throughout Scotland, details of which can be found on the internet, in the local Yellow Pages telephone directory or at www.yell.com. There are also some listed in the directory of suppliers. Most outside caterers will have a limited area they cover. If you want them to travel further, they may do this, but will charge extra to cover their travelling time and expenses. It is sensible to choose a local company wherever possible. As well as keeping costs down, the food will have less far to travel and so be in better condition when it arrives!

When using outside caterers, you will need to inform them of the kitchen facilities available on site. Remember that a formal meal for a fairly large party will require quite a large kitchen and adequate oven space. Although the caterers may have portable cooking facilities, this may not be suitable for what you have in mind if there is just not enough kitchen space at your chosen venue. In such a case you may be better opting for a buffet meal.

Alternatively, you could go for the quirky – some enterprising couples have gone deliberately 'down-market' and offered their guests fish and chips or bangers and mash at their receptions. If you have a favourite meal, why not share it with your guests on your special day?

Buffet

When you are sent details of the wedding catering, whether this is in-house or from an outside caterer, there will generally be a choice between sit-down or buffet menus. Buffets are a very popular choice, for a number of reasons. They tend to suit the less formal style of wedding which is many modern couples prefer; they can work out cheaper per head than a multi-course meal, which is an important consideration if your budget is limited; and with a dozen or more dishes, including meat, fish and vegetarian options, you have a better chance of having something to suit all your guests' different tastes – no easy matter when you invite everybody from close friends of your own age to very young and very old members of your family.

There will be a variety of different options, to suit a range of budgets. Again the menu will be priced at so much per head. Within that price range you will be able to choose a specified number of dishes from a wide selection. Nowadays these tend to be very cosmopolitan, with dishes inspired by many different cuisines. You could have classic Scottish salmon alongside Indian samosas and Greek salad, for example.

There is normally also a choice between hot and cold buffets. After an outdoor ceremony in the spring or autumn, when it can get rather chilly in Scotland, a selection of hot dishes might please your guests more than cold cuts and salads, which are better suited for a summer wedding.

Drinks & Canapes

Some venues do not have the space or the facilities for a full reception with a meal, but do allow a small drinks reception after the ceremony. As alcohol on an empty stomach is not a good idea, you should consider also providing a small selection of finger food for your guests. This can make for a convivial, relaxed atmosphere after the excitement of the ceremony.

Where you are having a late morning/early afternoon ceremony, with a full reception in the evening, you will need to consider how to feed the guests attending the ceremony itself. They will need some sustenance to keep them going until the evening meal. Most outside caterers offer extensive and delicious canape selections, often including a set number of drinks per person depending on the option you choose.

Champagne or sparkling wine, with a non-alcoholic alternative, is the classic choice for a wedding reception, but popular alternatives are bucks fizz (champagne with orange juice); wine (provide a choice of red or white); mulled wine, especially for a winter wedding; whisky, for a real Scottish touch (although do provide an alternative for non-whisky drinkers); or, for a sophisticated wedding, cocktails – preferably with a skilled barman on hand to prepare them.

SAMPLE MENUS

A selection from the menus of a number of outside caterers in Scotland.

Canapes – £1.25 - £1.75 per item per head
  Smoked Salmon Roulade on Pumpernickel
  Tartlet of Prawns & Avocado
  Roasted Peppers & Basil Crostini
  Chicken & Bacon Roulade
  Breaded Haggis
  Mini Thai Fishcake and Pea Puree

Finger Buffets – £1.25 - £1.75 per item per head
  Traditional Sandwiches with Various Fillings
  Vegetable & Tomato Wrap
  Roast Venison, Pear & Rowanberry Tartlets
  Cajun Chicken on Spinach Tortilla
  Bagels topped with Smoked Salmon Pate
  Fried Seafood Selection

Evening Buffets

£7.95 per head
  Assorted Cocktail Sandwiches
  Sausage Rolls
  Mull Cheddar & Ham Quiche
  Tea or Coffee

£12.95 per head
  Chinese Vegetable Spring Rolls
  Assorted Cocktail Sandwiches
  Selection of Mini Quiches
  Chicken Satay
  Baby New Potatoes with Smoked Salmon & Cream Cheese
  Sausage Rolls
  Tea or Coffee

Dinner Menus

£28 per head
  Chicken Liver Parfait with Pear & Red Onion Chutney
  Gigot of Ayrshire Lamb with Roast Potatoes & Vegetables
  Citrus & Mascarpone Cheesecake with Passion Fruit Syrup
  Coffee & Little Sweets

£37 per head
  Local Smoked Salmon with Chargrilled Lemon & Black Pepper
  Corn-fed Chicken with Red Cabbage, Potato Rosti & Tarragon Cream
  Vanilla & Drambuie Panacotta with Raspberry & Lemon Curd Coulis
  Coffee & Fudge

Drinks Package – £19.50 per person
  Pigalle Brut Sparkling Wine or Fresh Orange Juice (3 glasses)
  Fortant Sauvignon Blanc or Fortant Merlot (½ bottle per person.)

Restaurants

Restaurants are worth considering for smaller weddings. In recent years the choice and quality of restaurants in Scotland has improved tremendously. If you are marrying in or close to one of the cities, there are many to choose from. In the Highlands and other rural areas there are some 'hidden gems' tucked away down remote side roads or accessible only by boat. If you fancy one of these, it might be best to book the restaurant first before you decide where the ceremony should take place, as they can get booked up long in advance, especially if you choose a place with an international reputation like the now world-famous *Three Chimneys* restaurant on Skye. This has been chosen as one of the top 50 restaurants in the world, so as you can imagine it is booked up for months in advance.

AWARD-WINNING RESTAURANTS

The Three Chimneys. Tucked away in an idyllic spot beside Loch Dunvegan on the Isle of Skye, this restaurant has won a raft of awards, including being voted one of the world's top 50 restaurants. Accommodation in six luxury suites available. **Colbost, Dunvegan, Isle of Skye, IV55 8ZT; tel 01470-511258; www.threechimneys.co.uk**

Braidwoods. A tiny restaurant in a converted two-room cottage. In addition to one Michelin star, it has won many awards and accolades over recent years, including the AA Best Restaurant in Scotland award. Locally caught seafood and the best Scottish lamb, deer and game-birds are staples of their ever-changing menu, but so are subtle use of more exotic herbs and spices. **Drumastle Mill, Dalry, Ayrshire, KA24 4LN; tel 01294-833544; www.braidwoods.co.uk**

Restaurant Martin Wishart. The eponymous chef learned his trade working with many of the world's top chefs, then returned to his native Edinburgh to set up his own restaurant, winning the city's first Michelin star in 2001. The restaurant is situated on the waterfront in the historic port of Leith. **54 The Shore, Leith, Edinburgh EH6 6RA; tel 0131-553 3557; www.martin-wishart.co.uk**

Michael Caines Restaurant. Located within the ABode Hotel, Glasgow, this fine dining restaurant has a light and fresh atmosphere and provides the perfect setting in which to enjoy the innovative and award-winning cuisine of Michael Caines, one of Britain's most talented and respected chefs. Winner Scottish Hotel restaurant of the Year 2006. **ABode Glasgow, 129 Bath Street, Glasgow, G2 2SZ; tel 0141-572 6000; www.michaelcaines.com/locations/glasgow**

Summer Isles Hotel. In a stunning setting in the far north west of Scotland, the hotel has views across to the Summer Isles and the Hebrides. Nearly everything you eat in the Michelin-starred restaurant is home produced or locally caught. Scallops, lobsters, langoustines, crabs, halibut, turbot, salmon, venison, big brown eggs, wholesome brown bread fresh from the oven - the list of real food is endless. **Achiltibuie, Ross-shire, IV26 2YG; tel 01854-622282; www.summerisleshotel.co.uk**

Pubs

Informal weddings are better suited to informal receptions, and in this case why not consider a pub (public house) for your lunch or evening meal? Whether in a countryside public house, the bar of a hotel, or in a city centre bar, the quality of bar food available in Scotland has improved tremendously in recent years, especially with the phenomenon of the 'gastro-pub' where the informality of bar meals is not seen as an excuse for cheap, bad quality food.

Pubs are an ideal place to sample local Scottish dishes, washed down with traditional Scottish ale or whisky. If that's not to your taste, however, don't worry – the best pubs now have varied menus with an international flavour, and have a good stock of wines and even champagne.

It is advisable to book ahead at the pub of your choice, although not all of them will reserve tables, some prefer to work on a 'first come first served' basis. Some may have a separate room which you can book, which may be a better solution for a larger party. However, the fun of Scottish pubs is the atmosphere created by the varied clientele, so shutting yourself away in a function room may not provide the full experience you're after.

PUBS

The following pubs are all recipients of good food awards from the Good Pub Guide.

Applecross Inn, Applecross, IV54 8ND (Highland); tel 01520-744262; www.applecross.uk.com/inn

Badachro Inn, Badachro, IV21 2AA (Highland); tel 01445-741255; www.badachroinn.com

Old Inn, Gairloch, IV21 2BD (Highland); tel 01445-712006; www.theoldinn.net.

Babbity Bowster, Blackfriars Street, Glasgow, G1 1PE; tel 0141-552 5055; www.taste-of-scotland.com/babbity_bowster.html

Glenelg Inn, Glenelg, IV40 8JR (Highland); tel 01599-522273; www.glenelg-inn.com

Steam Packet, Harbour Row, Isle of Whithorn, DG8 8LL (Dumfries & Galloway); tel 01988-500334; http://home.btconnect.com/steampacketinn/index.html

Burts Hotel, Market Square, Melrose, TD6 9PL (Scottish Borders); tel 01896-822285; www.burtshotel.co.uk

Plockton Hotel, Plockton, IV52 8TN (Highland); tel 01599-544274; www.plocktonhotel.co.uk

Wheatsheaf, Swinton, TD11 3JJ (Scottish Borders); tel 01890-860257; www.wheatsheaf-swinton.co.uk

Tayvallich Inn, Tayvallich, PA31 8PL (Argyll & Bute); tel 01546-870282; www.tayvallich-inn.com

Ailean Chraggan, Weem, PH15 2LD (Perth & Kinross); tel 01887-820346; www.aileanchraggan.co.uk

Do It Yourself

If you really want to make your wedding a 'home-made' affair, you could arrange to cook and supply your own food, maybe with the guests each bringing their own contribution to the feast. There should also not be a problem with supplying your own alcohol, as long as it is provided free for your guests. Any venue other than a community hall would almost certainly frown on you bringing your own food and drink.

Ready-made luxury foods suitable for weddings are available from the better quality supermarkets and food stores. Marks and Spencer have a branch in most towns in Scotland, some now dealing simply in food, hence the name of this offshoot 'Simply Food'. Their party foods, including wedding cakes, are also available online for delivery to your home address or direct to the venue.

Sainsburys also have a good range of quality foods, including cakes, which you can order online for delivery. You do need to check, for any online delivery service, that they deliver to the area of Scotland where you are marrying - some more remote rural areas are not covered.

Costs

As in-house or outside caterers always price per head, it is important that you know as accurately as possible how many people will be attending. You may be able to adjust numbers up to a point, but as you get nearer to the wedding this may not be possible. It is inevitable that a few people find for domestic or other reasons that they cannot make it, even if they had intended to.

If there does seem a lot of food left at the end of your buffet, ask the caterers if you can have it put in containers for you, or your family and friends, to take home. They can hardly refuse – you've already paid for it!

The Wedding Cake

Traditionally, the wedding cake was a three tiered affair, and was usually a rich fruit cake covered in marzipan (almond paste) and white icing (frosting), decorated with sugar paste decorations such as flowers and swags. The reason for choosing a dark, heavy fruit cake, laced with copious quantities of alcohol, was not just for the taste; it was customary to save the small top tier for the Christening of the first child, or for the first wedding anniversary. A heavy cake stuffed with dried fruits and alcohol could last for up to a year without ill-effect, if stored correctly – in fact, it would improve in flavour during that time as it matured.

Nowadays, of course, the deep freezer has made the storage of the cake much less of a hit and miss affair. Doubtless there were many occasions in the past when the Christening cake had to be replaced with a hurriedly made or purchased version, when it was discovered the stored cake had gone mouldy!

Types of Cake

Whether you wish to freeze your cake or not, nowadays wedding cakes come in all shapes, sizes and flavours. Sponge cakes filled with butter cream are just as popular as fruit cakes, and come in a range of flavours, chocolate and vanilla being the favourites. If you can't decide on one particular flavour, or wish to satisfy all your guests, each tier of the cake can be of a different type.

There is no reason why you have to have a three-tiered cake. For a small wedding with just a few guests, it would be far too big, and you'd be living on it for the first few months of your married life! Two tiers might be more suitable – and if you like the spectacle of a huge pyramid of cake, the largest 'cake' at the base can be artificial. For a massive wedding, or if you are cake-lovers extraordinaire, you can of course have more then three tiers – the sky's the limit!

And why just stick with white icing, or a conventional round or square cake? There are many different and more imaginative options. Here are some ideas.

- **Tiered cake.** Choose one with or without pillars supporting the tiers; go for unusual shapes, such as heart-shaped for the true romantics; decorate with sugar paste roses, tartan ribbons, or something more quirky reflecting your interests; have each tier a different type or flavour of cake; go for a dramatic dark red, chocolate or even tartan icing.

- **Single cake.** More suitable for a small wedding, a single cake can be just as beautifully decorated as a multi-layered one. Choose decorations which reflect the colour scheme and theme of your wedding. Fresh flowers, the same as those in your bouquet, rather than edible paste ones, give a wonderfully fresh and pretty look.

- **Designer cake.** To introduce some humour into the reception centrepiece, commission an individually designed cake which reflects your interests. Are you into sky-diving, country-dancing, stock car racing? Whatever it is, a cake can be made to reflect your hobby. If you're marrying in a beautiful ancient castle, have a cake made as a replica of the building, or if not, have a fantasy fairytale castle.

- **Individual cakes.** A modern innovation (which actually has it roots in the ancient practice of breaking small cakes over the head of the newly-married couple) is to have a stack of individual fairy cakes or cup cakes on a specially designed stand. The cakes can be in different flavours, with different decorations. It looks great, and guests can help themselves, avoiding the inevitably messy business of cutting the cake and passing it round.

- **Croquembouche.** This is a traditional French wedding cake made from profiteroles filled with crème patissière flavoured with liqueur. The profiteroles are caramel-glazed and stacked into a cone shaped cake, then the whole edifice is decorated with sugared almonds, marzipan or fresh flowers. For a final luxurious touch, the croquembouche may be served with chocolate sauce.

- **Cake toppers.** Traditionally, the cake is topped with a model of a bride and groom, but if that doesn't suit you, there are many alternatives: a pair of doves to symbolise lasting love; comedy/tragedy masks for a thespian couple; fresh flowers or fruits; a model of your classic sports car... use your imagination!

- **Chocolate fountain.** Why have a cake at all? A truly stunning centrepiece, and one which adds a sense of fun to the whole affair, getting your guests mingling beautifully, is to have a chocolate fountain. A cascade of dark, milk, plain or flavoured liquid chocolate fills the air with its tantalising scent and guests dip a range of treats including exotic fruits, marshmallow, profiteroles, biscotti, mini doughnuts and other sweets into the flowing chocolate.

Displaying the Cake

It is customary for the wedding cake to be displayed throughout the reception, as a focal point for the festivities. Generally it stands on its own table beside the table at which the bride and groom and the bridal party sit. The table is draped with a special tablecloth, and decorated with flowers, ribbons, balloons, or whatever suits the theme and colour scheme of the wedding.

To really highlight the cake it can be a dramatic touch to have a spotlight shining on it, but ensure that this will not affect the cake. It is not advised with a chocolate cake, for example, which might just melt!

To add to the sense of ceremony, a specially engraved and decorated knife is placed on the table for cutting the cake when the time comes. In some Scottish castles, you may even be offered a ceremonial sword with which to make the first cut in the cake.

Most venues or caterers will provide a suitable knife for cutting the cake, but you can buy special knives or swords for the purpose, which can be engraved with your names, the venue and your wedding date, and kept as a souvenir of the day. Rainbow Sugarcraft (www.rainbowsugarcraft.co.uk) sell knives with a Scottish flavour, one with a glass thistle design handle, and cake-cutting swords based on historic Scottish swords, including the Braveheart sword.

The wedding cake cutting should be announced in advance, to allow everybody to get ready with their cameras to catch the significant event, which historically was seen as the first action the bride and groom perform together as husband and wife. The bride takes the knife in her hand, her husband places his hand on hers, and they cut the wedding cake together. Traditionally the groom feeds the first slice to his bride, then she feeds him.

The cutting of the cake is purely symbolic, so the bride and groom aren't expected to cut up the rest of the cake. The catering staff should cut up the rest and serve it to the guests along with coffee or champagne. If everybody is too full to eat it then and there, it may be put in small boxes for the guests to take away with them. You may also wish to take or send portions to invited guests who could not attend on the day.

Costs

Wedding cakes are usually priced per portion, and this can range from £3 to £15 per guest, so for a large wedding it can be a substantial price. When counting up how many portions you need, don't forget to add on anybody who won't be attending the reception but you would like to send a piece to. And if you're intending to keep the top tier for your first anniversary, again don't forget to include this in the calculations.

It is wise to 'shop around' for your wedding cake supplier, because their prices can vary greatly. A small local baker, or somebody working from their home, may work out less expensive than a large confectioners. Sometimes a deposit needs to be paid for pillars, cake toppers and other reusable decorations, which is refunded on return of these items. Don't forget to ask whether the price includes transportation and setting up of the cake.

You may be expected to collect the cake from the bakers yourself, in which case, make sure you can transport it safely yourself. You must be able to place it upright in the vehicle. Never sit it straight on the back seat, as this is not a level surface. A board placed across for the cake box(es) to sit on – and with somebody sitting next to them to hang on when you go round corners! – is probably the safest way to get it there in one piece. A tiered caked with pillars should be carried unassembled, and erected only when at the reception.

If you are having caterers providing the rest of the food, ask if they can also provide a cake. This may work out cheaper than going to a separate supplier and they will also transport and set it up for you along with the rest of the food. Caterers are often reluctant to set up a cake ordered from another supplier, in case of accidents!

A budget way of getting a beautiful and unique cake is to make it yourself, or to ask a relative or friend who is skilled in baking to make it for you. Don't worry if fancy icing is beyond you, a plain iced cake can be decorated using fresh flowers, fruits, ribbons or even sweets. It is also possible to buy ready-made icing and sugar decorations from the supermarket.

Don't overlook the supermarket. There are some very reasonably-priced, good quality celebration cakes available to buy, either 'off the shelf' or personalised. In the UK, Sainsburys and Marks and Spencer offer a selection which you can buy online and have delivered to your home or the venue.

STORING YOUR WEDDING CAKE

If you choose to keep the top tier for your first anniversary, or your baby's christening, follow these simple instructions and it should stay as good as new in the freezer for up to a year.

- Remove the cake topper and any inedible decorations from the cake. Decorations made from icing or almond paste can be left on. If any of the decorations are particularly large, remove them and freeze separately if suitable.
- Place the cake on a foil-covered cardboard cake board or a plastic plate.
- Put it in the freezer for one hour, to harden the icing.
- Wrap the cake in cling film (plastic wrap), making sure that it is completely airtight.
- Wrap it in two layers of aluminium foil.
- Place it in a freezer container and freeze for up to a year.
- When you remove it from the freezer, unwrap it while still frozen and leave it to defrost slowly at room temperature.

Timing

Give plenty of time to order your wedding cake. It is best to decide on the design and place your order at least eight weeks in advance. Ask how long before the wedding the cake will be made. A sponge cake should be made as close to the wedding date as possible, allowing enough time for the icing and decorating to be done, of course. A fruitcake lasts far longer, and the recipe might require a couple of weeks for it to mature before it is iced and decorated.

If you are making your own cake, it is wise to practice first, in case your first attempts go awry. Once you have a perfect cake, you can freeze it before adding any fillings or decorations, and it will keep fine in a domestic deep freezer for a couple of weeks. Take it out and allow it to defrost thoroughly before filling and decorating it.

Flowers, Frills & Furbelows

Once you have sorted out the basics – the venue, the ceremony, what you're going to wear, what you're going to eat, and who you're going to invite – the rest is all just trimming. So have fun! The main part of your budget is accounted for, so you know exactly how much (or how little) you have to spend on flowers and other decorations. Don't worry if you don't have a great deal of money to play with here, this is an area where do-it-yourself solutions can really pay dividends. And if you arrange your own flowers, design and make your own invitations, place cards and favours, instead of buying them 'off the shelf', not only will your wedding be truly unique, but you will gain an enormous amount of satisfaction from it. Why not get your friends and family involved in making them too. A pre-wedding party where you make table decorations, fill favour bags, write out place cards, make buttonholes, could be a great social occasion, and far more productive than your average hen party!

Alternatively, if money is no object, there is now a huge selection of products available to make your wedding look out of this world. They can be commissioned and designed especially for you, or bought ready-made and personalised, where appropriate, both through websites and in high street shops devoted to the art of prettying up a party.

Bouquets

After you have decided on your wedding clothes and on the colour scheme for the bridesmaids dresses, you can begin to think about flowers. The style as much as the colour of your dress is important when choosing suitable flowers to carry. While a very formal wedding gown calls for a structured, formal bouquet, a simple flowing style of dress will be better enhanced with a simpler, more natural style of hand-tied bouquet. The florist you choose will wish to know as much as possible about your dress, in order to advise you on the flowers to include in your bouquet. If possible, provide the florist with sketches and fabric swatches of your dress, of the bridesmaids' dresses, and of any coloured fabrics (e.g. tartan or fancy waistcoat) the groom will be wearing. Even if you have a plain white or ivory dress, the florist will ask for a sample of the fabric if possible. It is surprising quite how much variation there can be between different 'whites', of fabrics and flowers.

Don't worry if gardening is not one of your hobbies, the florist will advise you on what varieties of flowers will be in season on your wedding day. If it is important to you to have specific varieties in your wedding bouquet, you may have to time your wedding for the correct season. An alternative is to have artificial flowers, or a mixture of fresh and artifical. There are beautiful silk flowers readily available, and modern techniques of drying and preserving fresh flowers are so successful that it can be hard to detect that the flowers you are carrying down the aisle weren't picked fresh that very morning! Artifical flowers also have the advantage that they won't have wilted by the end of the day, and can be kept as a memento of your wedding for years to come.

If having a historical theme, choose flowers and styles which are in keeping with that era. *Weddings and Flowers* (www.weddingsandflowers.co.uk) has lots of useful advice about choosing wedding flowers, including lists of flowers suitable for different historical eras.

For a real Scottish touch, especially good if your wedding has a tartan theme, go for heathers and maybe Scottish thistles. The Speyside Heather Centre (www.heathercentre.com) near Aviemore sells wedding bouquets, posies and buttonholes online if you cannot vist them in person.

Tradition says that the bride should toss her bouquet to the unmarried females at the wedding, and the one who catches it is destined to be the next bride. If you want to keep your bouquet as a memento but still want to abide by tradition, you should order a special 'bride's toss bouquet' in addition to the one you will carry.

WEDDING FLOWERS

It's normal to use the same flowers and/or colours as you have in your bouquet for any other floral decorations. These range from a simple buttonhole for the groom, to buttonholes and corsages for all the main guests, and flower arrangements in every conceivable nook and cranny of the venue. Here's an exhaustive list to pick and choose from, depending on your budget, your love of flowers, and your propensity to hay fever!

- **Bouquets:** bride; matron of honour; bridesmaids; bride's toss bouquet; mothers of bride & groom.
- **Hair Ornaments:** bride; matron of honour; bridesmaids.
- **Buttonholes:** groom; best man; ushers; fathers of bride & groom.
- **Corsages/Handbag Decorations:** mothers; other close female relatives
- **Ceremony:** main entrance; altar/table; pew/seat row ends.
- **Reception:** entrance; table centrepieces; staircases; buffet tables; wedding cake & cake table.

Headdresses

For a fresh natural look, a floral headdress, or simply a flower pinned in the hair, can be very effective for bride or bridesmaid alike. Silk flowers are a good choice here as they are more robust than fresh blooms.

Buttonholes & Corsages

Buttonholes are traditional wear for groom and groomsmen, normally a single bloom with a little foliage, or maybe a simple sprig of heather. A corsage is a similar floral decoration worn by women, and tends to be slightly bigger than a buttonhole, although it would normally include the same flowers and/or foliage. A corsage may be pinned on like a buttonhole, worn on the wrist, or attached to one's bag or purse.

Ceremony & Reception

Sometimes there are restrictions imposed by the venue on the decorations you can use, which may mean you cannot stick to the same floral theme throughout.

If your ceremony is taking place in a church, you may find that you are not permitted to provide your own flowers. In many churches the flowers are customarily arranged by members of the local congregation, and they may insist on doing so for your wedding. If you discuss the matter in advance, you may be able to request flowers which match your theme.

However, if there are other weddings in the church on the same day, the same flowers will be used for all the ceremonies. If you want something specific, you may have to choose a less popular day when only your wedding is taking place. There would not normally be a charge made for flowers provided by the church, but a donation would be gracefully accepted.

Some ceremony or reception venues provide flowers as part of the wedding package, while others charge extra, but in either case you should normally be able to request specific flowers or colour schemes. Some venues allow couples to provide their own floral decorations, and will be happy to advise the sort of arrangements which work well within the room.

Receptions in large halls or marquees generally benefit from lots of flowers and plants, as they can look rather bare and stark otherwise. On the other hand, an opulent dining room in a castle may not be conducive to too many, overly fussy and colourful floral arrangements. In this case, think simple: white lilies and deep green foliage in tall vases, for example, can be stunning.

Table Decorations

A floral centrepiece on each table is a nice touch – invite your elderly female relatives to take them home as a gift and you'll be in their good books for years! Alternatively, freeze dried flower petals or rose buds look fresh and pretty scattered over white tablecloths. These can also be filled into paper cones and used as confetti for throwing over the couple after the ceremony. Coventional paper confetti is banned by many churches and venues, as it is terribly difficult to sweep up and, even more seriously, can stain clothing, including that precious wedding dress, if it gets wet. Dried petals are natural, biodegradable and don't stain, so are a far better solution. Although rose petals are the classic choice, there is a wide choice available, including lavender and heather sprigs and grains, marigold petals, rose buds.

Timing

Book your florist as early as possible, at least three to four months in advance of the wedding date if possible, as they can only do so many weddings on one day and may be booked up if you leave it too late. They may ask you for a small deposit at that time, even if you are not ready to discuss your requirements. They will need to confirm the final details about six weeks before the wedding to ensure that everything will be available when you want it and that the venue is happy with those arrangements too.

As with any other suppliers, check out a few different florists, using personal recommendations where possible. They should be able to show you examples of what they can provide, and pictures of the flowers at weddings they have previously done.

Generally, a florist local to the venue is best: in addition to being able to deliver the flowers as fresh as possible, they may be familiar with the room where the reception will take place, and therefore will know what works best. Although any florist should be able to provide wedding flowers, some specialise in this area and may therefore be a safer choice. If you are not in a position to get local recommendations, the venue staff may be able to advise on which florists have done a good job in the past.

Costs

The flower budget can be adjusted very easily to suit your own circumstances. If money is tight, don't worry; a simple posy of spring flowers can look just as stunning as a grand cascading bouquet.

A small wedding at a register office can cost as little as £75, even if you hire a professional florist. At the other end of the scale, a large marquee may cost as much as £800 to decorate. Whatever your budget, always check that the florist can work within it to provide what you want.

If you really need to cut costs but don't want to go without flowers, you could use flowers cut from the gardens of your friends and family. Or go for foliage rather than flowers. Ivy garlands look lovely on white tablecloths, and are far cheaper than blooms.

When providing and arranging the flowers yourself, do bear in mind that most of the work will have to be done the day before and on the morning of the wedding. You will have to plan your time carefully. If you can, get your friends or family to help, to minimise the additional stress this may cause.

Decorative Touches

In addition to the flowers, there are many other ways of decorating your wedding venue. You can go for the co-ordinated look, and buy everything from a single range, starting with the invitations and acceptance cards and going through to the favours for your guests to take home. Alternatively, you can pick and choose from the many different products available. These include bth 'off-the-shelf' goodies and all the paraphernalia you might need to make your own designs of cards and so on for the personal touch. Personalisation with names and the date and veneu of your wedding can also be provided if required.

To produce a unique look for your wedding, one you know will not be similar to any other, stay away from the specialised wedding suppliers. Search general craft shops, the haberdashery section of good department stores, or specialist fabric and trimmings shops, for all the materials you could need to transform your wedding venue into a feast for the eyes!

It is fashionable to provide certain entertainments for your wedding guests at their tables. These things can certainly act as ice-breakers, especially where many of your guests do not know each other. These include fun things such as tiny bottles of bubbles to blow, old favourites like party poppers and paper streamers, disposable cameras (although everybody nowadays seems to have a digital camera so this may be a waste of money). And if you really think your guests might get bored, you can provide table games with a wedding theme!

You might like to provide a book for your guests to sign and leave their best wishes. This makes a wonderful memento of the day which will bring all those memories back in years to come.

If you let your imagination run wild, the possibilities are endless, but the best effects are often the simplest. It's best to choose a colour palette of two or three colours, and keep in mind the saying 'less is more' – it is possible to get carried away by the huge variety of options available, and end up with too many different choices, too many colours. Quite apart from spending a fortune!

It's a good idea to produce a checklist of what you want, and stick to it when you go shopping. Settle on a colour scheme, which for the best effect should complement your wedding costumes. Note down how many of each item you need.

ITEM	NUMBER
Stationery	
Invitations/acceptance cards	
Place name cards	
Thank you letters	
Table decorations	
Tableware	
Centrepiece	
Scatter petals	
Candles/candleholders	
Party poppers	
Disposable cameras	
Bubbles	
Table trivia/puzzles	
Favours	
Room decorations	
Flowers/plants	
Ribbons	
Balloons	
Congratulations banner	
Guest book	
Miscellaneous	
Car ribbons	
Umbrellas	
Confetti	

Wedding Gifts

The Couple

Some couples are unsure of etiquette regarding wedding gifts – understandably, they don't want to appear to be expecting gifts, even though they know that wedding guests will expect to buy them one. The best way to approach the issue is to accept that it is a well-respected custom for your guests to buy you a gift – indeed, even people you do not invite to your wedding, such as workmates, may wish to mark your marriage with a gift.

In the past it was generally the done thing to buy the couple items for their home; they would in almost all cases be moving into their first home together, so any household items would be useful. Today, however, with many couples having lived in their own homes, either together or separately, for years before their marriage, they are likely to have all the household goods they need. This poses a problem for the guests as much as the couple. What do you buy the couple who already has everything?

You can leave the choice of gifts totally to the guests, and just hope that you don't end up with too many things you don't like or would never use. To avoid this, a popular solution is to write a gift list, on which you itemise everything you would like (in an ideal world!) Guests choose which item they will buy and cross it off the list. Make sure there is a range of gifts on the list, so there's something to suit every budget. Or, if you do want a particularly expensive item, suggest that guests might like to club together to buy it. Add a discreet note in the invitations asking guests to contact to you if they wish to see your gift list. There should be no compulsion to buy from the list – some guests will prefer to buy you something they have chosen personally.

An alternative to the do-it-yourself gift list is to subscribe to a wedding list service. Many stores and websites now offer this facility, and allow your guests to shop for the items you put on your list in person, by phone or online. They should provide cards to go inside your wedding invitations giving details of how guests can buy from your list, and include a wrapping and delivery service.

Finally, some couples prefer to ask for presents in the form of cash, or gift vouchers from specific stores. This is perfectly acceptable, although some guests will still prefer to buy you a gift, and this is, of course, their prerogative.

Even if you receive most of your gifts in advance of the wedding day, there will undoubtedly be some guests who bring them along to the ceremony, so make sure you have a table available at the reception to display them on and make sure cards do not get separated from the gifts, so you know who to thank afterwards! You should always send personal thank you notes for all gifts received, either as you receive them, or after the wedding.

The Bridal Party

It is customary for the groom to buy thank you gifts for the main members of the bridal party, especially both mothers, best man, bridesmaids and page boys. The gifts should be something that reminds them of the occasion, and maybe something that can be worn on the day. Cufflinks for the men, items of jewellery for the women, are popular, as are items such as champagne glasses or tankards, which can be engraved with a personalised message including the date of the wedding. Gifts for younger children can include such things as personalised teddy bears, bags and money banks.

As you are having your wedding in Scotland, it is a nice touch to have Scottish themed gifts for your bridal party. Items such as presentation quaiches, thistle brooches, celtic design jewellery and ceramics, even hadn-carved wooden spurtles (porridge stirrers) are available from a number of websites.

Favours

So that nobody feels left out, you can provide a small gift for every guest at your wedding. These are known as wedding favours and can range from the fun and frivolous to the practical to the longlasting. Sugared almonds are a traditional choice, but the options are endless: chocolates or jellybeans; miniature bottles of wine or spirits; small items of costume jewellery; packets of seeds or flower bulbs to plant and become a lasting reminder of the day; scented candles; small toys... your imagination and your budget are the only restrictions! Present the favours in beribboned packages or pretty boxes, and place one at each guest's place at the reception. Choose appropriate women's, men's and children's gifts.

Favour bags and boxes, and the favours to fill them, can be bought from wedding shops and websites, or make your own favour bags using pretty fabric or paper squares tied with ribbon and fill them with gifts of your choice.

Arrive In Style

Cars

When you're dressed in your beautiful wedding clothes, you need something just as showy to arrive in. Classic cars are the usual choice, something large and luxurious, both for the grand entrance, and for the practical reason that your average saloon car may just not be roomy enough nor the doors wide enough for you to travel and dismount without your dress being creased or crumpled. After spending maybe hundreds on your dress, you want it to appear at its best, so your mode of transport is an important consideration. Classic cars, with a uniformed chauffeur, also show to best advantage on the wedding photos.

The most popular choice of wedding cars are the Rolls Royce, Bentley, Daimler, Jaguar or Mercedes. Choose the car to match or complement your dress, both colour and style, and the overall theme of the wedding.

A historical theme demands a form of transport suitable to that era. For a thirties style wedding, for example, hire a vintage car from the correct period to complete the look.

For a less formal wedding, why not hire a taxi cab? The so-called 'London taxi' is now widely used in Scotland too. Cab firms have special white and silver cabs, which will be decorated with all the standard bridal trimmings. Alternatively, choose the classic black cab, or a more unusual livery, such as a tartan taxi.

If you want to transport yourself and your whole wedding party in style, a fun option is to hire a stretch limousine. There are a number of different companies now hiring these throughout Scotland – they are increasingly popular for all sorts of celebrations, including weddings. For the sophisticated look, go for a classic silver 31 foot American limousine, or if your tastes are more kitsch, they also come in shocking pink or Royal Stewart tartan. If you fancy a real monster of a machine, that can seat up to 16 passengers, you can go for a stretch Hummer.

Whatever your choice, the striking exterior of these vehicles is overshadowed by what you'll find inside. They include a range of luxury features, including plasma screens, DVD, music and karaoke systems, mirrored ceilings, fibre optic and neon lighting, laser disco balls, smoke machines, and champagne on ice.

Costs

Hiring a wedding car is not cheap: it is likely to cost you between £250-£400 to hire a classic car; taxi prices vary depending on distance, so you must get an individual quote. Prices for stretch limos vary, although given the number of passengers they can take, this can work out cheaper per head than the other options.

It is traditional for the bride to arrive in one car with her father or whoever is giving her away; don't forget that you also need to arrange transport for the bridesmaids and the mother of the bride, and for the groom and best man. The costs can all add up.

To keep costs down, use your own car(s), or a standard rental car if you're visiting Scotland. Decorate them with ribbons and other trimmings and you can make a striking entrance for a fraction of the price.

On Foot

When you are staying at, or very close to, the ceremony venue, there may be no need for a special bridal car. Why not walk, in traditional Scottish fashion? Hire a bagpiper to lead the way, with the bridal party walking behind. If there is any distance to walk, make sure your shoes are suitable – some castles or outdoor venues have uneven terrain to reconnoitre. Consider having a flat pair of shoes for the walk, and give your stillettos to a member of your party to carry.

Horse & Carriage

Love & marriage, love & marriage,
Go together like a horse and carriage...

For the truly romantic fairytale touch, or to give your historical-themed wedding authenticity, a horse and carriage is a popular choice. There are companies throughout Scotland who hire out various styles and vintages of horse-drawn carriage together with experienced coachmen and liveried attendants.

Alternatively, arriving at and leaving from the venue on horseback might be your dream, an option which is only advised for experienced horseriders. You don't want the wedding pictures to show the bride falling off her horse in her wedding dress or, even worse, the groom showing off what he actually has on under that kilt!

Flights of Fancy

Maybe you fancy arriving at your wedding from the sky? Small aeroplanes and helicopters can be hired by the hour, an adventurous choice that may also be very practical if your wedding is taking place in a remote area of the Highlands.

Check that there is a suitable place for the aircraft to land. As helicopters are regularly used for medical emergencies in the Highlands and Islands, you should find that there is a designated landing point in the area. Some hotels have their own landing points too.

Another unusual option, especially if you are marrying by a lochside, is to arrive by seaplane. Loch Lomond Seaplanes can be chartered to anywhere in Scotland, and can set down on both land and water.

Boats

With a coastline of over 6,000 miles (9,900 km), and 653 square miles (1,692 sq. km) of inland waters, your Scottish wedding is likely to take place close to water. So why not consider arriving by boat? There are boats of all shapes and sizes to hire, from rowing boats to luxury yachts. And, as long as your celebrant agrees, the ceremony can even take place on board.

Your entire wedding can take place on the water, if you wish. Jacobite Cruises have several well-appointed cruise boats, two of which are licensed for civil ceremonies, and you can have your reception and dance on board while you cruise Loch Ness.

If Music Be the Food of Love...

Nothing helps to set the atmosphere for your wedding better than the appropriate music, during both the ceremony and the reception. Whether your tastes are for classical orchestral music or the lastest hip hop, the music should sum up your personality and set the tone for the day.

Music for the Ceremony

If your ceremony is taking place in a church, there will probably be a church organist available to play before, during and after the ceremony. A large church may have its own choir who could be hired to sing on the day. You will normally have to pay a fee for the services of the organist or choir.

When your ceremony takes place at another venue, they are unlikely to have musicians 'on tap', although they may be able to put you in touch with musicians who have played there previously. Scotland is a country bursting with musicians, so it should not be difficult to find the right people to play for you, whether you prefer a string quartet, a traditional celtic harp, or anything else. If you have hired a bagpiper to pipe you to and from the ceremony, remember that pipe music is very loud and is at its best played outdoors. It is not generally appropriate for playing during the ceremony itself. This is a time for something more gentle, either religious or romantic, or a mixture of the two. As an alternative to live musicians, most venues will either have their own equipment to play your chosen selection of music on, or will allow you to bring along your own.

Plan the music carefully so you have the appropriate tunes for different parts of the ceremony. Some gentle classical or traditional music playing quietly in the background is helpful while your guests are arriving and taking their seats. Then play a tune that is important to you for your processional up the aisle or equivalent. Music is played during the signing of the register, and again for the recessional or progress out of the church or wedding room after the ceremony. If you are having a Christian ceremony, you will also want to choose some hymns for the congregation to sing during the service. Make sure in advance that your musicians know and can play all the tunes you have chosen.

Classical: There are certain pieces of classical music which are 'old-favourites' for weddings, perhaps the most famous being the wedding march from *Lohengrin* by Wagner (commonly known as *Here Comes the Bride*.) Some of the most popular classical music for these parts of the ceremony is listed at www.weddingguide.co.uk/articles/wordsmusic/musicwedding/musicforyourwedding.asp

Celtic: If you have hired traditional Scottish musicians, including bagpipers, you will probably prefer them to play a selection of traditional tunes. There are many favourite celtic tunes which are appropriate for weddings, including *Come to Mairi's Wedding,* which every wedding piper has in his or her repertoire. There is a list of suitable traditional wedding tunes at www.standingstones.com/wedding.html

Don't feel, however, that you can only have Celtic music. A good band should be able to play their versions of standard classical tunes or popular songs. Discuss your ideas with them in advance so they are well-prepared on the day.

Popular: If your musical tastes are more contemporary or unusual, you could always record your own selection of music to play, but bear in mind that your elderly aunt may not appreciate you walking up the aisle to Led Zeppelin. The minister too might draw the line at that!

However, there are plenty of beautiful love songs which would set the right romantic and emotional ambience. Because these popular songs are well known by most people, your guests will appreciate the sentiments and even be able to sing along, if this is appropriate!

Music for the Reception

At the reception you may want to have music playing, live or recorded, as the guests arrive and maybe throughout the meal, up to the beginning of the speeches. And then, of course, you will want music for your evening dance, disco or ceilidh if you have one.

To hire one or more groups of musicians for the whole day, from the start of the ceremony to the end of the evening party, can of course work out very expensive. A way of minimising on the costs is to use recorded music for the ceremony and during the meal, with the live musicians only making their appearance later. Or you could have just a piper, or a harp player, for the ceremony, with a full ceilidh band being hired for the evening.

Discos are always popular for weddings. They allow for a wide range of music to suit all ages of guests. It may also be a less expensive option to book a disco for the evening dance, and usually the DJ will provide lighting and even organise party games, if required.

You need to consider your mix of guests when deciding what sort of music and/or dancing you want at your evening reception. A ceilidh is a lively way to end the wedding, but it may not be everybody's cup of tea. Some people are fairly reserved when it comes to dancing, and although after a few glasses of champagne they may be brave enough to take to the floor in the low lighting of a disco, they may be far less happy about taking part in a Scottish reel in a brightly-lit room, especially if they have never done that type of dancing before. Nothing falls flatter than a ceilidh where nobody will get up and dance, so do think carefully about this option. However, if your guests are game for a laugh and a new experience, do try it. A ceildih band will always help the dancers to 'walk through' the steps first, and call out the steps as they dance so everybody can muddle and giggle their way through. It is certainly a very sociable form of dancing and makes the ideal ending to a strongly Scottish themed wedding.

It is traditional for the bride and groom to signal the start of the evening dance by taking to the floor for the the first dance. Ideally this should be to a song or tune which is special to you both in some way, so decide in advance what this should be and ensure that the DJ or musicians can play it for you.

Sourcing Musicians

Most active musicians, bands or individuals, have a presence on the internet. Typing 'ceilidh bands scotland' into Google, for example, brings up 437,000 results, while 'string quartets scotland' produces 345,000 hits.

It is, of course, risky to pick musicians 'blind' in this way; if you can, get personal recommendations. If not, ask bands if they have any testimonials from previous wedding couples, or if they have a CD or downloadable music files of them performing.

The venue may be able to recommend musicians who have played previously, or if you are really stuck, you could try contacting a wedding planner. They may agree to put you in touch with musicians they work with regularly. You will probably have to pay a fee to the wedding agency for this service, but you can be confident that they would not recommend anybody they have had bad feedback about in the past.

Costs

Musicians' charges vary tremendously. The fees will vary depending on how well-established they are. A new band will probably perform far more cheaply in order to get the exposure they need to build their profile. A single musician, or a duo, is likely to cost less than a five piece band.

Bagpipers generally charge a flat fee for performing at a wedding, but make sure what you are getting for this. One tune as you go into the ceremony and another as you come out might not strike you as good value for money, so why not ask the piper to give you and your guests a 'recital' of his favourite tunes while the photographs are taken or as you drink champagne after the ceremony?

If possible, try to pick musicians who do not have too far to travel to your venue, as their travelling costs, and the costs of any overnight stay, may be added on to your bill.

Keep a Record

When you've put all that effort into organising a day that you and everybody else will remember for years, a good photographic record of the day is a must. Quite apart from the fact that the mind is fallible, and things which you expect to be imprinted on your memory forever will inevitably fade with time, there will be parts of the day at which you, or your partner, or your guests, will not be present. Digital photography and videography mean that a complete record of the day is possible, from the moment you get up in the morning to when you go to bed after the last dance, if that's what you want!

You don't have to spend a fortune to get all that recorded in one form or another – and if you were to pay professionals to be on hand to take capture all those moments, it *would* cost a fortune. Many people have digital or home video cameras, so you could ask your friends or relatives to take pictures or film during the day. You will inevitably find that, even if you have hired a professional wedding photographer and videographer, there will be numerous guests taking their own shots, so you can get copies of their pictures to 'fill in the gaps' that the professionals didn't catch or weren't present at.

Bear in mind, however, that the quality of your guests' pictures are unlikely to be of the standard of an experienced professional , so it is worth paying for them to cover the ceremony and the reception up to the first dance (most basic photography and videography packages cover this period.)

Photographs

Media: The introduction of digital technology has made a dramatic change to wedding photography in recent years. Where once wedding photographers would use either medium format or 35mm film, now all of them, pretty much without exception, are now using digital cameras. If you choose a professional photographer using high-end equipment this should make no difference to the quality of the pictures you will receive, and it gives you a far greater choice of the media in which you receive those pictures.

Wedding photographers now offer you your pictures on a CD or DVD as part of their standard package. Because of the comparatively low cost of digital pictures, this may be as many as 100-200 shots. Some packages include a set number of prints chosen from these, presented in an album. Others allow you to order additional prints of various sizes at a cost per print. You can usually choose to have these presented in an album, or to buy your own album and frames for mounting them.

You may be able to upload the pictures to your own computer and print them out from there. With a good quality printer and photographic computer paper you can get some very good results. However, do be aware that these may not be as long-lasting as the traditional prints obtained from conventional film. Depending on the inks, paper, and printer used, this can be anything from 5 to 50 years. If you use very expensive equipment and archival quality paper they may last as much as 100 years. But all photographs, conventional or digital, will fade eventually. To make your prints last as long as possible, keep them covered by plastic or glass (i.e. in an album or a picture frame) and hang or stand pictures in frames out of direct sunlight.

However, if you do want some prints of your pictures, don't worry about them fading over the years; as long as you retain the original electronic files on a good quality CD or DVD which you store in a dark place, you can reprint them, good as new, whenever you want to.

Wedding photographers normally also provide additional electronic means of viewing your pictures, including displaying your pictures in an online wedding album on their website. They may also be uploaded to commercial websites such as Photobox (www.photobox.co.uk) which allow your friends and family to view the pictures and order prints of those they would like. It is also possible to have a short film made of your wedding pictures on a DVD.

One of the simplest ways of displaying your pictures electronically is to upload them to your computer and set up your screensaver to show a slideshow of your own pictures. Then every time your computer goes to screensaver mode, your wedding photos will be displayed in random order.

Style: The days are past when wedding photographs were formal and carefully posed, including a standard selection of shots – bride with bridesmaids, groom with best man, bride and groom with bride's family, ditto with groom's family... This resulted in eveybody's wedding album looking pretty much like everybody else's. With the far wider variety of wedding styles and venues today, and the flexibility of digital photography, which does not require the use of a tripod to get decent shots, and allows for good quality informal or candid shots to be taken at the click of a button, you can choose from a far wider range of styles.

'Reportage' or 'documentary' style is particularly popular, where there are few if any formal posed shots taken; the photographer instead takes many hundreds of candid shots during the day, recording the 'story of your wedding' from beginning to end. This can produce some magical intimate shots of the couple and their guests, often of little things that the bride and groom just didn't get the chance to see themselves.

If you prefer formal posed shots, check that the photographer is happy to do these – most will. A mixture of formal and informal shots, in both colour and black and white, is a solution which provides some nice contrasts of style.

Costs: Prices vary considerably depending on the length of time the photographer spends at your wedding, the number of pictures taken, the number and size of prints you choose, whether an album is included, and so on. A less experienced photographer would generally charge less, as may one who works from home rather than having the additional overheads of a shop to cover. Bear in mind too that, even if they are only at your wedding for a couple of hours, there are many more hours work involved in uploading, developing and printing your pictures, the production of an album and so forth.

As a very broad guideline, you will have to pay a minimum of £500 and probably more like £700-800 for coverage up to your first dance on a standard package; if you choose a more comprehensive package, you will be paying well over £1000.

Where money is tight, you may be able to negotiate a 'budget package' with a limited number of pictures taken over a shorter period. If your wedding is very small, with just you and your witnesses or a couple of guests, you should be able to get a nice selection of shots for a reasonable price. Anyway, a full package offering 100 or more shots, if there are just a handful of you at the wedding, would just not be appropriate – the photographer would be hard-pressed to get a varied enough selection of shots, and you and your guests would be worn out having your pictures taken from every conceivable angle! So even where standard packages are quoted, you should always discuss your own requirements if the standard package doesn't suit. If one photographer won't comply with your request, another surely will.

How to Choose a Photographer

- The best way to find a good photographer is through personal recommendation. If this isn't possible, compare what is being offered by several different photographers and pick one who will provide what you want, at a price you can afford.
- If you can arrange a personal visit, or at least a phonecall, this is a good idea, as it is important to choose someone you can get along with. A good photographer should be able to make you and your guests feel relaxed and happy, in order to get the best pictures.
- Ask to view a portfolio of their pictures, ideally from a single wedding rather than the best individual shots chosen from a number of different occasions.
- Check what is included in the price quoted: number of shots taken; whether you get a CD or DVD to keep; how many prints of what size, and so forth. Ask if there is any restriction on what you can do with the pictures on the disk: some photographers try to prevent you from printing them out yourself, or taking them to a high street printer, in order to charge you extra by forcing you to go to him/her for your prints. Generally speaking, it is unreasonable for a photographer to prevent you from using the electronic files however you want for your personal use: commercial exploitation of those images is a different matter, however.
- Discuss with the photographer what sort of shots you want and ensure that this is the kind of photography they are comfortable with. Some prefer candid shots, others like to take the more formal route, while yet others go for 'arty' shots. Do make sure that their style fits your preferences. If not, find another one whose style suits you better.
- Ask whether the photographer has taken pictures previously at your chosen venue. It is best if they know the venue well: they will be aware of the best 'photo opportunities' there, both outdoor and indoor, and

should know, or be able to check with the venue and the celebrant, as to whether there are any restrictions on taking pictures in certain places. Bear in mind that some National Trust for Scotland and Historic Scotland properties have prohibitions on indoor photgraphs being taken, in order to protect the artefacts as well as avoiding any commercial exploitation of their properties.

- There is a website with a database of some 70 wedding photographers in Scotland listed in the *Directory of Suppliers* below. Many, although not all of them, will belong to a professional association of wedding photographers. Contact details of their members are available through the websites.

Video

A good video should offer comprehensive coverage of the day, including both the formal parts such as the ceremony itself and the wedding speeches, and informal shots of you and your guests enjoying the day. The venue itself should also feature prominently. If you have put a lot of time and money into finding a historic castle or other beautiful setting for your wedding, make sure this is captured on film just as much as the dress and the wedding cake. Professional videos can look as impressive as a Hollywood film, with music, titles, camera tricks and slick cuts between scenes.

Media: The digital revolution has hit videography as much as photography, to the extent that most, if not all, UK videographers now offer your wedding film on DVD, rather than video tape. The assumption is, of course, that everybody has DVD players rather than video players in their homes. There are strong signs in the UK that video is going to be completely obsolete over the next few years, totally replaced by DVD. So if you want to be able to watch your wedding film for years to come, embracing the DVD technology is essential.

However, if you are coming from abroad to marry in Scotland, you may have a different situation in your home country, with video still widely available. If this is the situation you are in, don't despair – even a video taken on a digital camera can be transferred to video tape with the right equipment. Make sure that the videographer you choose is able to do this for you and, most importantly, can produce it in the correct video format for your country.

Costs: A video record of your wedding is likely to cost between £500 and £1500, depending on how much coverage is included and whether one or more videographers are used. Some companies offer a full 'movie'style' service where two or more camera operators are involved, to allow 'reverse shots' of key moments of the day.

To cut down on costs, you could ask a friend or relative to video your wedding, although it is best to choose somebody who has taken home videos previously. You may not end up with a polished professional video, but this can be a fun record of the highlights of the day. It is also possible to send the raw footage off to a professional company for them to edit it and add music and titles. If you choose to do this, it is best to ask your videographer to turn off the sound, except when recording the important words of the wedding service and maybe the speeches. This means you won't end up with a running commentary or lots of extraneous noise, and the professional editor can add music of your choise as a soundtrack.

How to Choose a Videographer
Many of the comments above regarding choosing a photographer are equally relevant when choosing a videographer. To summarise:

- Check what is included in the packages offered by various videographers. Ask how many DVDs/video tapes are produced and how much they charge for extra copies.
- Ask to see sample wedding videos, again being suspicious of 'edited highlights' of a number of weddings.
- How much of your wedding will they cover – to the first dance, or all the way through to the last?
- Will they edit the raw footage to include music of your own choice, titles and so forth, and is there an extra charge for this?
- Do they know the venue?
- Are they are a member of the Assocation of Professional Videomakers? For details of this organisation and of other videographers in Scotland sees below in *Directory of Suppliers*.

Where to Stay?

Bride & Groom
It is traditionally deemed to be bad luck for the bride and groom to see each other in the hours before the ceremony, so if you intend to abide by that custom, you will need accommodation in separate places the night before the wedding. Unless you are setting off on your honeymoon immediately after the wedding, you will also need a double room for your wedding night, either at the reception venue or nearby.

A simple solution, if you are both marrying at a distance from your homes, is for the groom to stay in a bed & breakfast the night before, while the bride stays in your wedding accommodation the night before the wedding, and both of you staying for the wedding night. This means minimum disruption, having to move wedding dresses and all the other paraphernalia from place to place, and provides the ideal surroundings for the bride to dress up in her finery in a relaxed atmosphere before the wedding. Or maybe you choose to have a standard room for the night before the wedding, and the bridal suite just for the wedding night. This both cuts down on costs and makes your wedding night even more special. Hotel staff should be happy to move your belongings from one room to another while the wedding is taking place.

Most good quality hotels have a bridal suite, but they are likely to be booked up well in advance, so it is important to arrange your accommodation early. If you are having a large wedding, anyway, you must always discover the availability of accommodation for yourself and your guests in conjunction with choosing your venue. There is no point paying a deposit for a venue on a certain date, and then finding that there is just not enough accommodation locally for all the guests who will need it. In order to avoid any difficulties, you need to be in the position to book accommodation for yourselves and the main members of the bridal party at least, at the same time as you book your venue.

Where your wedding venue has enough accommodation for you and your guests, this will all be booked at the same time, of course, making the whole process far simpler. But even if there are rooms available for everyone, you may prefer to spend your wedding night away from your guests, so again you need to ensure that there is other accommodation nearby.

When booking your accommodation, always tell the establishment that it is for your wedding night or honeymoon. This should ensure they offer you the best rooms they have available and they may even throw in some extras like a bottle of champagne in your room!

Bridal Party & Guests

If you want accommodation at your wedding venue for yourselves, the bridal party and your guests, you will need to check what is available at the earliest stages. Many castles do not have any accommodation, while others have a limited number of bedrooms. They often have additional accommodation in the grounds, in such buildings as converted stable blocks or cottages. If you want a large wedding where everybody can stay under the same roof, you will be restricted to a hotel, although some establishments classing themselves 'castle hotels' can give you the best of both worlds. You do tend to find, though, that although a castle hotel with a large number of bedrooms may look like a genuine castle on the outside, in order to provide all the facilities required of events such as large weddings and conferences, the alterations to the interior make it look and feel far more like a good quality corporate-style hotel than an ancient stronghold with ghosts and dungeons!

If you choose a venue with limited accommodation, guests may stay at local hotels, guest houses or b&bs. The venue may have a list of these, or you could contact Visit Scotland, via their website or by telephone, for their listings. Contact details are listed in *Directory of Suppliers* below.

You need to decide at an early stage whether you will be paying for accommodation for any or all of your guests. To avoid any embarrassment it is essential to make it clear at the outset whether guests are expected to make arrangements for their own accommodation. If they are paying, it is a good idea to give them a list of suggested places to stay, with a range of different prices to suit qall budgets. It is generally safer to give them all the details and ask them to book accommodation themselves, then you won't be left in the position of having to pay cancellation fees on behalf of guests you have booked in but do not turn up on the day.

Accommodation Choices

Hotel: Hotels normally charge for accommodation on a room-only or bed and breakfast basis. Some better class hotels do half- or full-board options, including lunch and/or evening meal, or you can pay separately for any meals you take within the hotel.

Hotels are available at different standards throughout Scotland. Most of them are graded through one tourism scheme or another which will give you a guide to the facilities you can expect, but the safest guide is price. The cheaper it is, the more basic it will be.

Prices range from £35-£50 per room per night for a basic standard hotel, up to several hundred pounds per night for a five star luxury suite.

LUXURY SCOTTISH HOTELS

If you want to really indulge yourselves on your wedding night, here is a selection of top quality hotels around Scotland. There are more hotels listed in *Directory of Venues*.

- **Banchory Lodge Hotel**, near Aberdeen. www.banchorylodge.co.uk
- **Skibo Castle**, Dornoch, Highland. www.carnegieclub.co.uk
- **The Balmoral Hotel**, Edinburgh. www.thebalmoralhotel.com
- **Hotel du Vin at One Devonshire Gardens**, Glasgow. www.hotelduvin.com/Hotels.aspx
- **Isle of Eriska Hotel**, near Oban, Argyll. www.eriska-hotel.co.uk
- **Kinnaird Estate**, Dunkeld, Perthshire. www.kinnairdestate.com
- **Rufflets Country House**, St. Andrews, Fife. www.rufflets.co.uk
- **De Vere Cameron House**, Loch Lomond, near Glasgow. www.devere-hotels.com/our-hotels/cameron-house/the-hotel
- **Glenapp Castle**, Ballantrae, South Ayrshire. www.glenappcastle.com
- **Blair House**, Dalry, North Ayrshire. www.blairestate.com

---

Guesthouse: A guesthouse is a small hotel, usually family-run. Bedrooms usually, but not always, have en suite or private bath or shower room. Breakfast is provided in the price of the room, and evening meals may be available.

Prices charged vary quite widely, but on average you can expect to pay around £30-£40 per person per night, with extra for an evening meal.

Bed & Breakfast: A bed & breakfast establishment (B&B) offers accommodation in a private house. You may have to share a bath or shower room, although many have en suite facilities. Breakfast is served, while some also offer evening meals.

Prices charged vary quite widely, but on average you can expect to pay around £20-£30 per person per night, with extra for an evening meal.

Self-catering cottage: As a truly private retreat for that romantic wedding night or honeymoon, there are some delightful country cottages available to let throughout Scotland. They are usually let on a weekly basis, although if your wedding is out of the summer season, you may be able to rent a cottage for a weekend or mid-week short break of two to four nights.

Apartment: Another alternative, especially if you are staying in a city, is to rent an apartment.

- **Serviced apartments** offer the facilities of a good hotel, with the flexibility of self-catering. They are fully self-contained, with well-equipped kitchens and bathrooms and nicely furnished living areas and bedrooms. There is usually a receptionist or concierge to help with any queries or requests you have, and maid service is provided, so the flat is cleaned and bed linen changed on a daily basis. These tend to be expensive, often over £100 per night.
- **Self-catering apartments** are generally a cheaper option. They don't have receptionist or maid service, but they have all the same facilities within the apartment. They are available at various standards, from the cheap and cheerful to the luxury penthouse. You can expect to pay the equivalent price of a standard hotel room, £60-£80 per night.

How to Source Accommodation
- Ask the wedding venue if they know of any local accommodation.
- Seach the internet for 'accommodation in Scotland'.
- Telephone Visit Scotland (the Scottish tourist board) and ask for a brochure of local accommodation, or go to www.visitscotland.com
- See *Directory of Suppliers* below for useful websites and addresses.
- If all else fails, a wedding planner may be able to recommend somewhere to stay. They may charge you a fee for passing you this information. (See *Using a Wedding Planner* for contact details.)

Get it Covered

Wedding insurance

Planning and carrying off even the simplest of weddings can be a complex business. There are many aspects of the day where something just might go wrong. Considering the amount of time, effort and money you are putting into it, it is sensible to take out wedding insurance. A comprehensive policy starts at around £50, a small price to pay when you consider how much money could be lost if the unthinkable happens, not to mention the emotional distress this could cause.

Your venue and suppliers should have their own insurance, in the event of you making a claim against them. However, if their failure to satisfy your requirements is due to their bankruptcy, you may find yourself out of pocket.

RISKS COVERED BY WEDDING INSURANCE

A standard wedding insurance policy should cover reimbursement of expenses, including loss of deposits, caused by the following:

- cancellation and /or rearrangement of wedding and/or reception
- loss of or damage to: wedding attire; wedding gifts; wedding rings; flowers; attendants' gifts; wedding cake
- failure or non-appearance of wedding transport
- loss of or damage to photographs and videos
- failure of suppliers
- essential document indemnity
- personal liability
- personal accident
- legal expenses

The normal exclusions are:

- circumstances known to you when you took out the policy
- you or your partner calling off the wedding due to a change of heart
- lack of funds (unless due to redundancy after the policy is taken out)
- the first £25 of each claim

Check the policy carefully for any other exclusions.

You should take out any insurance policy as soon as you have set a date and chosen the venue, to ensure that you are covered for the loss of any deposits paid out early in the process.

There are generally different levels of cover and premiums payable, depending on the overall cost of the various items. Ensure that you have sufficient cover.

An additional premium may need to be taken out to cover cancellation of or damage to hired marquees or gazebos.

Travel Insurance

If you are travelling from abroad for your wedding in Scotland, you should also take out travel insurance, as this will not be covered by your wedding insurance.

Where you are bringing expensive items with you, such as wedding attire, jewellery, wedding rings etc. you may find that your travel insurance will not cover you for loss of or damage to these while in transit. You may need to ensure them separately. Your household insurance may cover you for personal possessions in transit but check if you need to pay an additional premium.

DON'T TAKE ANY CHANCES!

Whatever services you arrange, make sure you get everything confirmed in writing, and double-check that the date, time and venue are correct on all documents.

It's a good idea to ring the register office, the venue(s) and all your suppliers a few days beforehand to ensure that they have you programmed in and that there are no problems.

OUR WEDDING

A Personal Wedding Story

Julie Macgregor, 29, married Graham White, 43, at The Park Lodge Hotel, Stirling on Saturday 19th August 2006. Julie tells their story:

'We wanted to organise it all ourselves. The idea of using a wedding planner wasn't one we even considered. There are several reasons why this was the case. Firstly, the fact that we wanted a simple wedding, with the emphasis on our marriage and us committing to spend the rest of our lives together rather than it being about one day. Secondly, it was an expense that we would have been unwilling to pay for. Thirdly, the whole process was so much fun that I can't imagine wanting to go through it with a stranger as opposed to our friends and family.

The Planning Process

We decided we would marry in August to give us enough time to organise things, while allowing us to have a summer wedding. The exact date was the only Saturday in the month our celebrant and our hotel were both available.

We started about 17 weeks before the date and it took us about three weeks to organise everything except our invites. That included one week of false starts on plans for a marquee wedding which we abandoned.

We both wanted a simple, meaningful wedding without most of the paraphernalia which go along with many weddings. We listed our priorities and basically started at the top and worked down. We decided to try to keep our budget as low as possible – we didn't want to spend vast sums of money on things 'for show'. We budgeted for our celebrant, a venue, a meal and drinks for the day guests, a simple buffet for the evening, and our outfits. And we both wanted to have a wonderful honeymoon to start our married life together.

I had attended a funeral conducted by a humanist and was very taken with the notion of humanism. The ceremony was entirely personal to us and we even wrote our own vows. The civil weddings I have attended seem to have a less personal feel and seem to be more about the legalities of getting married. Our ceremony was the best part of the day, the way it should be! It was very emotional – I think the celebrant was the only person with a dry eye.

It was very easy to find a humanist celebrant to perform the ceremony. We used the internet as a starting point and got our local humanist celebrant's details from there. We contacted her to establish when she would be available, this allowed us to set our date.

Originally we wanted to get married in my parents' garden, and have our reception in a marquee. Unfortunately this proved to be too expensive for our budget, so we enquired about availability at hotels in our home town. Luckily, of the four we tried, two were available on our date. They were both lovely but very different.

We opted for The Park Lodge Hotel, a small family run hotel, as it has a beautiful garden which would allow us the option to be outdoors, weather permitting! It also struck us what a lovely setting the garden would be for the wedding photographs. We were delighted to find the manager of the hotel was very experienced with weddings. He has been doing them for over 20 years and is very passionate and enthusiastic about making sure the day runs smoothly. And the location of the hotel couldn't be more convenient as it is just at the end of the street where we live!

Graham had his best friend Danny as best man, my friend Tricia was my bridesmaid, and my dad gave me away.

We knew who we wanted to invite, so we just needed to produce invites and hope that everyone would turn up on the day! We wanted to keep it small and intimate so we invited about 40 guests to the wedding itself and another 50 or so to the reception. I made the invitations myself which took longer than expected so we sent out our invites just four weeks before the wedding.

The legislative procedures were very easy. Our humanist celebrant gave us all the information we needed, although it is also readily available on the internet. We had to complete our marriage notices then attend for a meeting with the registrar which took about 20 minutes. Missing birth certificates can easily be found by the registrar on-line.

As for all the other aspects of the wedding, we sourced things in a number of different ways, virtually all starting with the internet. As a tool to get an idea of what is available and at what cost, it is invaluable.

I looked at dresses online and decided that I wanted something that would reflect my style and personality rather than a traditional gown. I bought my dress off-the-peg from a high street store, so that was easy!

The bridesmaids' dresses and my accessories we bought from a local shop that was advertising at a wedding fair. The service was first class, and although I detest shopping, the girls made the whole experience great fun. The staff there recommended a photographer who had taken the shots for their advertising. We were very impressed with his pictures and, even better, he offered a great choice at very reasonable prices.

We bought a plain white cake and decorated it with fresh flowers. Again, this was readily available on the high street for a fraction of the cost of a specially ordered wedding cake. My colleagues and I are lucky enough to have very nice company cars, so we have a fleet of matching Mercedes at our disposal at no charge! We decided what kind of music we wanted for our reception and booked a band through a local agency.

Throughout the process, we tried to balance cost with having exactly what we wanted. We were fortunate enough to source everything relatively inexpensively because things like a cake, flowers and stationery aren't particularly important to us. At first I planned to visit Glasgow or Edinburgh to find a dress, cake etc. as there would be more choice, but I cannot recommend highly enough the service we have received from local suppliers. Word of mouth recommendations and service are more important than designer labels! Shopping around was beneficial as we have saved lots of money on the first quotes. Another benefit of using small local suppliers is that you can find something a bit different, like the beautiful handmade tiara I wore on my wedding day.

My dress was from Monsoon: a calf-length ivory coloured dress with a fitted bodice and a 'swirly' skirt, decorated with ivory piping in floral shapes and tiny beads and sequins. I tried on a few 'proper' bridal gowns, but I didn't feel like me in them. Besides, all that material dragging around behind me all day would just annoy me – I like to dance uninhibited! It was the first dress I tried on and I felt like a real princess. My mum and bridesmaid agreed with my choice. In fact, my bridesmaid started crying! Most bridal gowns take months to order, so I didn't have time to get one anyway, but it just goes to show that you can have a dream dress without spending a fortune. With it, I wore a veil edged in tear-drop crystals, with tiny crystals scattered down the back. I spent the money I saved on my dress on a wonderful crystal tiara and very high heeled but very comfortable shoes.

Graham and his best man both wore full Highland dress in Royal Douglas tartan. Both of these were hired.

The bridesmaids' dresses were made to order. They chose chocolate brown dresses so I made chocolate brown and pink invites and carried pink flowers.

We decided against a wedding list as I don't feel comfortable with telling people what to buy us as a gift.

We didn't have a timetable for the wedding, apart from knowing that our ceremony was at two and the band started at eight. Other than that we figured it out on the day.

I have worked at lots of weddings as a waitress during my student years and things very rarely progress as planned. You should make sure the kitchen is flexible. I have seen many carefully planned meals ruined because the photographs took so long. A good piece of advice is to choose either a cold starter or soup, otherwise your food will be overcooked if you sit down to eat later than originally requested. Most chefs hate wedding photographers!

Everything was organised weeks before the wedding. I was feeling quite smug about how easy it was, in fact… Oh how wrong I was! There was a lull until about three weeks before, then all hell broke loose!

I admit that some of the problems were of our own making: we put our house up for sale two weeks before the big day, and I also decided to change my job. I had seven job interviews in the two weeks leading up to the wedding, as well as having to decorate and re-carpet our house and get it on the market in the same time period.

In the midst of all this, there was a problem with the bridesmaid's dress. It was made in America and arrived two weeks before the wedding but was the wrong size. Another one was rushed to us, leaving just enough time for alterations.

I changed my plans about flowers at the last minute. I had wanted to do them myself but we just didn't have enough time. I ended up with two days left to book a florist, however it all turned out just fine. Our florist produced stunning flowers for virtually the same price it would have cost for me to buy the flowers and arrange them myself. I gave the florist some pictures of things I liked, my colour preferences and a budget, but I didn't know what I was getting until the night before when we went to collect them. I was delighted with everything. My bouquet was hand-tied, with a mixture of light and deep pink roses and eucalyptus, with the same on the tables, mixed with pale green hydrangeas. They had the casual, just picked, country garden look that I wanted and they went perfectly with the country house feel of the hotel. I wrapped the bouquets in the spare material from my bridesmaid's dress.

With all that going on, I'm afraid I barely had time to eat, and in fact had to pin myself into my dress after losing so much weight in such a short time! So despite being relatively unfazed about the wedding itself, I ended up being exceptionally stressed after all!

The Wedding Day

The night before the wedding, I stayed at home with my bridesmaid. My mum joined us in the morning along with our hairdresser and make-up artist. Graham stayed with his best man in Glasgow.

We booked a room in the hotel for ourselves for the wedding night. Several people stayed at our house, which is a few minutes walk away from the hotel, and most of the other guests got a taxi home.

The day itself was perfect. Despite torrential rain the day before, the sun came out just as we were leaving the house and stayed out all day. We were married in a lovely room overlooking the garden and the ceremony was wonderful. The rest of the day was just as good: the meal was perfect and everyone had a ball.

What are the images that stay in my mind? Sunshine, tears and lots of smiles. Glasses of champagne. White linen tables with flowers. People dancing. Memories being made...

My advice for other couples arranging their own weddings:

- The biggest problem we came across in planning it ourselves was finding the time to do all the small things. Booking the big stuff initially was easy, but trying to save money by doing lots of things ourselves was stressful at times. It was scary planning something with no experience or advice when you want it to be perfect. It was impossible to know what would work and what wouldn't – we had lots of unusual ideas that we ended up discarding as too risky with no one to advise us.
- Despite that, I would recommend doing it yourself. It's great fun, even if it is time-consuming. The bonus of using a wedding planner would be someone with a huge amount of experience advising on what works and what doesn't – there is an element of hoping for the best when you do it yourself.
- Don't be influenced by other people – do things the way *you* want to.
- Don't get caught up in the 'hype'. The day should be emotional and meaningful. I bought several bridal magazines which would all have you believe that if you don't have a certain lipstick or a dress by a certain designer you won't look beautiful. Or if you don't have a five tier cake you just haven't made the effort. Being happy on the day is far more important.
- The more details you have, the more things there are to go wrong.
- Don't get hung up on everything having to be perfect, it will only set unrealistic expectations and make you stressed out.
- Make time to spend with your future spouse in the weeks before the wedding – and *don't* talk about the day.
- Don't assume that the supplier charging the most is necessarily the best. Our excellent photographer was proof of this.

- Make sure all your honeymoon arrangements are made and everything is ready (including packing) at least one week before.
- Don't be frightened to delegate.

Post Script:
Although we enjoyed every minute of our wedding day, after the stresses and strains of the final couple of weeks, it was such a relief to get on a plane and fly off for three weeks. Oh, and the honeymoon was wonderful!'

WEDDING RESOURCES GUIDE

Sources of Information

Whatever the romantic connotations surrounding marriage, the undeniable fact is that getting married or registering a Civil Partnership is, first and foremost, a legal process surrounded by rules and regulations. This means that, inevitably, you will have to deal with official bodies and public officials, even if only to access the relevant information for your own particular requirements.

In addition, and especially if you are intent on organising every single aspect of your own marriage yourselves, you will need to be able to source all kinds of information. In order to do this, you will need to know who to contact about particular bits of information as they become necessary to your plans.

Public Bodies

The General Register Office for Scotland (GROS) is located in Edinburgh and is headed by the Registrar General. The main laws relating to registration and marriage are:

- Registration of Births, Deaths and Marriages (Scotland) Act 1965.
- Marriage (Scotland) Act 1977.

GROS is part of the devolved Scottish Administration and is responsible for, among other things:

- The registration of births, marriages, civil partnerships, deaths, divorces and adoptions.
- The statutes relating to the formalities of marriage and conduct of civil marriage.
- The running of the national Census and the publication of information about population and households.
- The maintenance of family history records.

Contact details: *General Register for Scotland:* New Register House, 3 West Register Street, Edinburgh, EH1 3YT; tel 0131-314 0380; www.gro-scotland.gov.uk

The Scottish Government is based in Edinburgh. Scottish law relating to marriage is different from that in England and Wales, this being one of the areas of government devolved to the Scottish Parliament.

The department dealing with the law relating to marriages and Civil Partnerships is The Justice Department:

Contact details: *The Justice Department:* St Andrews House, Regent Road, Edinburgh, EH1 3DG; general enquiries tel 08457-741741 or 0131-556 8400; ceu@scotland.gsi.gov.uk; www.scotland.gov.uk

The Home Office UK Border Agency (UKBA) is responsible for Immigration control. www.ukba.homeoffice.gov.uk

For matters relating to entry to the UK for the purposes of marriage or Civil Partnership, see www.ukba.homeoffice.gov.uk/visitingtheuk/gettingmarried

For information about visas, see www.ukvisas.gov.uk

If you are overseas, visa applications should be made to a visa application centre in your own country. These are listed at www.ukvisas.gov.uk/en/howtoapply/wheretoapply

Historic Scotland is responsible for over 3000 buildings and sites in Scotland which are culturally significant. Many of those sites are spectacular and suitable as wedding venues. Some of them are identified in the *Directory of Venues*.
Contact details: *Historic Scotland:* Longmore House, Salisbury Place, Edinburgh, EH9 1SH; tel 0131-668 8973; hs.weddings@scotland.gsi.gov.uk; www.historic-scotland.gov.uk

The National Trust for Scotland is the conservation charity that protects and promotes Scotland's natural and cultural heritage for present and future generations to enjoy. With over 270,000 members it is the largest conservation charity in Scotland. It is the guardian of many of the nation's magnificent heritage of architectural, scenic and historic treasures, some of which are ideal as wedding venues. The *Directory of Venues* includes a selection of National Trust properties.
Contact details: *The National Trust for Scotland,* Head Office, Wemyss House, 28 Charlotte Square, Edinburgh, EH2 4ET; tel 0844-493 2100; from the USA (toll free)
1866 211 7573; functions@nts.org.uk; www.nts.org.uk.

Visit Scotland is the national tourism agency for Scotland. It has local and regional offices throughout the country. An invaluable source of information about Scotland, where to stay, what to see and what to do, in addition to the facility to book accommodation online.
Contact details: *VisitScotland:* Ocean Point One, 94 Ocean Drive, Edinburgh EH6 6JH; tel: 0131-472 2222 or 0845-2255121; info@visitscotland.com; www.visitscotland.com

Wedding Professionals

The VOWS Awards: These are designed to recognise the best suppliers in the Scottish wedding industry. VOWS (Voted Outstanding Wedding Supplier) Awards are voted for by the wedding couples themselves, so if you have received outstanding service from any of the many suppliers involved in your Scottish wedding, go to the website to nominate them.

There are also details of previous winners on the site, which may help you in your own choice of suppliers. www.vowsawards.co.uk

Wedding Advice Websites

Electric Scotland: Online Scottish Wedding Guide.
www.electricscotland.com/weddings
Guides for Brides: 'The Wedding Information Website' with links to suppliers of all sorts throughout Scotland. www.guidesforbrides.co.uk
Hitched: 'The definitive wedding site', packed with information and advice. www.hitched.co.uk
Pink Products: Advice and listings of Civil Partnership related services and products. www.pinkproducts.co.uk
Pink Wedding Days: Wedding planning guide for gay and lesbian couples. www.pinkweddingdays.co.uk
Scottish History Online: Lists clans, clan societies and Caledonian clubs in Scotland and around the world. www.scotshistoryonline.co.uk
Scottish Wedding Planners: Supplier directory.
www.scottishweddingplanners.co.uk
The Best Scottish Weddings: Advice and directory of venues and suppliers throughout Scotland. www.thebestscottishweddings.co.uk
The Scottish Wedding Directory Online: Advice and links to venues and suppliers throughout Scotland. www.scottishweddingdirectory.co.uk
Wedding Guide UK: Online discussion forums, articles, advice, gifts and more, all about weddings in the UK. www.weddingguideuk.com
Wedsite Scotland: Directory of wedding service providers in Scotland. www.wedsitescotland.com

Wedding Magazines

The Best Scottish Weddings: Quarterly magazine available from newsagents or online. Peebles Media Group, Bergius House, 20 Clifton Street, Glasgow G3 7LA; tel: 0141-567 6000 www.thebestscottishweddings.co.uk
The Scottish Wedding Directory: Quarterly magazine available from newsagents or online. Unit 26, 6 Harmony Row, Glasgow G51 3BA; tel 0141-445 5545; www.scottishweddingdirectory.co.uk

Wedding Shows

United Kingdom: *Gay Wedding Show:* Regular shows throughout the UK. www.gayweddingshow.co.uk
Scotland's Exclusive Wedding Event: Glasgow Royal Concert Hall. For full details and dates see www.scotlandsweddingevent.co.uk
The Best Scottish Weddings Exhibition: Regular two-day exhibitions at Braehead Arena Scotland. A wide range of suppliers exhibiting, with bridal wear fashion shows. www.thebestscottishweddings.co.uk/exhibition
The Scottish Wedding Show: 'The UK's biggest wedding show'. Scottish Exhibition & Conference Centre, Glasgow. www.scottishweddingshow.com

International: *Association for Wedding Professionals International:* Listing of bridal exhibitions throughout Europe, USA & Canada. www.afwpi.com/europe/index.html

Bridal Show Producers International: Wedding shows throughout USA & Canada. www.bspishows.com

Wedding Planners

There are an increasing number of wedding planners specialising in weddings in Scotland. They may be able to help you with information and advice, or put you in contact with suppliers, even if they aren't arranging your wedding. Remember, they may make a charge for this service. Contact details of a number of wedding planners in Scotland can be found below in *Using A Wedding Planner.*

Books

Getting Married in Scotland, Iona McGregor (National Museums of Scotland, 2000). An historical overview of marriage ceremonies in Scotland.

Handfast: Scottish Poems For Weddings And Affirmations, Lizzie MacGregor (Polygon, 2005). Those seeking memorable words for their ceremonies of marriage or commitment, or who simply want to take delight in an anthology of love poems, will find in this collection old favourites and brand new poems, in English, Scots, and Gaelic, all with a Scottish flavour.

In Search of Ancient Scotland, A Guide for The Independent Traveler, Gerald M Ruzicki, Dorothy A Ruzicki, Dodie Ruzicki (Aspen Grove Publishing, 2000). The Guide is full of common-sense evaluations, advice, and remarkably precise directions about where to find Scotland's ancient monuments, especially its prehistoric stones, brochs and castles.

Making the Bridegroom's Speech: Etiquette, Jokes, Sample Speeches, One-liners, John Bowden (How To Books, 2000). Providing examples, tips and hints for confidence, this wedding speech guide is written exclusively for the bridegroom. It covers conveying feelings to guests; adding a little humour; finding the ideal beginning and ending; putting it all together; and getting the delivery right.

Scotland For Dummies, Barry Shelby (For Dummies, 2005). Down-to-earth trip-planning advice, what you shouldn't miss, and the best hotels and restaurants for every budget.

Scottish Love Poems: A Personal Anthology, Antonia Fraser (Hippocrene Books, 1995). A carefully chosen collection of poems, 'to be embraced, experienced and treasured'.

The Illustrated History of Scotland, Chris Tabraham, Colin Baxter (Oyster Press, 2004). Baxter, with dozens of books of Scottish landscape photos to his credit, loads the pages with one stunner after another, alongside several dozen fine old paintings and period photos.

Directory of Wedding Service Providers

Ceremony & Reception Venues
Comprehensive advice and information on choosing your venue, together with a *Directory of Venues* divided by type and geographical area, can be found in *Choosing A Venue.*

Engagement and Wedding Rings
Baxters Jewellers: Scottish, Celtic and Mackintosh Jewellery and gifts. P.O. Box 8631; Saltcoats; Ayrshire; KA21 5YF; tel 01294-469241; www.baxtersjewellers.com
Ortak Jewellery: Orkney-based Scottish and Celtic design jewellery. Retail outlets in UK and USA. Hatston, Kirkwall, Orkney, KW15 1RH;
tel: 01856-872224; www.ortak.co.uk
Ortak USA: 1050 Main Street, 2nd Floor, River Edge, New Jersey 07661;
tel Toll Free: 1-866-257-3182; email drc5@juno.com
Pure Jewels: Online suppliers of jewellery, watches and gifts. tel 0208-4701221; www.purejewels.com
Walker Metalsmiths: Handmade celtic design rings and jewellery, based in USA. One Main Street, PO Box 706, Andover, NY 14806, USA;
tel Toll Free USA or Canada: 1-800-488-6347; www.celtarts.com

Wedding Stationery
Piccolo Press: Specialist printers and diestampers. 90 Harbour Street, Nairn, IV12 4PG; tel 01667-454508; www.piccolopress.co.uk
Wedding Stationery Etc: For all wedding and Civil Partnership stationery. Newcombe Design Limited, Mansfield Cottage, Cranford Avenue, Exmouth, Devon EX8 1RS; tel 01395-268638; www.weddingstationeryetc.co.uk

Clothing
Belmont Bridal Studios: Brides' and bridesmaids' dresses, near Aberdeen. First Floor, Carlton House, 32/36 High Street, Banchory, AB31 5SR;
tel 01330-820822; www.belmontbridal.co.uk
Beverley Wedgewood: Formal wear for men and boys. Online shop. www.beverleywedgwood.co.uk/html/mens_hire.html
Catherines of Partick: The perfect wedding outfit for the Mother of the Bride and Matron of Honour. 106-114 Dumbarton Rd, Glasgow, G11 6NY;
tel 0141- 339 1351; www.catherinesofpartick.co.uk
Caroline Castigliano: High class bridal wear in Edinburgh. 6 Waterloo Place, Edinburgh; tel 0131-558 3355; www.carolinecastigliano.co.uk
Clan Gatherings: Tartan clothing for women, including silk tartan wedding gowns. 167 Maxwell Avenue, Bearsden, Glasgow, tel 0141-576 4007; www.clangatherings.com
Ebay: Online auction including new and used wedding clothing and accessories. www.ebay.co.uk; www.ebay.com

Exclusively Bridal: Bridal wear in Inverness. Exclusively Bridal, 20 Market Brae Steps, High Street, Inverness, IV2 3AB; tel 01463 718171; www.exclusivelybridal.com

Harman Hay: Bespoke historical clothing for weddings and civil partnerships. Mercury House, Shipstones Business Centre, Northgate, New Basford, Nottingham, NG7 7FN; tel 0115 8402454; www.harmanhay.co.uk

June Brides Ltd: Brides' and bridesmaids' dresses, tiaras and accessories in Glasgow. 325-329 Eglinton Street, Glasgow, G5 9SP; tel 0141-429 4162; www.junebrides.co.uk

Kirk Wynd Highland House Ltd: For kilt hire and purchase in the St Andrews area.149a Market Street, St. Andrews, KY16 9PF; tel 01334-473268; www.kilt-shop-scotland.com

Sara's Attic: Vintage wedding gowns and accessories. Tel 07980-497326; www.sarasattic.co.uk

Slater Menswear: Highland dress and formal wear to buy or hire, including two exclusive tartans. Branches countrywide – see website for store locator. 165 Howard Street, Glasgow G1 4HF; tel: 0141-552 7171; www.slaters.co.uk

Stewarts of Helensburgh: Men's morning and dinner suits for hire. 30 West Princes Street, Helensburgh, Dunbartonshire, G84 8TD; tel 01436- 671543; www.stewartsclothing.co.uk

Viva La Frock: Vintage wedding gowns and accessories. www.vivalafrock.co.uk

Caterers

Braveheart Banqueting: Caters for weddings nationwide. Tel: 01236-794274; www.braveheartbanqueting.com

Encore Creative Catering: Exclusive caterers for Glasgow city council venues. Tel: 0141 353 9148; www.encorecatering.co.uk

Marks & Spencer: Branches throughout Scotland, see store finder on website. Online order and delivery service also available. www.marksandspencer.com

Prestige Scotland: Has exclusive contracts with many leading venues. Viewforth House; 31 The Loan; South Queensferry, Edinburgh, EH30 9SD; tel 0800-3281373; www.prestigescotland.co.uk

Sainsburys Supermarket: Branches throughout Scotland, see store locator on website. Online order and delivery service also available. www.sainsburys.co.uk

The Sizzling Piggy Baa-B-Q: Barbeque whole pigs and lambs plus a host of other roasts. Will cater for weddings anywhere in Scotland. Tel 01896-752413; www.sizzlingpiggy.co.uk

Tuck-In Outside Catering: Experienced caterers for weddings. Tel 0131-467 2599; www.tuckin.co.uk

Restaurants

Edinburgh Restaurateurs Association: Links to member restaurants. www.edinburghrestaurants.co.uk

Glasgow Restaurateurs Association: Links to member restaurants. www.graonline.co.uk

The UK Restaurant Guide: Listings of restaurants across Scotland recommended by major guides or food writers. www.restaurant-guide.com

Wedding Cakes

Chocolate On Demand: Chocolate fountain hire. 3 Ewenfield Place, Ayr, Ayrshire KA7 2QU; tel 0870-760 7200; www.chocolateondemand.com

Rainbow Sugarcraft: Classic, contemporary and novelty wedding cakes for delivery throughout Scotland. New Hall, Traquair, Peeblesshire, EH44 6PY; tel 01896-833458; www.rainbowsugarcraft.co.uk

Top Tier: Wedding cake suppliers for Glasgow and the nation. Top Tier Designer Cakes, 76 Hyndland Road, Glasgow, G12 9UT; tel 0141-334 4244; www.toptiercakes.com

Wedding Cakes made in Scotland: Patricia MacGowan is a prize-winning cake designer and maker. 14 Wallace Gardens, Causewayhead, Stirling, FK9 5LS; tel 01786-464652; www.art2eat.co.uk

Wedding Decorations & Favours

Confetti: Suppliers of wedding decorations and favours as well as many other products. Stores in Glasgow, London, Leeds, Birmingham & Reading. Also sell their products online. Tel 0870-840 6060; www.confetti.co.uk/weddings

Guides for Brides: An index of wedding decoration and favours suppliers in Scotland. www.guidesforbrides.co.uk

Rainbow Sugar Craft: Sweet favours for delivery anywhere in Scotland. Rainbow Sugarcraft, New Hall, Traquair, Peeblesshire, EH44 6PY; tel 01896-833458; www.rainbowsugarcraft.co.uk

V V Rouleaux: Gorgeous ribbons and trimmings. Shops in UK and online. 94 Miller Street, Merchant City, Glasgow, G1 1DT; tel 0141-221 2277; www.vvrouleaux.com

Florists

Daisy Rue Flowers: Highlands-based florist with online ordering. 29 High Street, Dingwall, Ross-shire, IV15 9RU; tel 01349-862390; www.daisyrue.co.uk

Flowers by McDowell: Edinburgh based florist with online ordering. 556 Gorgie Road, Edinburgh, EH11 3AL; tel 0131-443 1512; www.flowersbymcdowell.co.uk

Martins Dried Flowers: Longford Farm, Longford, Market Drayton, Shropshire, TF9 3PW; tel 01630-638295; www.martinsdriedflowers.co.uk

My Florist: Online florists for selection and delivery of flowers anywhere in Scotland. www.myflorist.co.uk

The Flower Preservation Studio: A fresh and modern approach to 3D bouquet preservation. 6 Little Fallow, Lychpit, Basingstoke, RG24 8UN; tel 01256-769658; www.theflowerpreservationstudio.co.uk

Wedding Gifts

Pure Jewels: Online jewellery, watch and other gifts retailer. Pure Jewels, 294 Green Street, Forest Gate, London E7 8LF; tel 0208-470 1221; www.purejewels.com

Scotch Corner: Online index of Scottish jewellery, clothing and gifts suitable for weddings. www.scotch-corner.com

Made in Scotland: Top quality clothing, food, knitwear, jewellery and accessories at Beauly, just a short drive from Inverness or available online. Station Road, Beauly, Inverness-shire, IV4 7EH; tel 01463 782821; www.madeinscotland.co.uk
Fripperies: John O'Groats based retailer with a large range of keepsakes and other gifts. Unit 4 Business Centre, John O'Groats, Caithness, KW1 4YR; tel 01955 611445; www.fripperies.com
Scotweb Store: Scottish gifts. Online and telephone ordering. Units 3-4, 14 Springvalley Gardens, Edinburgh, EH10 4QG; tel 0800-634 8640; www.scotwebstore.com

Gift Lists

Emma Bridgewater: Designer items for the home. Stores in Edinburgh, London and Stoke on Trent. Online gift list service. Tel 020-2371 5489; www.emmabridgewater.co.uk
John Lewis: John Lewis Department Stores in Edinburgh and Glasgow with online facilities for gift lists. www.johnlewis.com

Hairdressers & Beauticians

Access Place: Listings of service providers in Scotland.
Hairdressers: www.accessplace.com/hairdresser.scotland;
Beauty Therapists: www.accessplace.com/beauty-therapist.scotland

Transport
Cars

Ashton Cars: Supplying wedding cars to western and central Scotland. Ashton Cars, Sunnybeach Coach House, Midge Lane, Strone, Argyll, PA23 8RX; tel 0845-006 6333; www.ashtoncars.com
Ecosse Classic Wedding Cars: Classic weddings cars for Edinburgh and the Lothians. Unit 13A, Newbattle Road, Dalkeith, Midlothian, EH22 3LL; tel 0131-663 2796; www.ecosseclassiccars.co.uk
Glasgow Taxis: Taxi House, 140 Boden Street, Glasgow G40 3PX; tel 0141-429 7070; www.glasgowtaxisltd.co.uk
Platinum Limos: American stretch limousines, branches throughout Scotland. Tel 08700 135466; www.theplatinumlimocompany.com
Stretch Hummers: Available for hire in Central Scotland. Tel 01698-375900; www.clydevalleylimousines.co.uk
Tartan Limos: 'Glasgow's only tartan stretch limo'. Tel 07891-844290; www.tartanlimos.co.uk

Horse-drawn Carriages

Carriages For All Seasons: A West Lothian provider of Victorian coach and team of horses in Scotland. 10 Redburn Road, Blackridge, West Lothian, EH48 3RU; tel 01501-752309; www.carriagesforalloccasions.co.uk
Elegant Carriages: Horse and carriage for weddings based in England but will travel to weddings anywhere in Scotland. Tel 01536-761095; www.elegantcarriages.co.uk

Aircraft

Balloons Over Britain: Hot air balloons to hire in Scotland. Aerosaurus Balloons Ltd, National Booking Office, Southbrook House, Southbrook, Whimple, Exeter, Devon, EX5 2PG; tel 01404-822733; www.balloonsoverbritain.com

Loch Lomond Seaplanes: Flying out of Helensburgh close to Glasgow, Loch Lomond. Seaplanes are available for charter to anywhere in Scotland. PO Box 26613, Helensburgh, Argyll and Bute, G84 9YG; tel 0870 2421457; www.lochlomondseaplanes.com

Premiair: The UK's largest helicopter charter company. Tel 01252-890089; www.premiair.co.uk

Tayside Aviation: Private aircraft hire. Fife Airport, Goatmilk, Glenrothes, Fife, KY6 2SL; tel 01592-753792; www.taysideaviation.co.uk/fleethire

Boats

Charterworld: Luxury yacht charter in Scotland. www.charterworld.com/index.html?sub=scotland-yacht-charter

Jacobite Cruises: Luxury cruises on Loch Ness, boats licensed for civil weddings. Tomnahurich Bridge, Glenurquhart Road, Inverness IV3 5TD; tel 01463-233999; www.jacobite.co.uk

Loch Lomond Leisure: Luxury boat hire for special occasions. Marchfield House, 1b Marchfield Grove, Edinburgh, EH4 5BN; tel 07973-354707; www.lochlomond-scotland.com/special.htm

Undiscovered Scotland: Links to boat hire throughout Scotland. www.undiscoveredscotland.co.uk/uslinks/cruising.html

Musicians

Janet Annand: Harpist and clarsach player from West Lothian available for weddings in central Scotland. Linlithgow, West Lothian, EH49 6BG; tel 01506-842702; www.weddingharpist.co.uk

Pipe Major Jim Brown: Available for weddings throughout Scotland. Druimbeag, Balquhidder, Perthshire, FK19 8PA; tel 01877-384678; www.incallander.co.uk/scottishpiper.htm

Roddy The Piper: Based in Edinburgh but willing to travel anywhere in Scotland. 3F3 5 Merchiston Grove, Edinburgh, EH11 1PP; tel 0131-346 8393; www.roddythepiper.com

The Gold Ring Duo: Traditional Celtic music for weddings & receptions. Tel 07780-938046; www.celticweddingmusic.co.uk

Wedding Music Scotland: For musicians and entertainers of all types throughout Scotland. Tel 01631-730469; www.wedding-music-scotland.com

Photographers

Our Wedding Memories: Online index of wedding photographers throughout Scotland. www.ourweddingmemories.co.uk/files/areas/scotland.htm

Society of Wedding & Portrait Photographers: SWPP, 6 Bath St, Rhyl, LL18 3EB; tel 01745-356935; www.swpp.co.uk/wedding_photography/index.htm

Videographers

Association of Professional Videomakers: 7 Nether Grove, Shenley Brook End, Milton Keynes, Bucks, MK5 7BQ; tel 01908-522145; www.apv.org.uk

Scotsmart Scottish Directory: Online index of videographers available for weddings in Scotland. www.scotsmart.com/c/wedding-video.html

Accommodation

Glasgow City Flats: Luxury apartments for weddings and honeymoons in Glasgow city centre. Tel 07983-647125; www.glasgowcityflats.com

Scotland's Best B&Bs: 4 & 5 star bed and breakfast accommodation throughout Scotland. www.scotlandsbestbandbs.co.uk

Scotland's Personal Hotels: Independent hotels across Scotland. Mark Linklater, 58 Whitehouse Road, Edinburgh, EH4 6PH; tel 0800-056 1870 or 0131-476 1590; www.scotland-hotels.com

Scottish Holiday Cottages: Listings of holiday cottages, apartments, castles and mansions throughout Scotland sleeping 2-20 people. Tel 01738-451610; www.scottish-holiday-cottages.co.uk

VisitScotland: Graded accommodation of all sorts throughout Scotland. www.visitscotland.com

Wedding Insurance

Confetti Wedding Insurance: Online insurance cover from wedding specialists. www.confetti.co.uk/shopping/insurance/default.asp

Weddingplan Insurance: Online insurance cover for all eventualities in connection with weddings. 1 Prince of Wales Road, Norwich, Norfolk, England, NR1 1AW; tel 0844-412 3115; www.weddingplaninsurance.co.uk

Marks and Spencer: Online wedding insurance from one of the UK's best known high street names. www.marksandspencer.com

Stag & Hen Nights

Chillisauce: For stag/hen nights and weekends anywhere in Scotland. Tel 0845-450 8269. www.chillisauce.co.uk

ReleaseTravel: Tel 0871-2233331; www.releasetravel.co.uk

Travel Quest: www.travel-quest.co.uk/tqstag.htm

Honeymoons

Highland Country Weddings Ltd.: An online index of honeymoon travel and transport links. www.highlandcountryweddings.co.uk/honeymoons.htm

USING A WEDDING PLANNER

The Wedding Planner's Role

A good wedding planner will help and advise you on every aspect of your wedding, including suggestion of suitable venues, completion of paperwork, venue and accommodation booking, kilt and dress hire, pipers and other musicians, meals, champagne, flowers, transport, hair and beauty treatments, complementary services and pampering, the wedding cake, photographs and videography. If you want to extend their help beyond the day itself, they may also be able to arrange sightseeing tours, sporting activities, or anything else you fancy, to entertain yourselves and your guests while you are in Scotland.

All these things should only be arranged after detailed discussion with the planner. You want your day to be unique, so beware of anybody who seems to be trying to give you an 'off the peg' service. If you come across the words 'wedding package' in the literature provided by the weddings agency or venue, always clarify exactly what this means. Some planners will provide a 'bespoke' service, in which every detail is planned specifically to your requirements, but they may also have a number of wedding packages using certain venues and accommodation and including a limited number of services, at a fixed price. If your budget is limited, this can be a way of getting your wedding in Scotland at an affordable price, so may be worth investigating.

If you are organising your wedding from a distance, most agencies can be contacted by email, phone or fax. If you prefer a face to face meeting some time before the wedding they should also provide this as part of the service.

Quite a number of the larger venues, such as hotels and castles, now employ their own in-house wedding planners. You may find that they do not allow independent agencies to arrange weddings at their venue, and it is probably a cheaper option to allow them to arrange it for you in-house, as there may be no extra charge for this. So this could be the easiest and most cost-effective solution if you are settled on that particular venue. However, if you do decide to go with the in-house planner, look out for restrictions on your choice, such as the requirement to have your wedding ceremony, the reception and accommodation all in the one venue, or in places they stipulate. If you wish to be married in a castle, have your reception at a nearby award-winning restaurant and stay in the honeymoon suite in a luxury hotel in the next town, with accommodation for your guests arranged elsewhere, you would probably be better hiring an independent wedding agency to dovetail all the arrangements for you.

If you are having a very small wedding, with just you and your partner present, you will need two people to attend as witnesses in order to make the wedding legal. A wedding planner will be able to arrange this for you.

In addition to making all the pre-wedding arrangements, the planner should also be there on the day, to ensure that everything goes without a hitch and to take care of such things as paying the minister and piper, taking the signed marriage schedule back to the registrar after the ceremony, returning kilts to the hire shop and so on.

Most agencies will also organise civil partnership, renewal of vows or commitment ceremonies.

Costs

It is extremely difficult to give an idea of how much a wedding agency will charge; theirs is a very competitive business and they are reluctant to give details of standard charges. They tend to say that, as every wedding is unique, they do not have standard charges. However, as a guide, a typical wedding planner is likely to charge 15%-20% of the total cost of the wedding, with a minimum fee of £500. Others just charge a fee which is incorporated into the final contract price – it may be difficult here to find out exactly how much the fee is. The normal way of working is for a deposit to be payable when the contract is issued. This will be after the basic details of the wedding have been decided between you and the planner. A typical deposit amount is 35% of contract total, with the balance due a number of weeks prior to the wedding date.

Remember that wedding planners may be able to secure discounts for some of the services, so it may be money well spent. In addition, there are other factors to take into account.

Joanne & Craig Dickson from the USA found hiring a wedding planner was money well spent

We realised that legal requirements, and also the logistics of organising all the details from the US, might be better handled by someone who knew the venue and various services available. While we could research much of that online, it seemed better to let someone with experience, relationships and local contacts to advise us and suggest possibilities based on our needs and budget. What I discovered was that it did not cost us more than doing it ourselves. In fact they made all the planning more efficient and cost-effective, having contacts and relationships with various services we could not have from the States.

Both Joanne and I made separate searches and inquiries, then compared notes, and discussed what we found. It was interesting that in some cases we had both written to the same planners and got quotes for the same exact thing with different prices, and the differences were significant. We inquired for a detailed break down of that total package price; none of the planners we contacted initially were willing to break it down.

The couple are expected to pay for almost everything prior to their wedding day. An exception is the drinks provided for the reception. They normally pay the hotel/venue direct, unless they have picked out a 'drinks package' ahead of time. Many couples have 'open bar' where they provide free drinks for their guests, so it is difficult therefore to pre-pay on this. If they have a 'pay bar', of course, guests will pay for their drinks as they buy them.

If the couple or their guests want extra reprints of photographs, they would liaise directly with the photographer and pay for these.

There is no doubt that it is likely to cost more for you to hire a wedding planner than to do the job yourself, but don't forget that your time actually has a cost as well. There are many hours work involved in planning and organising a wedding, and if you are working full-time you may find that you just don't have the time to spare. If you need to take time off work to make arrangements or visit venues or suppliers, you should really charge this at the cost per hour you would earn at work. In this case, hiring a wedding planner could be cost-effective.

In addition, don't forget to factor in the cost of phone calls to suppliers and service providers, postage costs and so on, if you do the organising yourself. These administrative costs all mount up. A wedding planner will take these costs into account in setting their fees, so bear this in mind when studying their quote. The amount they charge is not all profit to them – don't forget they have to cover their overheads.

You should also bear in mind that an established wedding agency should be able to negotiate discounts on the price of hiring certain venues and other services, discounts that they may pass on to you, whereas if you were organising the wedding yourself you would have to pay the full price of any hire charges.

If you have a limited budget, you may find that a wedding planner is especially cost-effective, even taking their fees into account. They will have knowledge of a wide number of venues and service providers, some of which will be prepared to do a budget package which they may not advertise to the general public. For instance, most 'high street' photographers charge very high prices for wedding photography, offering packages which may include expensive wedding albums and sometimes insisting on keeping the negatives or digital files themselves, so if you want any reprints you have to have them done at the high price charged by that particular photographer. A wedding agency, however, may be able to offer you a 'budget' photography package, where the photographs are of just as high a standard, but the photographer agrees to take a limited number of shots, and allows you to order reprints for your guests from a high street photo shop.

A good wedding planner should always stick to *your* budget rather than encouraging you to spend more than you can really afford. They will also know whether your initial ideas are achievable within your budget – it is a well-known fact that brides and grooms always underestimate the cost of their dream wedding. If you are organising it yourself, you may be halfway through the process before you realise that your £5,000 wedding is actually going to cost you £8,000 or more – and you will be tempted to spend the extra money, which could be bad news for your credit card! Wedding planners are the experts, and they will be able to advise you from the outset whether your requirements are achievable within your budget. If it is not, they can help you to hone your wish list, ensuring you get best value for money in all aspects of the wedding, so you get a beautiful day to remember that doesn't break the bank.

If you wish to organise some of the wedding yourself, but are having difficulty organising a specific aspect of the wedding, most wedding planners are happy to organise just part of the day for you. Or they may be prepared to pass on contact details of service providers for you to contact them yourself. This way you can be certain that the venue or the supplier, whether a minister , a photographer, a florist, or whatever, have been vetted by the wedding agency and will give you a good service. This can save you time and put your mind at rest, which could be well worth the fee charged by the wedding planner for sourcing services and passing on the information.

If you wish only to have a simple ceremony arranged for you, without any reception or accommodation, you can find wedding planners who will do this for as little as a £50 administrative fee, plus the fee for the registrar, minister or celebrant.

Emma & Mark Goodjohn from England did it themselves
It's hard to judge, but we reckon we saved thousands of pounds by organising our own wedding. However, not knowing the area or having local contacts, it took a lot of time and effort to get it right, but it was worth it.
Our recommendation is, money depending, if you've got loads of cash use a wedding planner, just make sure they organise what you want and not just some carbon copy of everyone else's wedding. Alternatively, do it yourself and save the money.

How To Choose Your Wedding Planner

Finding a Planner
Anybody serious about wedding planning will undoubtedly have their own website. If you use a search engine such as Google to find 'wedding planners in Scotland', bear in mind that internet search engines organise the 'hits' that come up on the basis of how long the website has been in existence and how many hits it receives, so this may mean that some of the newer ones are way down the list. One way to find these is to look on the directory sites which have a database of wedding agencies and other suppliers.

Kerry & Steve Pantony from England searched on the internet for a weddings agency
We chose to go with a wedding planner because we wanted remembrance of our wedding to be dominated by pleasure rather than the hassle of organisation. Also because we were a bit vague about what we wanted and what was required by law. We looked up "weddings in Scotland" on the internet – the number of hits that that phrase brings is very scary. But we eventually went for more specific locations in Scotland.
I don't think we could have arranged it on our own – we relied quite heavily on their advice. It may be different if you live in the area. However, I do feel that we were incredibly lucky in our choice of wedding planner as there was a certain amount of randomness involved.

TO USE OR NOT TO USE?

Wedding Planner

- They can arrange every detail of your big day, removing the stress of organising a complex wedding.
- You can sit back and let them do all the work – all you need to do is enjoy the day when it arrives.
- If you have a demanding job or are very busy with other commitments, you may not have time to do a thorough job yourself.
- If you live abroad, using a planner in Scotland with local contacts will make the whole process easier.
- The wedding planner may have an agent in your home country who speaks your language.
- They will arrange as much or as little of your wedding as you wish.
- They will stick to your agreed budget.
- They will advise you on all the legislative and administrative requirements.
- They can advise you on such things as customs forms you need to complete if you wish to send your dress or anything else to the UK from abroad.
- They will collect your dress when it arrives and ensure it is looked after and pressed before the big day.
- They will have detailed knowledge of a wide range of recommended venues and other service providers, and can find just what suits you and your pocket.
- You may save on costs due to discounts the wedding planner can negotiate with venues and service providers.
- Some venues have their own planners who will do an 'in-house' job included in the cost of venue hire.
- The planner will know the area and can more easily source local service providers and accommodation.
- If you have a specific venue or accommodation in mind, they can visit it for you in advance and give an honest appraisal of the standard and quality of service you are likely to receive.
- As their reputation depends on feedback from satisfied wedding couples, you can be sure that they will only recommend venues and other service providers who have done a good job in the past.
- If you are looking for something very special or unusual, but don't know exactly what, they will be able to advise you and suggest ideas you may not have thought of.
- They will act as mediator between venue and clients wherever there is dispute.
- They will be personally contactable from the moment you arrive in Scotland to iron out any difficulties, to help you with any problems, and to ensure that everything you have asked for turns up in the right place at the right time.

- They will be there on the day to deal with any last minute hitches.
- They will be the focal point for your, or your guests', requests so that you have no need to speak with the bar manager to arrange drinks, the chef to arrange the meal, the booking clerk to arrange the room, and so on.
- They can arrange accommodation for your other guests outside of the sometimes expensive wedding venue.
- They will keep in contact with you every step of the way, advising you on how to complete the legal paperwork and confirming ALL arrangements before booking them. So, all you need to do is show up at your ceremony!

Plan It Yourself
- Probably less expensive.
- You keep control over your wedding.
- Although it is hard work to arrange it yourself, it can also be a great deal of fun and give you a sense of satisfaction.
- You can get your friends and relatives involved in the planning, making it a real combined effort.
- You may be able to use venues and service providers who do not work with wedding planners.
- You will be sure your wedding is totally unique.
- You can use your friends and relatives to provide the services where appropriate: your sister can make the dress, your mother can bake the cake, best friend Joe can take the photographs, cousin Mary can play the harp and so on.
- You have to arrange to send forms and personal documents to the registrar yourself, and to collect the marriage schedule from them. A planner isn't allowed to do this for you, so why pay them for this as part of their service?
- You can be far more flexible, especially if it's just the two of you: you may choose to arrange accommodation, book meals and so forth once you arrive in Scotland and can examine these places yourself.
- Very little need be paid for in advance.
- You will have an active rather than a passive role in every aspect of your wedding.
- If you have a very definite idea of where you want to get married and exactly what other facilities you want, there may be little advantage in having a planner organise it for you.
- You will be able to speak direct with all wedding service providers so that they understand fully your wishes rather than have them mediated by a wedding planner.
- You will have the satisfaction of knowing that every aspect of your wedding was the result of your own hard work.

Another source of information about wedding planners is via one of the many weddings magazines available in newsagents or through subscription. For a list of Scottish Wedding Planners, see the list below. There are listings of wedding magazines and other suppliers in *Sources of Information* below.

The information given on the wedding planner's website, and the way it is laid out, should be your first guide. Generally, if it is a well-designed, user-friendly and informative website, there is a good chance that they will be efficient, approachable and easy to work with. Some websites give very little information about who they are or what they can do for you, are difficult to navigate around and don't give a clear explanation of the range of services they offer. This might raise alarm bells about how approachable and transparent they will be if you employ them to plan your wedding. By the nature of their profession, they will all offer similar services, so it is important that you feel you can work well with them.

Your Initial Enquiry

Once you have drawn up a shortlist of those which give you a positive first impression, you should email or ring them with a brief enquiry regarding your wedding. Include the basic details you know, such as when (roughly) it would take place, how large or small it would be and whether you have any specific desires at this time, e.g. it must be in a castle, or in the Highlands. If you have not decided anything other than it should be in Scotland, tell them this, and invite them to suggest the various options available to you.

Kerry & Steve were impressed by the helpfulness of their wedding planner

They suggested a few places for the wedding itself.. We wanted accommodation not too far away and we were happy to be guided by their suggestions... We wanted flowers – I had a vague idea but again it was their input – and the result was gorgeous. They arranged the celebrant (humanist) and we were able to have vows that suited us. They told us what documents they thought we would need and gave us contact details of the relevant registrar – but they were very clear that we needed to send those documents directly to the registrar (which we did). What we had to do was very clear and very easy and the registrar was great.

Their Response

Make a note of how quickly the different agencies respond to your query. Did they reply instantly to your email? Did you manage to get through on the phone immediately or, if you were asked to leave a message, did they get back to you within the day? If you had to wait several days for a reply, this doesn't bode well for their future efficiency. Having said which, some may be very efficient when it comes to getting your business, but once you have signed a contract, you may find the level and speed of service declines, so their initial response time is not a foolproof guide.

Many wedding agencies will send you a questionnaire to complete in response to your initial enquiry. You may find that you receive several very similar – in some cases identical – questionnaires back. This is a useful tool for both you and the planner – it allows you to state clearly and systematically what your wedding might entail, and allows them to assess how much it might cost. The downside is that at this stage in the process it may be difficult for you to answer the questionnaire in as much detail as they need to give you an accurate quote. If you wish to discuss the options further before you complete the questionnaire, don't be afraid to tell them – a good wedding planner should be prepared to do this.

Assess the quality of any letter or email they send to you. Does this appear to be a 'form letter/email' sent out to all enquirers, or is it a personal note to you, which refers to your original query and shows that they have read it and are responding to your specific request?

Kerry & Steve were put off one wedding planner because they did not tailor their response to their specific situation
The decision re which wedding planner to use was easy and was entirely due to the quality of response that we got. We're both quite realistic and we accept that in the scheme of things that it is probably far more profitable for a wedding planner to do a big wedding and that we were really small potatoes. But it's your wedding – you don't want to feel that you're not very important. We told both wedding planners that it would be just the two of us (and that we'd need witnesses). [One] grasped this immediately. The other wedding planner said that they did but then immediately emailed us a standard form, two thirds of which seemed to be about the size of the wedding party and the number of guests. So we re-informed them that there would only be the two of us. We then asked them specific questions about the number of photographs – the answer included information about how the photographer would come to the bride's home and get all those shots with the bride's family. We informed them that there would only be the two of us. We asked for more information re accommodation – we were told it depended on the size of the party. At this point we stopped giving them the benefit of the doubt and gave up.

Testimonials
Some wedding agencies have a 'testimonials' page on their website which has quotes from a number of their previous clients saying what a fabulous day they had and what a wonderful service the company provided. Of course, these need to be taken with a pinch of salt – who knows how many complaints they have had from other clients. But if there's a goodly number of endorsements, it is a better sign than if there are only one or two, or none at all.

SAMPLE WEDDING/CIVIL PARTNERSHIP QUESTIONNAIRE

Personal Details:
Name
Address
E-mail
Telephone
Citizens of which country
Prospective Ceremony Date: (Month/Year)
Type of Ceremony:
Religious/Non-religious/Humanist
Civil/Registrar
Religious blessing/commitment ceremony
Civil Partnership
Requirements:
Number of guests
Do you require witnesses?
Do you require a photographer?
Do you require video coverage?
Approximate Budget
Area of Scotland
Venue Type:
Castle/Stately Home
Church/Chapel/Cathedral
Hotel
Other
Preferred overnight accommodation:
At the venue
Nearby hotel or guesthouse
Number of nights accommodation.
How many guests require accommodation?
Dress Hire for Groom and Groomsmen:
Kilt
Morning suit
How many required?
Preferred tartan
Type of photographs:
Formal
Informal
Mixed
Transport:
Vintage car
Horse & carriage
Limousine
Taxi/Black Cab
Other

Flowers:
Bride's Bouquet
Bridesmaid's Bouquet(s)
Flowers for hair
Corsage/Buttonhole(s)
Room displays
Reception Table Displays
Beauty Treatments:
Hairdresser
Makeup
Manicure/Pedicure
Facial
Massage
Other
Wedding cake:
Traditional Fruitcake
Sponge
Chocolate
Chocolate Fountain
Other
Drinks:
Champagne
Cocktails
Sparkling Wine
Soft Drinks
Canapés
Budget per person: £10 - £15   £15 - £20   £20 or more
Meal:
Buffet
Sit-down meal
Budget per person: £20 - £30   £30 - £40   £40 or more
Music for ceremony:
Bagpipes
Harp
Organ
Recorded music
Other
Music for reception:
String Quartet
Gaelic Singer
Harp
DJ
Scottish Ceilidh Band
Other Live Band
Other
Any additional information about your wedding

It is a good idea to ask the various planners you are considering if they would put you in touch with previous clients so you can ask them their opinion of the service they had. Again, you would obviously only be put into contact with those who had a good experience, but if a planner is reluctant, or refuses altogether, to allow you to speak or write to any of their previous clients, this may give you pause for thought.

Of course, you want to be sure that your own confidentiality will be observed once you sign up with a wedding agency, so again, if a planner immediately says, 'oh yes, you can talk to so and so and here's their contact details,' think again. The professional way for them to approach your request is to say of course you can speak to their previous clients, as long as they agree. They should then sound out those clients and ask them if they are prepared to talk to you, and if they can pass on their contact details to you. This way you can be sure that your own privacy as a client would be respected in future.

Check Their Services

Before you sign a contract with an agency, ensure that you know exactly what they will and won't do. Use the 'To use or not to use' list above as a guide. If there is anything in the above list which your wedding planner won't provide as part of their service, look for another who will.

In addition, ask them if they have their own insurance to cover them for any failures on their part. Some may also be able to provide wedding insurance for you, through a reputable insurance company.

Check whether they are able to arrange your flights or other transport to Scotland. They may not – this is really the province of a travel agent, and it may be that you can book cheaper transport yourself. However, they may work with a travel agent who can give you a good deal.

Clarify exactly how much the deposit will be and when it and the balance should be paid. Ensure that you are given a contract that itemises all the services they will be providing, and check it carefully before you pay any money. Bear in mind that you may add extra services, or change certain details, once the deposit is paid. In this case, you should always be sent an amended contract indicating any change in price.

What To Look Out For

With the growth in the wedding planning industry in recent years, it seems to have become a pretty cut-throat business, with some sharp practices going on here and there. Without wishing to take the gloss off the romantic of organising your wedding, it is wise to be aware of some of the less appealing aspects of the weddings business. These are the things to be wary of:

- It appears that some wedding agencies have tried to confuse prospective clients by using similar URLs, and in some cases identical wording on their webpages. One wedding agency even has a warning sign in bright red letters on their homepage, *Warning -Beware of copycat wedding sites.*
- In another case, a wedding agency found that their company name was advertised on Google Ad Words, using a very similar URL which

actually pointed to a competing website. They found there was little they could do to correct this situation without going through lengthy legal battles and Google investigations.

- Some wedding agencies claim to offer a full service but fail to deliver. Some may not show up to a wedding unless it's a certain size, or may charge extra for their attendance rather than including that as standard in their basic price.

- Some agencies set out to appeal to the elite, those for whom money is no object. Look for phrases like 'high end' services. The service providers they use will charge equally high prices, for example with photographers charging upwards of £5000. There is no suggestion that these people will not do an excellent job, but you may receive just as good a service for a much lower price by going to a different wedding agency.

- Your wedding is possibly one of the most expensive purchases you will make during your lifetime, so do be aware that, in such a lucrative trade, there may be a few people who try to take advantage of that and over-charge or give a bad service. You can avoid this by ensuring that you are happy with the general approach of the company and that all the costs you will be charged, and the services that will be provided, are explained clearly when you sign your contract. There will almost inevitably be changes made after you have signed. You may want to alter the number of guests, or add an extra service you didn't include initially; the agency may find that, due to circumstances beyond their control, they will have to change supplier for one or more of the services. As long as it is clearly stated on your contract that any changes in arrangements or costs will be always agreed between you and the wedding agency in advance, you should not receive any unpleasant surprises.

Having said this, with thousands of weddings being arranged each year by professional companies, any problems are a tiny proportion of the total. The vast majority of weddings go off without a hitch, and most wedding planners genuinely want to organise the perfect day for you. They go into the business because they love weddings, not because they want to make a fortune.

To quote one wedding planner who was affected by sharp practice from a competitor
While this is annoying, we do realise that it is but a 'flea in our ear' type of annoyance because in the end, you can try to copy anything you like – even Coca Cola – but the 'real thing' is the real deal!

CASE STUDY FROM A WEDDING AGENCY

Highland Country Weddings (HCW) was formed in February 2005 by Janis MacLean and Natasha Honan. Although the agency was newly-formed, the two women had worked together at a former wedding planning agency and had combined experience of 18 years planning weddings exclusively in Scotland.

'We wanted to take the Scottish Wedding planning business out of the 'one-woman-one area in Scotland' type business and truly make it international, with agents in different countries servicing local brides and grooms, in their own language, in their own time zone. We wanted to provide the best service possible, with a central office in Scotland, a US office in California to deal with our many American clients without the difficulty of conflicting time zones, and multi-lingual agents in other European countries.

We also wanted to cover the whole of Scotland and wanted to take weddings where no weddings had been before! Up a mountain, on Loch Ness – whatever and wherever the couple desired. We wanted an agency with fast and efficient communication, where no email enquiry or phone call is left unanswered for more than a day. We wanted to make a Scottish wedding available for any size of wedding and for all budgets.

Ambitiously, we formed the first agency with agents working exclusively for us in other countries. We currently have international agents, speaking the local languages, for Holland and Belgium; France; Italy, Switzerland and Germany; USA and Canada. Our website can be read in Dutch, French, German and Italian as well as English.

We also formed the first Scottish Gay wedding website, to coincide with the introduction of the new Civil Partnership legislation in December 2005.'

Initial enquiry

Natasha, HCW's American Director, takes us through the planning of a typical wedding:

'This is typical of the email enquiries we receive:

Hello,

My fiancé and I would like to get married in Scotland, and we are writing to enquire about locations and get some cost estimates. We would like to get married in a castle or large manor house with nice gardens, sometime in the summer of 2007. Our guest list isn't set but we expect to invite about 40 people, who would be coming from the United States, England, and Scotland. We would like to be married near Aberdeen, since it is the city where me met, but we don't have any strong preferences yet. We both live in the United States right now (I am American, my fiancé is English) so we think that it would be good to hire a wedding planning service since we won't be in Scotland to preview locations and it would be good to have someone there who can help us out.

Thank you very much in advance, Jane Shapiro

Our Response

As soon as this mail arrives, I respond, sometimes within seconds of it being received. We aim to get the process started and progressed in efficient, friendly and personalized fashion. Janis in Scotland also answers e-mail enquiries as quickly as possible. The couple have no idea of the kind of service they will get from the wedding planner until they receive their first response: wedding planning agency websites all look pretty good, although some are more professional-looking than others, some with better information than others. Plus there are all the castles/venues with their own wedding planning operation. This adds up to a confusing amount of information for the prospective couple. We want to make it simple for them and we want to have everything under one roof, even their honeymoon planning and favours, if that's what they require.

I send a personal letter or email in response. I attach the HCW questionnaire and we mail our letter introducing Highland Country Weddings and its directors: we work on all weddings together, wherever they may originate. I am based in Southern California and can be reached 24/7. I am at my desk, on the computer and on the phone most days. I am approachable and reachable, as is Janis in Scotland – we freely give out our mobile phone numbers. I also attach our 'Choices' document which outlines all the services we can arrange for the couple.

Follow-Up

I make a note of their e-mail address and date received, and if I don't hear from them in a week or so, I will enquire whether they received my mail and whether they require any more assistance with their wedding plans. I almost always receive an excited email back within a day, usually with a completed questionnaire and their phone number. I usually respond by email and ask permission to ring them. I introduce myself and we work out the best day and time to ring. Most couples are reluctant just to make arrangements through email. They are reassured when they can talk to a human voice on the telephone. But email comes into its own when confirming detailed arrangements. Everything then is down in black and white, so no misunderstanding can creep in on either side.

A number of enquirers phone first, which allows me to introduce myself and run through the services we can offer. I would then normally email further information to them.

International Service

We have two directors on two continents and three other agents in Europe. If we have clients contacting us from Holland, Belgium, France, Italy, Switzerland or Germany we assign them to the relevant agent for their country. This makes the process so much easier for them as they can talk to, phone or email our agent in their own language.

Couples in the USA or Canada will be assigned to me, in the US, avoiding time-zone problems. I am available to deal with any questions during their waking hours. Janis will work with couples in the UK. Couples from outside Europe or North America will be assigned to either me or Janis.

The agents are responsible for communicating directly with their own clients, in their country. Each agent is assigned to one of the two directors so that communication is free-flowing from client to agent to director – often spanning several continents. Email is our greatest tool. There is usually someone working on an HCW wedding somewhere in the world at any hour of the day!'

The Planning Process

On the basis of the information the couple have provided in the questionnaire, I send a list of venues based upon their requirements. In this case, castles and other venues in and around the Aberdeen area plus some others that I think they might like. We send the client links to the specific websites. I explain that we at HCW have our own pictures and personal reviews on these venues. If there are any which look of interest to them, they can email us to ask for this specific information. The client chooses a venue – and off we go!

Over several months we are chatting on the phone, emailing back and forth about details of the wedding: the photographer, type of flowers, the legal paperwork issues, the timing for everything, the marriage visas that are required. I speak with the mother of the bride and the groom about the details. I arrange for baskets of Scottish goodies to be placed in every room that is booked at the Castle. I arrange for the Minister to chat with the bride and groom on the details of the ceremony.

The photographer also needs to know the type of pictures they would like, the numbers, the specific people in the group and so on. The cake is going to be specially made 200 miles down south, as the bride and groom have requested a specific tartan sugar paste to be draped down their four-tier stacked cake. Very few bakers have the specific equipment to make the tartan. The couple have requested an outdoor wedding in the gardens of the castle. We purchase several large white umbrellas, just in case.

There is a last minute hitch: the wedding dress, which had been sent over from America ahead of time, for us to have steamed and pressed, is held up at customs and we receive a letter from Parcelforce for £66.35 import duty, £108.38 VAT and £8.00 Parcelforce fee: £182.73 in total. Janis phones Parcelforce to explain the goods have no commercial value, the bride calls them too to explain, but to no avail. We are told that we would have to repackage and resubmit from point of departure. No time for that! We pay the fee and make a note to sort this out afterwards – probably the customs forms were filled out incorrectly, as normally there should be no duty to pay.

The Wedding Day

On the day of the wedding, the HCW representative is present from early in the morning, helping the bride to get ready or running errands. She will ensure that everything on the day is running to plan, and that everyone booked is there, on time, and in place. She will also ensure that all the necessary equipment is available: for example, we may need a CD player to play music for the processional; we may need to help the florist tie ribbons on the pews; quite often we deliver the floral requirements and the wedding cake (which we also set up); we deliver the kilts for the groomsmen.

Sometimes, if the couple chose to have no wedding transport provided, we will drive the bride and groom to the venue. We meet with service providers such as the videographer and photographer to introduce the key members of the bridal party and confirm final arrangements for the day so everybody knows what they are doing when.

We liaise with the celebrant and introduce him or her to the couple, if they haven't already met. We work as a team with hotel and catering staff to ensure all the events of the day are in place and running to plan. We take care of the marriage schedule and deliver it back safely to the registrar, who will then prepare the marriage certificate.

We help to keep the events to the planned time schedule, so that the day flows smoothly. We set up tables, move furniture, carry and hold bouquets, stick the bride's veil back into her tiara when it falls out, hand out tissues to those who cry, show people where to go and where to stand or sit.

On the day, we are there to ensure that the couple are not stressed, to make sure they enjoy their day and that they do not have to worry about any of the organisation. All the bride and groom have to do is to enjoy their wedding day.

Recommended Venues

We are very careful to select for our couples only those venues we can recommend as giving an excellent service both to us and our clients. This still leaves a long list to choose from!

We have used many different venues over the years, but if we have had a bad experience with them, we normally do not use them again. We have now narrowed our venue list to those that are truly easy to work with – efficient, kind and professional. We also only use venues that are first rate – gorgeous, clean and in a beautiful area – that we know will appeal to our national and international clients.

We know that when we make contact with one of our recommended venues we can expect a professional and instant response. We demand this of every venue and service provider we use. Efficient and timely communication has to be uppermost for us. We have couples anxious to confirm dates and venues who are literally at their phone or computer waiting with bated breath for our news.

Service Providers

Our relationship with the many service providers we use gives us great satisfaction. When we started out we wanted to find new service providers to inject some new blood into the Scottish weddings industry. Scotland is a hive of cultural activity with some very famous Schools of Arts, photography and so forth. We wanted to tap into this and see what was out there and now we can offer our couples a choice of photographer, videographer, florist and other suppliers in every region of Scotland. We work with our clients to find the best ones for them.

We started our agency in the year that Scotland gave legal rights to Humanist Society celebrants to perform non-religious wedding ceremonies throughout Scotland. We know most of these celebrants, and what a nice bunch they are – so happy and willing to fulfill all our client's wishes, however out of the ordinary. They are an enthusiastic bunch and so happy to have been given this privilege.

We have made friends with ministers too, some of whom are retired from the Church of Scotland but licensed to perform weddings. All are enthusiastic and willing and completely computer literate; some even have their own websites. All are intelligent, witty and open, liberal and fun and have remained friends with our couples too. They communicate with them well before the wedding, passing on information and pictures and ideas and so on.

Clients

It is sometimes difficult to predict how much work will be involved in a wedding. It may take us 30 hours of work or may take us 280 hours. We can usually judge by the size of the wedding and by the number of requirements at the beginning and we base our quote on these. However, more requirements may be added later as the couple get a clearer idea of what they want.

We never underestimate the psychological factors. Arranging a wedding can be a stressful time, and not just for the bride and groom – their parents too can become worried and anxious as they realise the choices that need to be made. It can become overwhelming for them, at which time we have to be good listeners and good counsellors. Janis and myself are always available to listen to our clients' worries and ensure that everything is sorted out to their satisfaction. This can take many extra hours of our time, which we have not priced into our quote, but we are happy to do this because we know that this sort of customer care is essential for a successful wedding day.

Budget

We ask prospective couples for their approximate budget on the initial questionnaire in order to guide us with the venue information we provide. Venues have vastly different charges so we are careful not to suggest a venue which is beyond the couple's reach.

A problem is that couples usually underestimate the cost of their requirements. Sometimes, we get asked for the moon – a tremendous list of requirements for a tiny budget. We tactfully point this out to the couple so that they do not waste their time looking for the unachievable. Most of them are then willing to compromise. We are very conscious of people's budgets and never attempt to go above this. If they are totally inflexible on their requirements we just have to say it cannot be done within their budget.

What we cannot do is give a detailed breakdown of every part of the wedding and our fees. Some clients will ask us for itemised costing and we point out that we can't really do this in a way that would make much sense, simply because we tailor a package for each client. There are too many variables and would confuse more than help the client. We take into account discounts that we may receive from venues and providers so that our own fees to the client are lower, and we are confident that in the end the couple will pay not much more than if they were to go direct to the venue and plan the wedding themselves (with all the hassle that involves).

All in all, we pride ourselves on providing the best service we can without breaking the bank. And most of all, we love what we do!'

Contact details: *Highland Country Weddings:* tel 07752-265833; USA/Canada enquiries: tel 866-794-3675 (toll free) or 310-457-4964 PST; European enquiries: tel 003902-90002055; www.highlandcountryweddings.co.uk
Gay Weddings in Scotland: tel 01355-246905; USA/Canada enquiries: tel 866-794-3675 (toll free) or 310-457-4964 PST; www.gayweddingscotland.co.uk

Wedding Planners in Scotland

As You Like It: Central Scotland agency. Roodwell House, Stenton, East Lothian, EH42 1TE; tel 01368-850675; www.asyoulikeitweddings.co.uk

Celebrate In Scotland: Based in Edinburgh, a complete events service. 20 Castle Avenue, Edinburgh, EH12 7LA; tel 0131-334 5005; email info@celebrateinscotland.com; www.celebrateinscotland.com

Highland Country Weddings: tel 07752-265833; USA/Canada enquiries: tel 866-794-3675 (toll free) or 310-457-4964 PST; European enquiries: tel 003902-90002055; www.highlandcountryweddings.co.uk

Gay Weddings in Scotland: tel 01355-246905; USA/Canada enquiries: tel 866-794-3675 (toll free) or 310-457-4964 PST; www.gayweddingscotland.co.uk*Litu:* Based in east Scotland. Aithernie, Leven, Fife, KY8 5NJ; 01333-439340; www.scottish-wedding-consultants.com

Scottish Wedding Consultants: 3 Morham Lea, Edinburgh EH10 5GL; tel 0131-445 1000; www.scottishweddingconsultants.co.uk

SW Scotland Events: Based in Dumfries and Galloway. Tel 01556-630403; www.swscotlandevents.co.uk

The Dream Wedding Planner: Based in Aberdeen, North-east Scotland. 34 Whitehall Terrace, Aberdeen, AB25 2RY; tel 07830-354456; www.thedreamweddingplanner.com

Utopia-Scotland: Located in Perthshire. Abbotsfield Gardens, Abbotsfield Terrace, Auchterarder, PH3 1DE; tel 01764-664424; www.utopia-scotland.com

THE PERFECT VENUE

Choosing Your Venue

There are so many possible locations for your wedding in Scotland, that the first step in choosing the one which is ideal for you is to narrow it down to a shortlist. Make a checklist of your essential requirements and discount all venues which don't fit the bill.

Checklist

- **Number of guests:** Ensure that the venue you choose is neither too big nor too small for your wedding party and guests. Although it is obvious that a venue which is too small will not be able to accommodate your wedding, it is just as bad to choose a large space where your small party will feel dwarfed by the surroundings. The ambience is always at its best where the room is full, without being crowded, so aim for a number of guests towards the maximum number the venue, or particular room within the venue, will hold.
- **Overnight accommodation:** How many rooms for overnight accommodation do you require, either within or close to the venue? If you are having a large wedding and it is important to you that both you and your guests all stay in the building where the wedding takes place, you may find that a large hotel is the only suitable option. Many castles have only a small number of bedrooms, while some have none at all.
- **Reception:** Do you want your wedding ceremony and reception to take place under the same roof, or are you happy to have your ceremony in one place, with your reception at a nearby restaurant or hotel? Some venues have their own chapel in the grounds, so you can have your ceremony there and the reception in the main building.
- **Type of ceremony:** If you want a civil ceremony, you will be restricted in the venues you can choose, as these can only take place in Register Offices or in Approved Places. No building which is, or has been, mainly used for religious purposes may be approved for civil ceremonies, nor can they take place out of doors. You have a far greater choice of venue if you decide on a religious or non-religious ceremony. A minister or celebrant can marry you anywhere at all in Scotland, subject to their agreement and that of the land or property owner.
- **Time of year:** Some venues are definitely better reserved for the warmer months of the year – a winter wedding is best in a nice warm hotel rather than a drafty castle ruin! And if you are intent on an outdoor wedding in the Highlands between May and September, do not underestimate the nuisance midges can cause if the weather is warm and still. Again, an outdoor venue can be ruined by rain, so it is advisable that there is an indoor alternative if the weather is not kind to you. Many venues will allow you to marry either indoors or in the grounds, a decision you can make at the last minute depending on the weather on the day.

- **Date:** Popular venues can be booked up months or years in advance, so it is important to fix on a date as soon as possible during the planning process. If you can be flexible on the date or the day of the week you marry, this will allow you more choice. Saturdays in June, July and August are most likely to be booked a long way in advance at popular venues, so if you can avoid these you will have a better chance of getting your first choice.
- **Theme:** If you have a specific theme in mind, check that the venue is suitable and that they are happy to accommodate your wishes. It may be best to choose the theme after you have chosen the venue, then you can make sure it is one which is appropriate to the age or style of the building and its facilities.
- **Budget:** The cost of hiring a venue varies enormously, from nothing for most outdoor locations, to a few hundred pounds for a castle ruin, to a top quality castle hotel which may charge you several thousand pounds just for the hire fee, with accommodation and food extra. When asking about cost, do ensure that you know exactly what is included in the quoted price.
- **Area of Scotland:** Do you want to marry in romantic isolation, in the remote highlands or islands, or do you want to be near to the bright lights of the towns and cities? You need to consider how accessible your venue will be for you and your guests. Bear in mind the distance from airports, if you are to be flying to Scotland, and the local road and rail provision.
- **Disabled access:** If you or any of your guests have mobility problems, do check with the venue that it is suitable. Some castles or other ancient monuments are in fairly inaccessible places, which involve walking over rocky or boggy terrain, or have many stairs to climb.
- **Facilities**: Do you want facilities such as hairdressing and beauty treatments to be available on site? Some hotels provide a complete wedding package where you have no need to leave the venue at all from the moment you arrive until your departure after the wedding night. Alternatively, check that all the facilities you require are available nearby, or that you can book a travelling beautician to come to your accommodation.

Questions to Ask

- Once you have narrowed your search down to a shortlist, contact each venue to compare what they are offering and to assess how pleasantly and efficiently they deal with your queries.
- If at all possible, it is a good idea to visit the venue. Or if you can't visit in person, maybe you can ask a trusted friend or relative to give the place the 'once over' for you. Even if you can only make contact with the venue by telephone or email beforehand, be wary if their response seems less than helpful. If your emails or telephone calls are answered promptly and efficiently, and there is plenty of information provided, you can be far more confident that things will go without a hitch both before and during the wedding. If staff seem at all off-hand, unable to deal with your

queries, or unsure about who is the right person for you to speak to, you may be better off somewhere else.

- Don't be swayed by slick, persuasive advertising or websites into booking a venue without contacting them directly. You can glean far more from the way they deal with you on a one to one basis than you can from a glossy brochure.
- If the venue does not have accommodation, or not enough for the whole party, ask them if they can recommend anywhere nearby. Most places will keep a list of local good quality accommodation.
- If you are having a religious ceremony, ask the venue if they can provide or recommend a minister, a piper or any other local suppliers you may need.
- Ascertain if they do their own catering or whether they either recommend or work with specific outside caterers. If the venue does not cater for receptions at all, they may be able to suggest local hotels or restaurants which will do so. This is particularly useful if you do not know the area yourself.
- If you want a particular caterer to do the food, or you wish to do it yourself, will they allow this? Not all venues are amenable to wedding parties bringing in caterers they do not know personally.
- Will they allow you to decorate the venue in the way you wish? Some churches have regular flower arrangers and may not allow you to do your own, or may specify how many arrangements of what size you may have. However, if you let them know the colour scheme, and the flowers that are in your wedding bouquet, they should agree to provide flowers to suit.
- If you have your heart set on a venue, but it isn't really big enough for your requirements, they may be able to provide a marquee. Do check the cost of this, however, before you agree, because marquee hire is very expensive, at least two thousand pounds for a fairly small one. Some venues have a marquee set up permanently during the summer months for weddings and other events, and this can bring the cost of hire down.
- Will the venue arrange any extras you might want – local excursions, sightseeing, adventure packages, special themes?
- An increasing number of venues now have their own wedding planner on the staff. He or she will work with you to provide exactly what you want for your special day. If you wish to hire your own wedding planner it is important to check with the venue that they will allow an outside agency to come in and arrange the day.
- If you wish to have exclusive use of the venue during your wedding, this is likely to cost extra and generally would only be cost-effective for the venue if you have a large wedding, If your wedding is very small, you should expect that other guests or visitors are likely to be around. It's always worth asking, however, if there will be any other weddings going on at the same time or on the same day as your wedidng. If there are others, make sure you won't feel that you are on a 'production line'.
- Get a definite price as early as possible. Ascertain how much deposit they need and when the balance should be paid. Also clarify whether there

will be anything extra to pay after the wedding. They should issue you with a contract which itemises everything to be included. Read your contract carefully before you sign it – once it is signed, you will be legally bound by it.

Directory of Wedding Venues

This is a careful selection of some of the most splendid, romantic and unusual venues for your wedding. Most are on the mainland, with a few on islands near to the west coast. Locations further afield have not been included due to difficulties of transport, and also because venues on the smaller, more remote islands, inevitably tend to be suitable only for very small wedding parties.

Either the author or her associates have personal and positive experiences of all the venues listed here. However, it was impossible due to lack of space to include all those we would have liked to. As a result, the directory is by no means exhaustive, and there are further suggestions of where to find your ideal venue below. Those listed here are divided into five categories:

- Castles
- Churches: including churche, chapels, abbeys and cathedrals
- Country Houses: including both stately homes open to the public, and a number of large private houses which can be hired for your wedding party on a self-catering or catered basis
- Hotels
- Miscellaneous: a number of quirky and unique venues

Details given for each venue include:

- Their location
- How many bedrooms they have, or where local accommodation may be found. (For further advice on arranging accommodation for yourself or your guests, see *Organise It Yourself* above.)
- Whether they are licensed for civil weddings and civil partnership ceremonies (all of them welcome religious and non-religious weddings)
- A brief description
- Full contact details including their website address

The venues are cross-referenced below by area, allowing you to easily find those in a particular region of Scotland.

Area	Town	Venue	Category
Dumfries and Galloway	Dumfries	Caerlaverock Castle	Castle
	Dumfries	Comlongon Castle	Castle
	Stranraer	Corsewall Lighthouse Hotel	Hotel
	Dumfries	Lincluden Collegiate Church	Church
	Dumfries	Sweetheart Abbey	Church
	Castle Douglas	Threave House	Country House

Scottish Borders	Peebles	Cringletie House	Hotel
	Melrose	Dryburgh Abbey	Church
	Melrose	Melrose Abbey	Church
	Kelso	Roxburghe House	Hotel
	Peebles	Traquair House	Country House
	Berwick-upon-Tweed	Wedderburn Castle	Castle

Fife	Dunfermline	Aberdour Castle	Castle
	St Andrews	Birkhill Castle	Castle
	Dunfermline	Culross Palace	Country House
	Cupar	Falkland Palace	Country House
	St Andrews	Kellie Castle	Castle
	St Andrews	Myres Castle	Castle

Argyll & Bute	Oban	Ardanaiseig Hotel	Hotel
	Tarbert	Balinakill Country House	Hotel
	Tobermory, Mull	Duart Castle	Castle
	Tobermory, Mull	Glengorm Castle	Castle
	Dunoon	Castle Lachlan	Castle
	Tarbert	Stonefield Castle Hotel	Hotel
	Tobermory, Mull	Torosay Castle	Castle

Strathclyde	Brodick, Arran	Brodick Castle	Castle
	Kilmarnock	Carnell Castle	Castle
	Millport, Great Cumbrae	Cathedral of the Isles	Church
	Glasgow	Corinthian	Miscellaneous
	Ayr	Culzean Castle	Castle
	Ayr	Enterkine Country House	Hotel
	Glasgow	Greenbank Garden	Miscellaneous
	Glasgow	House For An Art Lover	Miscellaneous
	Largs	Kelburn Castle	Castle
	Glasgow	Mackintosh Church	Church
	Glasgow	Mar Hall	Hotel
	Glasgow	Oran Mor	Miscellaneous
	Glasgow	People's Palace	Miscellaneous
	Glasgow	Pollok House	Country house

Forth Valley	Alloa	Alloa Tower	Castle
	Alloa	Castle Campbell	Castle
	Stirling	Doune Castle	Castle
	Dunblane	Dunblane Cathedral	Church
	Aberfoyle	Forest Hills Hotel	Hotel
	Alloa	Gean House	Country House
	Stirling	Church of the Holy Rude	Church
	Stirling	Kilbryde Castle	Castle
	Stirling	Park Lodge Hotel	Hotel
	Stirling	Stirling Castle	Castle
	Stirling	Wallace Monument	Miscellaneous

Tayside	Pitlochry	Blair Castle	Castle
	Dundee	Drumkilbo House	Hotel
	Arbroath	Ethie Castle	Castle
	Auchterarder	Gleneagles Hotel	Hotel
	Perth	Huntingtower Castle	Castle
	Perth	Murthly Castle	Castle

Lothian	Edinburgh	Borthwick Castle	Castle
	Edinburgh	28 Charlotte Square	Miscellaneous
	Edinburgh	Craigmillar Castle	Castle
	Edinburgh	Dalhousie Castle	Castle
	North Berwick	Dirleton Castle	Castle
	Edinburgh	The Dome	Miscellaneous
	Queensferry	Dundas Castle	Castle
	Edinburgh	Edinburgh Castle	Castle
	Edinburgh	Georgian House	Country House
	Edinburgh	Harburn House	Country House
	Edinburgh	Houstoun House	Hotel
	Edinburgh	Linlithgow Palace	Castle
	Edinburgh	Melville Castle	Castle
	Edinburgh	Rosslyn Chapel	Church
	Edinburgh	Royal College of Physicians	Miscellaneous
	Edinburgh	Oxenfoord Castle	Castle
	Edinburgh	Saint Michael's Parish Church	Church
	North Berwick	Tantallon Castle	Castle

Grampian	Aberdeen	Ardoe House	Hotel
	Peterhead	Cortes House	Country House
	Aberdeen	Crathes Castle	Castle
	Banff	Delgatie Castle	Castle
	Aberdeen	Drum Castle	Castle
	Stonehaven	Dunnottar Castle	Castle
	Elgin	Elgin Cathedral	Church
	Banff	Fyvie Castle	Castle
	Aberdeen	Castle Fraser	Castle
	Aberdeen	Glen Tanar Chapel	Church
	Ellon	Haddo House	Country House
	Banff	Hatton Castle	Castle
	Elgin	Innes House	Country House
	Aberdeen	Marcliffe Hotel	Hotel
	Ballater	Monaltrie House	Hotel
	Aberdeen	Pittodrie House	Hotel
	Aberdeen	Raemoir House Hotel	Hotel

Highland	Wick	Ackergill Tower	Castle
	Newtonmore	Ardverikie House	Country House
	Beauly	Beauly Priory	Church
	Thurso	Bighouse Lodge	Country House
	Nairn	Boath House	Hotel
	Forres	Brodie Castle	Castle
	Aviemore	Cairngorm Mountain	Miscellaneous
	Dornoch	Carbisdale Castle	Castle
	Inverness	Culloden House	Hotel
	Dornoch	Dornoch Cathedral	Church
	Kyle of Lochalsh	Eilean Donan Castle	Castle
	Isle Ornsay, Skye	Hotel Eilean Larmain	Hotel
	Portree, Skye	Flodigarry Hotel	Hotel
	Fort William	Inverlochy Castle	Castle
	Inverness	Jacobite Cruises	Miscellaneous
	Shieldaig	Loch Torridon Hotel	Hotel
	Fort William	The Moorings	Hotel
	Gairloch	Shieldaig Lodge Hotel	Hotel
	Portree, Skye	Skeabost Hotel	Hotel
	Dingwall	Tulloch Castle	Hotel
	Drumnadrochit	Urquhart Castle	Castle

153

Castles

There are over 2,500 castles and fortified sites in Scotland, ranging from ruins in remote glens to substantial fully-functioning buildings which have all the facilities you could require for a large wedding and reception. The most famous ones – Edinburgh Castle, Urquhart Castle and Eilean Donan Castle pre-eminent among these – are among Scotland's most popular tourist attractions , and they are equally popular for weddings. Others have found a new lease of life in the modern world as luxurious hotels. Of these, some have retained the historic look and feel of a castle both inside and out; others look satisfyingly like a fairy-tale castle on the outside, but inside the reception rooms and bedrooms have been modernised and can feel little different from a high quality modern hotel.

Before choosing a castle for your wedding, therefore, as well as finding out what facilities are available, it is wise to check the ambience: if the genuine 'castle' feel is important to you, you may be better opting for a castle which perhaps has less accommodation. If, on the other hand, you want a castle where all your guests can stay, you may have to accept that in order to provide that amount of accommodation, some historic authenticity may necessarily have been lost.

There are many small castles in Scotland which are owned and lived in by individual families. As the upkeep on the fabric of these ancient buildings is inevitably high, a number of them have now opened their homes for weddings. You can gain much in the way of informality and intimacy by hiring such a venue, but you need to bear in mind that this is somebody's home, and there may well be compromises on what they will or will not provide for your wedding.

Always find out from the staff whether there are any difficulties of accessibility either in getting to the venue or within the building itself. If there is difficult terrain to negotiate or many stairs to climb, adjust your wedding dress accordingly, and ensure that all your guests will be able to take full part in proceedings – if your aged grandmother has mobility problems, don't expect her to be able to climb a spiral staircase to the Grand Ballroom!

Just as the size of castles varies enormously, so too do the facilities available. Some may be a gorgeous place for the ceremony, and give scope for stunning photographs, but unable to provide for a reception or accommodation, which you will need to find nearby.

Check whether there any restrictions on where in the castle or grounds you can marry.

If you're having a civil ceremony, certain room(s) in the castle will have been 'approved' and you will not be able to marry elsewhere. If you're having a religious or non-religious ceremony, this could in theory be held anywhere in the castle or the grounds.

Some larger castles may offer you a number of different options as to which room(s) you use for your ceremony and reception. They may also give you the option of exclusive use of the castle for your party alone, but there may be an additional charge for this.

Some of the larger or more important castles have their own wedding planners who will help you to organise your day. Many of these are managed by Historic Scotland and they have a central wedding co-ordinator.

If you choose to marry at a famous castle which is also a tourist attraction may find you become part of the 'show' – expect to have uninvited guests looking on and asking to take photos of, or with, the happy couple. Edinburgh Castle and Urquhart Castle, for example, have weddings taking place during normal opening hours. Eilean Donan Castle schedule them in the evening, after they have closed for the day, so you get exclusive use of the castle and it is a far more private affair.

N.B. All castles are available for religious and non-religious ceremonies; some are also licensed for civil ceremonies.

Aberdour Castle
Location: Fife: 4 miles (6km) east of Dunfermline on the Firth of Forth
Accommodation: None, but plentiful in Dunfermline and Burntisland
Licensed for Civil Weddings: Yes
Capacity: Ceremony 60; Reception 120
A Historic Scotland property, Aberdour Castle stands on the northern shore of the Firth of Forth looking south across the water to Edinburgh. It was originally a 13th century fortified residence but, like many other such structures, was extended in the 15th, 16th and 17th centuries. To the south of the castle lie terraced gardens which were constructed in the 17th century and which are currently being restored to their former glory. This ruined castle provides a romantic and historic venue for a wedding ceremony.
Contact details: Historic Scotland, Longmore House, Salisbury Place, Edinburgh, EH9 1SH; tel 0131-668 8973 or 8916; hs.weddings@scotland.gsi.gov.uk; www.historic-scotland.gov.uk/weddings

Ackergill Tower
Location: Highland: just north of Wick
Accommodation: 17 bedrooms in the castle, 8 in the grounds
Licensed for Civil Ceremonies: Yes
Ackergill Tower is a magnificent 15th century Scottish castle, with accommodation, situated on the very edge of the sea. It is described as 'a home beyond 5 stars'. No bar, no restaurant, no reception, not a hotel, not a club.... just a glorious home for exclusive use. This Scottish castle with accommodation has 25 luxurious bedrooms to offer, each with its own personality but all furnished to the same exacting standards. Nearby is the UK's most northerly Opera House for music, an estate for sport and a wealth of local activities to entertain and enjoy. Local wildlife on both sea and moor make Caithness a naturalist's paradise.
Contact details: Ackergill Tower, by Wick, Caithness, Scotland KW1 4RG; Tel 01955- 603556; ruth@ackergill-tower.co.uk; www.ackergill-tower.co.uk

Alloa Tower

Location: Forth Valley: close to Alloa Town Centre
Accommodation: None but plentiful in Alloa
Licensed for Civil Weddings: Yes.
Capacity: Dinner 40; Drinks reception 60

A National Trust for Scotland property. Alloa Tower is a fully restored and furnished 14th century keep that has been in the hands of the Earls of Mar through the ages. The tower has seen a number of alterations over the centuries, but you can still see the medieval dungeon and magnificent oak roof beams. A sweeping Italian-style staircase was added in the early 1700s. Antiques lovers will appreciate the collection of portraits and silver on loan from the present Earl of Mar and Kellie. It has played host to many of Scotland's monarchs. According to legend, Mary Queen of Scots was reconciled with Darnley here.
Contact details: Alloa Tower, Alloa Park, Alloa, FK10 1PP; tel 0844-493 2129 or 0131-243 9405; functions@nts.org.uk; www.nts.org.uk/Functions/Venue/1

Birkhill Castle

Location: Fife: 15 miles (24km) inland from St Andrews
Accommodation: 10 double bedrooms and two single rooms
Licensed for Civil Weddings: Yes
Capacity: Reception 50 in the castle; Marquees by arrangement

Birkhill is the family home of the Earl and Countess of Dundee. Located on the shores of the River Tay a short distance from St Andrews, the castle is a most romantic venue for weddings. Set in glorious countryside, Birkhill was built in 1780. The house is surrounded by beautiful gardens and the interior has an old-style grace which creates the perfect, relaxed atmosphere for a traditional Scottish wedding ceremony and reception. Cooking is first class, using locally grown organic ingredients. Seats up to 20 people round the dining table, or for larger groups four tables of 8-10 can be provided.
Contact details: Birkhill Castle, Birkhill, Cupar, Fife, KY15 4QP;
tel 01382-330200; info@birkhillcastle.org.uk; www.birkhillcastle.org.uk

Blair Castle

Location: Tayside: Blair Atholl, between Perth and Inverness
Accommodation: None in the castle but estate lodges available and local accommodation plentiful
Licensed for Civil Weddings: Yes
Capacity: Library 40; State Dining Room 140; Ballroom 220

Blair Castle, with its roots in the 13th century, is one of the most northerly of Scotland's great houses and is certainly one of the most majestic. It is the largest house in the Highlands and is one of Britain's oldest continuously inhabited houses, dating in part from 1269. Glorious ceremonies can take place in a glittering array of outstanding facilities – from the more dignified and intimate Library for smaller weddings to the magnificent Ballroom where guests can gather for ceremony, celebration, dining and dancing in a truly highland Scottish ambience. The beautiful grounds offer ideal opportunities for photographs.
Contact details: Blair Castle, Blair Atholl, Perthshire, PH18 5TL;
tel 01796-481207; weddings@blair-castle.co.uk; www.blair-castle.co.uk

Borthwick Castle
Location: Lothian: 13 miles (20km) from Edinburgh Airport
Accommodation: 10 bedrooms, 2 of which are in the Gatehouse Tower
Licensed for Civil Weddings: Yes
Capacity: 75
For nearly 600 years Borthwick Castle has overlooked the gently rolling hills on the edge of the romantic Scottish Borders. One can easily imagine that Mary Queen of Scots looked from her bedchamber window onto a very similar landscape in the 16th Century. The Castle's long and illustrious history has romance and drama and the walls still bear the battle-scars of Cromwell's cannon. Nowadays, with central heating and en-suite bathrooms, the castle retains a medieval ambience which charms even the most seasoned travellers. Your wedding can take place in the castle or a short walk away at the beautiful Borthwick Parish Church.
Contact details: Borthwick Castle Hotel, North Middleton, Midlothian, EH23 4QY; tel 01875-820514; enquiries@borthwickcastle.com; www.borthwickcastlehotel.com

Brodick Castle
Location: Strathclyde: Isle of Arran, 1.5 miles (2.5km) from Brodick
Accommodation: None, but plentiful on the island
Licensed for Civil Weddings: Yes
Capacity: Garden 200; Dining room 30
Brodick Castle, its gardens and country park, stretch from the shore to the highest peak on Arran. Crossing from the mainland, the journey itself is memorable, with spectacular views of Goatfell from the ferry. The castle, ancient seat of the Dukes of Hamilton, was the home of the Duke and Duchess of Montrose until 1957 and there are reputed to be many ghosts who have shared the castle with the owners over its 800-year history. There are walled gardens, an 'Ice House', the Bavarian Summer House, and a licensed restaurant.
Contact details: Brodick Castle, Brodick, Ayrshie KA27 8HY; tel 0844-493 2152 or 0131-243 9405; brodickcastle@nts.org.uk; www.nts.org.uk/Property/13/Weddings

Brodie Castle
Location: Highland: 4 miles (6km) west of Forres, 24 miles east of Inverness
Accommodation: Self-catering cottage. Other accommodation plentiful in the Forres area
Licensed for Civil Weddings: Yes
Capacity: Drawing Room 50; Library 50; Dining Room 22; Stables 60; Marquee 250
Brodie Castle is a 16th century tower house set in peaceful parkland. It contains fine French furniture; English, continental and Chinese porcelain; and a major collection of paintings. The magnificent library contains some 6,000 volumes. The grounds are beautifully maintained and boast a carpeting of daffodils in springtime.
Contact details: Brodie Castle, Forres, Inverness IV36 2TE; tel 0844-493 2157 or 0131-243 9405; functions@nts.org.uk; www.nts.org.uk/Functions/Venue/2

Caerlaverock Castle

Location: Dumfries & Galloway: 7 miles (11km) south east of Dumfries
Accommodation: None, but plentiful in Dumfries
Licensed for Civil Weddings: Yes
Capacity: Ceremony only, 60

An Historic Scotland property, with its moat, twin-towered gatehouse and imposing battlements, Caerlaverock Castle is the epitome of the medieval stronghold. The castle's turbulent history owes much to its proximity to England which brought it into border conflicts. It is a quite fabulous ruin and one of the most striking in Scotland. It overlooks the Solway Firth and its present day condition owes everything to its regular battering in conflict since construction first began in the 13th century.

Contact details: Historic Scotland, Longmore House, Salisbury Place, Edinburgh, EH9 1SH; tel 0131-668 8973 or 8916;
 hs.weddings@scotland,gsi.gov.uk; www.historic-scotland.gov.uk/weddings

Castle Campbell

Location: Forth Valley: 1 mile (1.5km) north of the A91, East of Stirling
Accommodation: None. Some accommodation in Dollar, the nearby village, and plentiful accommodation at Tillicoultry (1 mile) and Alloa (3 miles)
Licensed for Civil Weddings: Yes
Capacity: Ceremony only, 60

An Historic Scotland property, Castle Campbell, originally known as Castle Gloom, is a grand and beautiful, partly ruinous structure, dramatically situated above Dollar Glen. Access to the castle interior is not suitable for those with physical disabilities and there is no vehicle access to the castle or immediate surroundings. The main building at the castle is the Tower House which looks out over the courtyard and terraced gardens.

Contact details: Historic Scotland, Longmore House, Salisbury Place, Edinburgh, EH9 1SH; tel 0131-668 8973 or 8916;
hs.weddings@scotland,gsi.gov.uk; www.historic-scotland.gov.uk/weddings

Carbisdale Castle

Location: Highland: overlooking the Dornoch Firth, close to Bonar Bridge
Accommodation: Maximum of 189 guests
Licensed for Civil Ceremonies: Yes
Capacity: Dining 100-120

Carbisdale Castle is a Youth Hostel standing on the south bank of the Kyle of Sutherland. It was built between 1906 and 1917 for the Dowager Duchess of Sutherland. This haunted Castle has a large art collection and a collection of Italian marble statues on display in a main gallery. It is set in an area of extensive natural beauty overlooking the River Shin. Local attractions include distilleries, castles, nature walks, and historic villages only a short drive away. Carbisdale Castle is open from March to Oct for individual parties and for exclusive hire from November to the end of February.

Contact details: Carbisdale Castle, Culrain, Sutherland, IV24 3DP;
tel 0870-004 1109; www.carbisdale.org

Carnell Castle

Location: Strathclyde: Hurlford, Ayrshire, 3 miles (5km) from Kilmarnock, 10 miles inland from Ayr
Accommodation: 10 bedrooms
Licensed for Civil Weddings: Yes
Capacity: Main house 30; Gardens 200

Carnell is a listed category B 16th Century Tower (with substantial additions in Neo-Jacobean style) and Mansion House with extensive gardens and parkland. Only five weddings are accepted per year to maintain exclusivity. The bedrooms are all en suite and each is individually decorated. The ground floor is very spacious and includes a Great Hall, Dining Room, Vaulted Dining Room, Library and Drawing Room. The kitchen uses produce grown on the estate.

Contact details: Carnell Estates, Hurlford, Ayrshire, KA1 5JS;
tel 01563-884236; carnellestates@aol.com; www.carnellestates.com

Comlongon Castle

Location: Dumfries & Galloway: 15 miles (24km) west of Gretna, 9 miles (14km) east of Dumfries
Accommodation: 14 bedrooms
Licensed for Civil Weddings: Yes
Capacity: 170

Comlongon is a restored 14th century castle and luxurious Baronial hotel with 14 individually themed luxury en suite four-poster bedrooms. It has two RAC awarded, oak panelled restaurants and a private residents' bar. Steeped in Scottish Border history, Comlongon Castle has fantastic displays of armour, weapons and banners. Set at the end of a mile long, tree-lined drive in its own 120 acre estate, it has sweeping manicured lawns, secluded gardens, ornamental carp-filled ponds, paddocks and woodlands. It is a perfect setting for a blend of history and luxury.

Contact details: Comlongon Castle, Clarencefield, Dumfries, DG1 4NA;
tel 01387-870283; reception@comlongon.co.uk; www.comlongon.com

Craigmillar Castle

Location: Lothian: 3 miles (5km) south of Edinburgh
Accommodation: None, but plentiful in Edinburgh
Licensed for Civil Weddings: Yes
Capacity: Ceremony only, 60

An Historic Scotland property. Craigmillar is a well preserved, unrestored medieval castle. Its story is linked with that of Mary Queen of Scots who stayed here in 1563 and 1566. The Tower House, from which there are unrivalled views, was built in 1400, and various sections were added right through until the 1700s, including the curtain wall and the inner courtyard. The Chapel and Dovecot now lie ruined but the Tower House Hall still provides cover. The inner courtyard now sports two trees but the whole structure retains its authenticity.

Contact details: Historic Scotland, Longmore House, Salisbury Place, Edinburgh, EH9 1SH; tel 0131-668 8973 or 8916;
hs.weddings@scotland,gsi.gov.uk; www.historic-scotland.gov.uk/weddings

Crathes Castle

Location: Grampian: 15 miles (24km) west of Aberdeen
Accommodation: An 19th-century Victorian gate lodge sleeping four in two bedrooms. Other B&B accommodation available in nearby Banchory (3 miles)
Licensed for Civil Weddings: Yes
Capacity: Great Hall 50; Marquee 1000
A National Trust for Scotland property since 1951, Crathes Castle is a magnificent 16th century tower house standing on an estate granted to the Burnett family in 1323 by King Robert the Bruce. Ceremonies can he held in the Great Hall which accommodates up to 50 guests, or outside in the beautifully tended gardens, or in a marquee. The surrounding estate is a haven for Scottish wildlife and makes a wonderful backdrop for wedding photographs.
Contact details: Crathes Castle Gardens and Estate, Banchory, Aberdeenshire, AB31 5Q3; tel 01330-844525; functions@nts.org.uk;
www.nts.org.uk/Functions/Venue/6

Culzean Castle

Location: Strathclyde: on the coast, 12 miles (19km) south of Ayr
Accommodation: The Eisenhower Apartment has six rooms, sleeping 12
Licensed for Civil Weddings: Yes
Capacity: Circular Saloon & State Dining Room 70; Home Farm Restaurant 100
A National Trust for Scotland property, Culzean Castle is a magnificent structure standing dramatically on cliff-tops with wonderful views across to the Isle of Arran. Robert Adam converted an old tower castle in the 18th century to produce the finest Georgian castle in Scotland. President Eisenhower was gifted the top floor in 1946 and this is now the Eisenhower Apartment. The Circular Saloon and Oval Staircase are masterpieces of design where wedding ceremonies are held. The castle stands in 560 acres of stunning parkland with a separate restaurant complex where wedding ceremonies may also be held.
Contact details: Culzean Castle, Maybole, Ayrshire, KA19 8LE;
tel 0844-493 2149 or 01655-884455; culzean@nts.org.uk;
www.culzeanexperience.org/weddings.asp

Dalhousie Castle

Location: Lothian: 14 miles (22km) south of Edinburgh Airport
Accommodation: 36 bedrooms
Licensed for Civil Weddings: Yes
Capacity: Ramsey Room 100; Sir Alexander Room 110
A fascinating 13th century fortress set within acres of wooded parkland on the picturesque banks of the River Esk. Whether relaxing in the fabulous Spa, enjoying one of the library's extensive collection of books and a drink from the 'secret bar' next to the open fire, dining in the ancient barrel vaulted dungeon or relaxing in a unique bedroom, Dalhousie Castle will impress. The charming private Chapel and Vestry provide a unique location for the wedding ceremony, and terrace doors lead onto the patio which overlooks lush green parkland and the meandering South Esk River.
Contact details: Dalhousie Castle, Bonnyrigg, Edinburgh, EH19 3JB;
tel 01875-820153; info@dalhousiecastle.co.uk; www.dalhousiecastle.co.uk

Delgatie Castle
Location: Grampian: 37 miles (43km) north west of Aberdeen
Accommodation: The Symbister Suite and the Hayfield Suite, both sleeping 6, provide accommodation within the castle. There are also nine self-catering units within the grounds
Licensed for Civil Weddings: Yes
Dating from about 1050, Delgatie is a uniquely Scottish Castle. It is the home of the late Captain and Mrs Hay of Delgatie, and is the Clan Hay Centre. It is set peacefully within an extensive estate, with gardens and many delightful walks for guests to enjoy. Some of the rooms still boast their original 16th century painted ceilings, which are considered some of the finest in Scotland. Strange animals are depicted, some with human heads thought to represent the actual inhabitants of the time.
Contact details: Delgatie Castle, Delgatie, Turriff, Aberdeenshire, AB53 5TD;
Tel 01888-563479; jjohnson@delgatie-castle.freeserve.co.uk;
www.delgatiecastle.com

Dirleton Castle
Location: Lothian: 2 miles (3km) west of North Berwick
Accommodation: None, but plentiful in North Berwick and surrounding area.
Licensed for Civil Weddings: Yes
Capacity: Ceremony 100; Reception 120
An Historic Scotland property famous for the beauty of its gardens, Dirleton Castle dates back to the 13th century when the first of three phases was built on a natural rocky outcrop. Ceremonies can be held in the Barrel Vaults whose ground level windows let in beams of natural light; the Chapel, a small intimate room built for the private use of the Halyburton lords; and the Great Hall (open air), the largest area situated in the heart of the castle with a grand dais overlooking the splendid gardens.
Contact details: Historic Scotland, Longmore House, Salisbury Place, Edinburgh, EH9 1SH; tel 0131-668 8973 or 8916;
hs.weddings@scotland.gsi.gov.uk; www.historic-scotland.gov.uk/weddings

Doune Castle
Location: Forth Valley: 10 miles (16km) north west of Stirling off the A84
Accommodation: None. Accommodation in Doune or nearby Dunblane (3 miles) or Stirling
Licensed for Civil Weddings: Yes
Capacity: Ceremony only – Lord's Hall 60; Great Hall 120
Doune Castle is a magnificent late 14th century courtyard castle. Its most striking feature is the 100ft high gatehouse. The Lord's Hall and the Great Hall (with musician's gallery) have been restored but much of the rest of the castle is unrestored. It is an impressive, imposing structure that gained fame as the location for the filming of Monty Python's Holy Grail.
Contact details: Historic Scotland, Longmore House, Salisbury Place, Edinburgh, EH9 1SH; tel 0131-668 8973 or 8916;
hs.weddings@scotland.gsi.gov.uk; www.historic-scotland.gov.uk/weddings

Drum Castle

Location: Grampian: Royal Deeside, 10 miles (16km) from Aberdeen
Accommodation: None. Plenty of accommodation available in Aberdeen
Licensed for Civil Ceremonies: Yes
Capacity: Library 70; Chapel 30; Marquee 300

The oldest intact building in the care of the National Trust for Scotland, Drum Castle is situated at the gates to Royal Deeside. It was the home of the Irvine family from 1323 to 1975 and consists of the original Tower built in the 13th century, the Jacobean Mansion, added in 1619, and the Victorian Extension, added in 1872. It is set in magnificent grounds with stunning gardens. Wedding ceremonies may be held in four locations: the Library, the Chapel, a Marquee or outside in the Rose Garden.

Contact details: Drumoak, Banchory, AB31 5EY; tel 0844-4932161 or 01330-811204; functions@nts.org.uk; www.nts.org.uk/Functions/Venue/10

Duart Castle

Location: Argyll & Bute: Isle of Mull, overlooking the Sound of Mull
Accommodation: None, but available locally on the island during the season from April through to October
Licensed for Civil Weddings: Yes

Set in a commanding position overlooking the Sound of Mull on the south eastern tip of this famous Scottish west coast island, Duart Castle is to this day the ancestral home of the Maclean Clan. Renovation of the structure has been ongoing for many years but the main repairs were completed in 1995. Wedding ceremonies can be held in the Banqueting Hall or the Sea Room, or outside by the single cannon below the keep, with wonderful views straight up the Sound of Mull.

Contact details: Duart Castle, Isle of Mull, Argyll, PA64 6AP; tel 01680-812309; guide@duartcastle.com: www.duartcastle.com

Dundas Castle

Location: Lothian: near South Queensferry, half an hour west of Edinburgh
Accommodation: 14 bedrooms featuring antique furniture and original paintings
Licensed for Civil Weddings: Yes
Capacity: Croquet Room 80; Pavilion Wedding Marquee 180; Stag Chamber 25; Great Hall 90

Dundas Castle is one of Scotland's most beautiful and historic castles. Built in 1818, the Castle is now a luxurious stately home. Secluded in the peaceful countryside of its own 1000 acre grounds, yet only 8 miles from Edinburgh, Dundas Castle offers all the comforts and high standards associated with the best of hotels. Religious ceremonies and receptions can be held in The Auld Keep, a fairytale tower with winding staircase. Civil ceremonies and receptions can be held in the Georgian Croquet Room or the Pavilion Wedding Marquee.

Contact details: Dundas Castle, South Queensferry, Edinburgh EH30 9SP, tel 0131-319 2039; enquiry@dundascastle.co.uk; www.dundascastle.co.uk

Dunnottar Castle

Location: Grampian: 2 miles (3km) from Stonehaven, 15 miles (24km) from Aberdeen

Accommodation: None, but plentiful in nearby Stonehaven and Banchory

Licensed for Civil Ceremonies: Yes

Capacity: Ceremony only, 60

Dunnottar Castle is a dramatic and evocative ruin perched on top of an enormous flat-topped rock with steep cliffs on three sides and the sea below. At its heart stands a 14th century Keep or Tower House, one of eleven separate buildings which include barracks, lodgings, stables, storehouses and the remains of a 13th century chapel. Because of access difficulties, this location is not suitable for the very young, very old, or the infirm.

Contact details: Dunecht Estates Office, Dunecht, Westhill, Aberdeenshire, AB32 7AW; tel 01330-860223; info@dunechtestates.co.uk; www.dunnottarcastle.co.uk

Edinburgh Castle

Location: Lothian: the heart of Edinburgh

Accommodation: None, but plenty of accommodation nearby

Licensed for Civil Weddings: Yes

Capacity: Jacobite Room 100; Gatehouse Suite 40; Queen Anne Building 120; St Margaret's Chapel (ceremony only) 25

Magnificent and imposing, Edinburgh Castle is Scotland's most famous landmark, perched high on the core of an extinct volcano dominating the skyline of the city. The castle has played a major part in the history of Scotland, and houses the Scottish Crown Jewels and the Stone of Destiny. Your ceremony can be held in a choice of areas throughout the castle. The simple, elegant 12th century St Margaret's Chapel is lovely for the smaller party.

Contact details: Historic Scotland, Longmore House, Salisbury Place, Edinburgh, EH9 1SH; tel 0131-668 8973 or 8916; hs.weddings@scotland.si.gov.uk; www.historic-scotland.gov.uk/weddings.

Eilean Donan Castle

Location: Highland: 6 miles (10km) from the Kyle of Lochalsh

Accommodation: A cottage in the grounds sleeps 4 people. There are a couple of hotels and some b&bs at nearby Dornie

Licensed for Civil Weddings: Yes

Capacity: Ceremony and champagne reception 90

Eilean Donan Castle is one of the quintessential images of the Scottish Highlands. It features on countless postcards, in countless paintings and in quite a few movies. It will not disappoint in real life. It is set at the meeting of three lochs, not far from the Isle of Skye and within sight of the Five Sisters of Kintail, the range of mountains that flank the majestic Road to the Isles. Wedding ceremonies can be held in several locations at the castle, both inside and out. There are no dining facilities but a champagne reception can be held there.

Contact details: Eilean Donan Castle, Dornie, by Kyle of Lochalsh, IV40 8DX; tel 01599-555202; eileandonan@btconnect.com; www.eileandonancastle.com

Ethie Castle

Location: Tayside: just north of Dundee and Arbroath
Accommodation: A maximum of 8. Other accommodation available nearby
Licensed for Civil Weddings: Yes
Capacity: 40

A warm welcome awaits you at the de Morgan family home, Ethie Castle. An ancient sandstone fortress dating from the 14th Century, Ethie is reputed to be Scotland's second oldest permanently inhabited castle. It was immortalised by Sir Walter Scott as Knockwinnoch in his novel *The Antiquary*. Roaring log fires on cooler evenings in the sitting room, a secret stairwell in the barrel vaulted Cardinal's Room, wood panelling and a tiny door to Cardinal Beaton's ancient chapel are some of the unique features in Ethie Castle. And there is home cooking, too, using ingredients from the castle's kitchen garden.
Contact details: Ethie Castle, Inverkeilor, By Arbroath, Angus, DD11 5SP; tel 01241-830434; email kmydemorgan@aol.com; www.ethiecastle.com

Fyvie Castle

Location: Grampian: about 30 minutes south of Banff on the Moray Firth, and 25 miles (40km) north of Aberdeen
Accommodation: The Preston Tower Apartment, self-catering for a maximum of 13 guests, furnished to a high standard with predominantly antique furniture
Licensed for Civil Weddings: Yes
Capacity: Castle 120; Dining Room 50; Raquets Court 110; Marquee 1000

A National Trust for Scotland property since 1984, Fyvie Castle is set in extensive grounds and is within easy reach of the Moray Firth, the city of Aberdeen, and Royal Deeside. With a history stretching back to the year 1211, it occupies a commanding position on the left bank of the River Ythan. The dark woods and the lake create an unmistakable air of mystery.
Contact details: Fyvie Castle, Turriff, Aberdeenshire, AB53 8JS; tel 0844-493 2182 or 0131-243 9405; functions@nts.org.uk; www.nts.org.uk/Functions/Venue/11

Castle Fraser

Location: Grampian: 16 miles (25km) west of Aberdeen
Accommodation: East Wing self-contained flat with own entrance, 3 bedrooms, sleeping 5 guests
Licensed for Civil Weddings: Yes
Capacity: 100

Acquired by the National Trust for Scotland in 1976, this 16th and 17th century structure has imposing granite walls and turrets as befits everyone's idea of a Scottish castle. As with all National Trust properties, there are magnificent, well-maintained gardens and extensive grounds. The interior is sumptuously furnished and many rooms are hung with portraits of the Fraser family ancestors. One of the most evocative rooms is the strikingly simple Great Hall, and one of the most fascinating is the working Victorian kitchen.
Contact details: Castle Fraser, Sauchen, Inverurie, Aberdeenshire AB51 7LD; tel 0844-493 2164 or 0131-243 9405; email castlefraser@nts.org.uk; www.nts.org.uk/Functions/Venue/4

Glengorm Castle

Location: Argyll & Bute: Isle of Mull, its northern tip near to Tobermory
Accommodation: Five double rooms inside the castle. Self-catering also available: two flats, one of which is in the castle, and six cottages in the grounds
Licensed for Civil Weddings: Yes
Capacity: Library 20; Hall 50; Dining Room 40
Glengorm Castle overlooks the Atlantic and has views over 60 miles to the Outer Hebrides and Islands of Skye, Rhum and Canna. The Castle was built in 1860 and sits at the headland of Glengorm's vast area of coastline, forestry, lochs and hills. The interior is splendidly dark-panelled with the Library, the Dining Room and the Hall available for your wedding.
Contact details: Glengorm Castle, Tobermory, Isle of Mull, PA75 6QE; tel 01688-302321; email enquirieis@glengormcastle.co.uk; www.glengormcastle.co.uk

Hatton Castle

Location: Grampian: a 30 minute drive north west of Aberdeen and a 15 minute drive south of Banff on the Moray Firth
Accommodation: Sleeps 16 in eight en suite bedrooms
Licensed for Civil Ceremonies: Yes
Capacity: Hallway 60; Dining Room 25; Marquee 200
Home of the 12th Laird, David James Duff, and his wife Jayne, the castle dates back to the 14th century and has been the country seat of the Duffs since 1709. Looking more like an enormous country house than a traditional castle, the elegant interior has been restored to provide warm, welcoming and comfortable accommodation. With luxurious bedrooms, magnificent furniture and stunning artwork inside; beautiful gardens and sporting estate grounds outside, Hatton Castle is an ideal wedding venue.
Contact details: Hatton Castle, Turriff, Aberdeenshire, AB53 8ED; tel 01888-562279 or 563624; email: duff@btinternet.com; www.hattoncastle.com

Huntingtower Castle

Location: Tayside: just west of Perth
Accommodation: None, but plentiful in Perth
Licensed for Civil Weddings: Yes
Capcity: Ceremony only, 80
The unrestored Huntingtower Castle lies just outside Perth. Dating from the 15th century, it is famous as the place where Mary Queen of Scots and Lord Darnley stayed during their Honeymoon. The State Room is the ceremony location. It is an impressive and bright room on the upper floor within the West Tower. The modern day bride is urged not to follow the reported antics of Dorothea, an Earl's daughter, who leapt the gap of over nine feet between East and West Towers, known as the Maiden's Leap, to avoid discovery by her angry mother in her lover's room.
Contact details: Historic Scotland, Longmore House, Salisbury Place, Edinburgh, EH9 1SH; tel 0131-668 8973 or 8916; hs.weddings@scotland.gsi.gov.uk; www.historic-scotland.gov.uk/weddings

Inverlochy Castle

Location: Highland: four miles north of Fort William
Accommodation: 17 bedrooms, including three suites, and the Gate Lodge
Licensed for Civil Weddings: Yes
Capacity: 80

Inverlochy Castle nestles in the foothills around the mighty Ben Nevis amongst some of the country's finest scenery. It was built in 1863 and is now one of Scotland's finest country house hotels, and is the winner of many awards. Ceremonies can be held in the Great Hall or the Drawing Room. A dance floor is also available for exclusive use weddings. Inverlochy Castle is an opulent and romantic venue in a dramatic and romantic setting.

Contact details: Inverlochy Castle, Torlundy, Fort William, PH33 6SN; tel 01397 702177; info@inverlochycastlehotel.com; www.inverlochycastlehotel.com

Kelburn Castle

Location: Strathclyde: on the coast, close to Glasgow and just south of Largs
Accommodation: Eight double en suite bedrooms and seven with shared facilities
Licensed for Civil Weddings: Yes
Capacity: Dining room 50; Pavilion 150;

Kelburn Castle, the home of the Earls of Glasgow, is in a commanding position, beside a spectacular glen and waterfall, half a mile from the sea, overlooking the islands of the Firth of Clyde. The ceremony can be held in the Castle itself, in the grounds or in the Country Centre. There is a beautiful eighteenth century walled garden (The Plaisance) and a Secret Forest at the Centre that have proved popular in the past. Alternatively, there is a purpose-built Pavilion in the grounds.

Contact details: Kelburn Country Centre, Kelburn Estate, Fairlie, Largs KA29 0BE; tel 01475-568595; maggie@kelburncastle.com; www.kelburncastle.com

Kellie Castle

Location: Fife: 15 miles (24km) south of St Andrews.
Accommodation: None, but plentiful at the village of Pittenweem (three miles) or St Andrews
Licensed for Civil Weddings: Yes
Capcity: Castle 60; Marquee 300

Kellie Castle, completed around 1606 and restored by the Lorimer family in 1878. The oldest tower, dating back to 1360, is said to be haunted, but today the castle is a tranquil spot with magnificent plaster ceilings and panelling, and furniture designed by Sir Robert Lorimer. There is a magical Arts & Crafts garden filled with the scents of old roses. Unlike many a grand castle it looks like a family home, with toys and a rocking horse in the nursery and cooking pots in the kitchen.

Contact details: Kellie Castle, Pittenweem, Fife KY10 2RF; tel 0844-493 2184 or 0131-243 9405; functions@nts.org.uk; www.nts.org.uk/Functions/Venue/20

Kilbryde Castle

Location: Forth Valley: 15 minutes from Stirling
Accommodation: Garden Apartment sleeping 6. Extra accommodation available locally in Dunblane, Bridge of Allen and Stirling
Licensed for Civil Weddings: No
Capacity: Chapel 65; Dining room 12-30; Marquee 180
Home to the Campbell family since 1659, the building was originally a traditional Scottish Tower House. It is situated on the side of a gorge which the River Ardoch flows through encircling the castle on three sides. There is a small Chapel, a mile away, which can accommodate up to 65 guests for a wedding. Alternatively, the wedding can take place at the castle itself. The Dining Room seats only 12 but up to 30 guests can be catered for if a buffet is selected.
Contact details: Kilbryde Castle, Dunblane, FK15 9NF; www.kilbrydecastle.com

Castle Lachlan

Location: Argyll & Bute: on the eastern shore of Loch Fyne
Accommodation: The castle sleeps 15 in 4 doubles, 2 twins and 1 single
Licensed for Civil Weddings: Yes
Capacity: Small weddings in house; larger weddings in marquee
The Old Lachlan Castle was bombarded from the sea by the English in 1746 following the defeat of the Jacobites. The New Castle started life as a Queen Anne style house at the end of the eighteenth century. At the end of the nineteenth the Scottish baronial transformation was undertaken. It boasts a beautiful drawing room and dining room, and even has a full-sized billiard table. Outside, there are gardens with a tennis court and a surrounding estate with three miles of shoreline. It is let on a self-catering basis.
Contact details: Castle Lachlan, Strathlachlan, Cairndow, PA27 8BU; tel 01369-860669; euanmaclachlan@castlelachlan.com: www.castlelachlan.co.uk

Linlithgow Palace

Location: Lothian: 10 miles (16km) west of Edinburgh, just off the M9 at Linlithgow
Accommodation: None but plentiful in and around Linlithgow
Licensed for Civil Weddings: Yes
Capacity: Great Hall 60; Undercroft 60
An Historic Scotland property, the magnificent ruins of Linlithgow Palace are set in a park beside Linlithgow Loch. All of the Stewart kings lived at the Palace. The present structure is now roofless. Access to the ground and some first floor levels is possible but shelter is limited. Historically important because of its royal connections, the palace was razed in 1746 by Cumberland after Bonnie Prince Charlie had used it for refuge the year before. The Palace is the birthplace of Mary Queen of Scots.
Contact details: Historic Scotland, Longmore House, Salisbury Place, Edinburgh, EH9 1SH; tel 0131-668 8973 or 8916; hs.weddings@scotland.gsi.gov.uk; www.historic-scotland.gov.uk/weddings

Melville Castle

Location: Lothian: 6 miles (10km) south of Edinburgh City centre
Accommodation: 30 bedrooms, some of which are family rooms
Licensed for Civil Weddings: Yes
Capacity: Ballroom 80; Arniston Room 35

Melville Castle has been restored and refurbished to provide a superb luxury hotel. The castle is set in a secluded situation on the bank of the North Esk river within a fifty acre wooded estate. It was built in 1786 on the site of the old medieval castle for the first Viscount Melville. Each of the castle's 30 comfortably furnished bedrooms is unique. The passenger lift gives access to the dining and boardroom and four levels of bedrooms including luxury four-poster rooms, 6 Gallery and 2 Spa bedrooms. The range of public rooms includes a ballroom, a boardroom, sitting room and study.

Contact details: Melville Castle Hotel, Gilmerton Road, Midlothian, EH18 1AP; tel 0131-654 0088; enquiries@melvillecastlehotel.com; www.melvillecastlehotel.com

Murthly Castle

Location: Tayside: 10 miles(16km) north of Perth
Accommodation: None, but plentiful in the immediate area
Licensed for Civil Weddings: Yes
Capacity: Castle 60; Chapel 200

Murthly Castle and the 17th century Chapel of St Anthony the Eremite are in the heart of Scotland, occupying a spectacular position overlooking the River Tay, near the historic town of Dunkeld. The approach to the castle and chapel is one of the most breathtaking that you will see, with a two mile (3km) long drive lined with impressive trees that reach heights of up to 140ft. A marquee can be hired for the walled garden for larger weddings. Both the chapel and the castle interior are breathtakingly beautiful locations for a romantic Scottish wedding.

Contact details: Murthly Castle, near Dunkeld, Perthshire PH1 4HP; tel 01738-494121; info@murthly-estate.com; www.murthly-estate.com

Myres Castle

Location: Fife: between Edinburgh and St Andrews
Accommodation: Nine distinctively different double bedrooms
Licensed for Civil Weddings: Yes
Capacity: Castle 18; Marquee 150

Myres Castle is set within a 44 acre estate in the Kingdom of Fife, only 45 minutes drive from Edinburgh. The castle, recently refurbished, has exceptional charm and its dedicated staff create an atmosphere of quality and discretion. The castle is set on a rise with panoramic views from the battlements over the surrounding countryside. Dining at Myres is unique: choose the simplicity of a family supper around the solid oak table in the Victorian Kitchen or the formal setting of the magnificent dining room. The traditionally furnished public rooms are perfectly complemented by the deep comfort of the individually designed, en suite bedrooms.

Contact details: Myres Castle, Auchtermuchty, Fife, KY14 7EW; tel 01337-828350; www.myrescastle.com

Oxenfoord Castle

Location: Lothian: 12 miles (19km) south of Edinburgh
Accommodation: None but available locally and details supplied by the Castle.
Licensed for Civil Weddings: Yes
Capacity: Dining Rm 80; Library 100; Drawing Rm 100; Smoking Rm 30
In the midst of glorious park and woodland, yet only 12 miles from the centre of Edinburgh, the Castle is beautifully situated. The original core of the castle is the old tower of the MacGills. The interior of the principal floor boasts a magnificent Library and Drawing Room on the south side. There is a Dining Room to the west with carved woodwork dating from 1750 and an ornate Robert Adam ceiling. The Drawing Room has glass doors which open out onto the lawns to the south and west of the castle.
Contact details: Oxenfoord Castle, Pathhead, Midlothian, EH37 5UB;
tel 01875- 320 844; enquiries@oxenfoord.co.uk; www.oxenfoord.co.uk

Stirling Castle

Location: Forth Valley: the centre of Stirling
Accommodation: None, but plentiful accommodation in Stirling itself
Licensed for Civil Weddings: Yes
Capacity: Great Hall 300; Chapel Royal 200; Queen Anne Garden 300
An Historic Scotland property, Stirling Castle is one of Scotland's grandest castles and is the perfect venue for a Scottish wedding. This stunning location is ideal for wedding ceremonies and receptions. There are three locations available for the ceremony: the Queen Anne Garden; the Chapel Royal; and the Great Hall. Stirling Castle towers over the surrounding countryside in the heart of Braveheart country. You can follow in the footsteps of Kings and Queens of centuries past and celebrate your wedding in this prestigious venue.
Contact details: Historic Scotland, Longmore House, Salisbury Place, Edinburgh, EH9 1SH; tel 0131-668 8973 or 8916;
hs.weddings@scotland,gsi.gov.uk; www.historic-scotland.gov.uk/weddings

Tantallon Castle

Location: Lothian: 3 miles (5km) east of North Berwick
Accommodation: None, but plentiful in North Berwick and surrounding area
Licensed for Civil Weddings: Yes
Capacity: 100
An Historic Scotland property, and essentially a ruin, Tantallon Castle is a formidable stronghold set atop cliffs on the Firth of Forth It was the seat of the Douglas Earls of Angus, one of the most powerful baronial families in Scotland. Tantallon served as a noble fortification for more than three centuries and endured frequent sieges. A spectacular and unusual location for a wedding ceremony, it is open all year, although with restricted access during the winter months. It is not ideal for those with limited mobility but would ensure a spectacular backdrop for the wedding photographs.
Contact details: Historic Scotland, Longmore House, Salisbury Place, Edinburgh, EH9 1SH; tel 0131-668 8973 or 8916; hs.weddings@scotland.gsi.gov.uk;
www.historic-scotland.gov.uk/weddings

Torosay Castle

Location: Argyll & Bute: Isle of Mull, 1.5 miles (2.5km) from Craignure
Accommodation: 2 self-catering cottages sleeping 2 and 4
Licensed for Civil Weddings: Yes
Capacity: Smaller weddings
In the style of a mansion house, rather than a traditional castle, Torosay Castle is surrounded by 12 acres of spectacular gardens including formal terraces which are covered with roses and other climbers. There is an impressive statue walk which consists of 19 life-size limestone figures, sculpted by Antonio Bonazza. The castle itself was completed in 1858 All the rooms are finished in Scottish baronial style. The principal rooms include the front hall dominated by a collection of red deer stag antlers, and the library with its impressive collection of books.
Contact details: Torosay Castle and Gardens, Craignure, Isle of Mull, PA65 6AY; tel 01680-812421; info@torosay.com; www.torosay.com

Urquhart Castle

Location: Highland: on the northern shore of Loch Ness, 15 miles (24km) from Inverness
Accommodation: None, but plentiful in nearby Drumnadrochit
Licensed for Civil Ceremonies: Yes
Capacity: Great Chamber Cellar 100; Old Kitchens 60; Visitor Centre 75
Urquhart Castle, on the banks of Loch Ness, remains an impressive stronghold despite its ruinous state. Once one of Scotland's largest castles, Urquhart's remains include a tower house that commands splendid views of the famous loch and Great Glen. Urquhart witnessed considerable conflict throughout its 500 years. These days, it is more famous for its association with the Loch Ness Monster. Nessie has been 'sighted' many times in and around Urquhart Bay. The Visitor Centre restaurant may be used for your reception.
Contact details: Historic Scotland, Longmore House, Salisbury Place, Edinburgh, EH9 1SH; tel 0131-668 8973 or 8916; email hs.weddings@scotland.gsi.gov.uk; www.historic-scotland.gov.uk/weddings

Wedderburn Castle

Location: Scottish Borders: 13 miles (20km) west of Berwick-upon-Tweed
Accommodation: Up to 22 adults and 6 children in 12 bedrooms
Licensed for Civil Weddings: Yes
Capacity: Dining Room 50; Ballroom 80
Wedderburn is in its element when hosting a wedding and reception. The castle has four spacious and elegant reception rooms, together with the gallery and the stair hall. The sweeping stone stairs provide a dramatic entrance. There are also two small historic churches that couples may choose for their wedding before returning to Wedderburn for a reception. If you marry in the castle itself, the ballroom is a fitting place to hold your wedding ceremony. Smaller wedding parties sometimes choose the stair hall for the ceremony.
Contact details: Wedderburn Castle, Duns, Berwickshire, TD11 3LT; tel 0136-188 2190; enquiries@wedderburn-castle.co.uk; www.wedderburn-castle.co.uk

Churches

This section includes a range of religious buildings, from small private chapels to large cathedrals, with a couple of ruined abbeys which would provide a wonderfully atmospheric setting for your wedding.

Large or small, ruined or complete, none of these venues is licensed for civil weddings because the law states that a civil ceremony will not be allowed to take place in any place that is, or has been, used solely or mainly for religious purposes.

Obviously, if you wish to marry in a church, there will be no provision for reception or accommodation, so this will need to be found nearby. However, as most churches are in a village or town, this shouldn't be a problem.

Some of the chapels listed are in the grounds of castles or stately homes, and generally you should be able to have your reception and/or accommodation in the main building.

Most churches have a resident or regular minister who will perform the ceremony for you. This may not be the case where a church or chapel is no longer used regularly for services, in which case you will need to source a minister prepared to travel to officiate at your wedding.

Working churches which hold regular services and other ceremonies will generally not make a charge for your wedding, but it is good form to make a donation to the church, which is always gratefully received.

Most Scottish denominations are fairly relaxed about the form of the ceremony which you decide on, in consultation with the officiating minister. An exception to this is if you are a Roman Catholic; in this case your wedding must take place in a Catholic Church using the regular service. Sometimes your priest may insist it should take place in your home church. In any event, you should always consult him about your intentions before booking anywhere. If you wish to have a Catholic wedding service in a beautiful Scottish venue, a possibility is Traquair House (see below in *Country Houses*) which has its own Catholic chapel in the grounds.

It is important to check beforehand whether the minister will allow photographs or videos to be taken during the ceremony itself – many of them are happy to allow this, as long as it does not disrupt the service too much and the solemnity of the occasion is retained. However, the minister is perfectly entitled to forbid any picture-taking during the service.

If you wish to have music during your wedding service, check if there is an organ and organist available. Alternatively, ask whether the minister is happy for you to provide your own music, either with your own choice of musicians or by bringing in a CD player or other form of recorded music.

Beauly Priory

Location: Highland: 10 miles (16km) west of Inverness
Accommodation: None, but plentiful in Beauly and Inverness
Licensed for Civil Weddings: No

An Historic Scotland property, the beautiful, ruined Beauly Priory was founded in about 1230 by the lords of the Aird to the west of Inverness for the Valliscaulian order, later transferring its allegiance to the Cistercians. The structure has been much altered and added to over the years. In 1564 Mary, Queen of Scots stopped at Beauly Priory on her way to Dingwall, the modern day county town of Ross-shire. She is alleged to have said: "Oui, c'est un beau lieu," ("Yes, it is a beautiful place"), a pun on the name of Beauly.

Contact details: Historic Scotland, Longmore House, Salisbury Place, Edinburgh, EH9 1SH; tel 0131-668 8973 or 8916; hs.weddings@scotland.gsi.gov.uk; www.historic-scotland.gov.uk

The Cathedral of the Isles

Location: Strathclyde: Island of Great Cumbrae, just off Largs
Accommodation: None, but plentiful in Millport on Great Cumbrae
Licensed for Civil Weddings: No

Reachable by short ferry crossing from Largs, the island of Great Cumbrae is the location of the Cathedral of The Isles, which is the smallest cathedral in Great Britain and probably in Europe, seating barely 100 people. The nave is only 40 by 20 feet, but it boasts a 123 foot steeple. The nave is relatively plain, the chancel and sanctuary are rich in colour and detail with brightly coloured tiles and rich stained glass windows. Representations of the island's wild flowers can be seen in the multi-coloured stencilling, not only on the walls and floor but also extensively on beams, pillars and exquisitely painted ceiling.

Contact details: The Cathedral, Millport, Isle of Cumbrae, KA28 0HE; tel 01475-530353; tccumbrae@argyll.anglican.org; www.argyllandtheisles.org.uk/cumbrae.html

The Church of the Holy Rude

Location: Forth Valley: Stirling, adjacent to the castle
Accommodation: None, but plentiful in Stirling
Licensed for Civil Weddings: No

Begun in the early 15th century and still with its original oak roof beams, the Church of the Holy Rude is a stunningly beautiful building with the dimensions of a small cathedral. It is situated at the Top of the Town adjacent to Stirling Castle. Mary Queen of Scots worshipped here, and it was here in 1567 that the Coronation of her son, James VI, took place while she herself was a prisoner in Lochleven Castle. The Church also boasts one of the finest Romantic organs in Europe, which along with the beautiful stained glass windows, and the intimacy of the architecture, makes the Church of the Holy Rude such a favourite choice for brides.

Contact details: Mrs. Margaret Davidson, 47 Forth Park, Stirling FK9 5NK; tel 01786-834805; HolyRudeChurch@aol.com; http://holyrude.org/index.html

Dornoch Cathedral
Location: Highland: Dornoch
Accommodation: None, but plentiful in Dornoch
Licensed for Civil Weddings: No
Standing in the centre of Dornoch, the Cathedral dominates the small town and is most famous as the place where Madonna and Guy Ritchie's baby was christened. Bishop Gilbert started work on the cathedral at his own expense in 1224 and it experienced many changes and disasters over the next six centuries, being almost razed to the ground on several occasions. The building was finally rebuilt and restored in 1837. The Reverend Susan Brown, whose ministry the cathedral now is, was the first woman in Scotland to take charge of a cathedral. Its stained glass windows are magnificent.
Contact details: Rev. Susan Brown, The Manes, Cnoc-an-Lobht, Dornoch IV25 3HN; tel 01862-810296; revsbrown@aol.com; www.dornoch-cathedral.com

Dunblane Cathedral
Location: Forth Valley: Dunblane, 5 miles (8km) north of Stirling
Accommodation: None, but plentiful in Dunblane
Licensed for Civil Weddings: No
Dunblane Cathedral, built upon a Christian site first established by Saint Blane around the year 600, is one of the few surviving medieval churches in Scotland. It is home to a congregation of over 1200 members. It serves the parish of Dunblane and the surrounding area. Dunblane Cathedral is part of the Church of Scotland and Presbyterian in its constitution. On the outside, the Cathedral is impressive, but its true beauty lies within where towering pillars and archways of weathered stone are overlooked by colourful religious icons of stained glass and woodcarvings.
Contact details: Dunblane Cathedral, The Cross, Dunblane, Perthshire, FK15 0AQ; tel 01786-825388; www.dunblanecathedral.org.uk

Dryburgh Abbey
Location: Scottish Borders: close to Melrose
Accommodation: None, but plentiful in Melrose
Licensed for Civil Ceremonies: No
An Historic Scotland property, Dryburgh sits by the Tweed River. Its remarkably complete medieval ruins makes it easy to appreciate the attractions of monastic life. The abbey buildings were destroyed by fire three times and ravaged by war on four occasions but fine examples of ecclesiastic architecture and masonry remain, and its chapter house reveals plaster and paintwork dating back to its inception. There is a palpable air of seclusion about the location and the ruin that lends itself to the intimacy of a wedding ceremony.
Contact details: Historic Scotland, Longmore House, Salisbury Place, Edinburgh, EH9 1SH; tel 0131-668 8973 or 8916; hs.weddings@scotland.gsi.gov.uk; www.historic-scotland.gov.uk

Elgin Cathedral

Location: Grampian: Elgin, Moray
Accommodation: None, but plentiful in Elgin
Licensed for Civil Ceremonies: No

An Historic Scotland property, the magnificent ruin of Elgin Cathedral is one of Scotland's most beautiful medieval buildings, much of it dating back to the 13th century. The finest remains are those at the east end of the church. There are richly decorated tombs and carved effigies in the vaulted choir chapels and there is a beautiful 15th century octagonal Chapter House, unique in Scotland. An exquisite location for an outdoor wedding ceremony and for wedding photographs.

Contact details: Historic Scotland, Longmore House, Salisbury Place, Edinburgh, EH9 1SH; tel 0131-668 8973 or 8916; hs.weddings@scotland.gsi.gov.uk; www.historic-scotland.gov.uk

Glen Tanar Chapel

Location: Grampian: 35 miles (56km) west of Aberdeen
Accommodation: Five self-catering cottages within the grounds
Licensed for Civil Ceremonies: No

Situated in the grounds of the Glen Tanar Estate, the historic and unique Chapel of Saint Lesmo is available for weddings. The Chapel is a registered independent Scottish Episcopal Chapel. However, the Trustees encourage the ecumenical movement and services conducted by any of the recognised churches are welcomed. It is only a short walk away from the estate's elegant Victorian, oak-floored ballroom where the reception and subsequent festivities can be held. It has a beautiful, intricately beamed ceiling decorated with over 600 stag antlers.

Contact details: Glen Tanar Estate, Aboyne, Aberdeenshire, AB34 5EU; tel 01339-886150; ballroom@glentanar.co.uk; www.glentanar.co.uk

Lincluden Collegiate Church

Location: Dumfries & Galloway: the western outskirts of Dumfries
Accommodation: None, but plentiful in Dumfries
Licensed for Civil Ceremonies: No

An Historic Scotland property, Lincluden is the remains of a collegiate church and the accommodation for its canons founded in 1389 by Archibald the Grim, 3rd Earl of Douglas on the site of an earlier nunnery. The splendid chancel was probably added by his son Archibald, the 4th Earl, and houses the exquisite monumental tomb of his wife, Princess Margaret, daughter of Robert III. It lies next to the Cluden Water, near to its confluence with the River Nith.

Contact details: Historic Scotland, Longmore House, Salisbury Place, Edinburgh, EH9 1SH; tel 0131-668 8973 or 8916; hs.weddings@scotland.gsi.gov.uk; www.historic-scotland.gov.uk

The Mackintosh Church

Location: Strathclyde: Queen's Cross, central Glasgow

Accommodation: None but plentiful in Glasgow

Licensed for Civil Weddings: No

The Mackintosh Church is a hidden treasure that shows characteristic symbolism and creative detailing as well as providing a beautiful and flexible space. Architect Charles Rennie Mackintosh, famous for his version of Art Nouveau which became known as 'The Glasgow Style', constructed Queen's Cross Church in Glasgow 1897-1899. He started working on it shortly after completing his competition design for the Glasgow School of Art. The church is on a small plot of land close to the junction of Garscube Road and Maryhill Road. It is not in use as a church any more and is now the home of the Charles Rennie Mackintosh Society.

Contact details: The Mackintosh Church, Queen's Cross, 870 Garscube Road, Glasgow, G20 7EL; tel 0141-946 6600; trish@crmsociety.com; www.crmsociety.com

Melrose Abbey

Location: Scottish Borders: Melrose

Accommodation: None, but plentiful in Melrose

Licensed for Civil Ceremonies: No

An Historic Scotland property, Melrose Abbey is a magnificent ruin on a grand scale with lavishly decorated masonry. The Cistercian Abbey is thought to be the burial place of Robert the Bruce's heart, marked with a commemorative carved stone plaque within the grounds. There is also a small museum housing a display of artefacts found within the abbey. The delicacy of carved stone is remarkable. The visitor can spend hours finding carved images and decorative details, some of it high up and thus well preserved.

Contact details: Historic Scotland, Longmore House, Salisbury Place, Edinburgh, EH9 1SH; tel 0131-668 8973 or 8916; hs.weddings@scotland.gsi.gov.uk; www.historic-scotland.gov.uk

Rosslyn Chapel

Location: Lothian: 5 miles (8km) south of Edinburgh centre

Accommodation: None but plentiful in the area.

Licensed for Civil Ceremonies: No

Made world-famous by the book and film, *The Da Vinci Code*, Rossyln Chapel attracts thousands of visitors each year. It was founded in 1446 by Sir William St Clair, third and last St Clair, Prince of Orkney. It is in fact only part of the choir of what was intended to be a larger cruciform building with a tower at its centre. Rosslyn is a unique and beautiful building whose mystery is apparent in the intricate carvings, including that of the Dance of Death. The stone arched roof is finely decorated in squares with five pointed stars, ball flowers, tablet flowers, roses, and a dove with an olive branch.

Contact details: Rosslyn Chapel, Roslin, Midlothian, EH25 9PU; tel 0131-440 2159; e-mail mail@rosslynchapel.com; www.rosslynchapel.org.uk

Saint Michael's Parish Church

Location: Lothian: 12 miles (19km) west of Edinburgh
Accommodation: None, but plentiful in the immediate area
Licensed for Civil Ceremonies: No

Situated close to Linlithgow Palace, St Michael's Parish Church is a vibrant, working example of one of the country's finest mediaeval churches. With its distinctive tower, the top of which has been likened to a wigwam without its cover, St Michael's dominates the town of Linlithgow. Although there is evidence of a church on this site in the 12th century, the structure that exists today derives from some 400 years later. It has many beautiful and unique features including magnificent stained glass windows. *'St Michael is kinde to strangers'* says the ancient town motto.

Contact details: St Michael's Parish Church, Cross House, Linlithgow, EH49 7AL; tel 01506-842188; www.stmichaelsparish.org.uk

Sweetheart Abbey

Location: Dumfries & Galloway: 12 miles (19km) south of Dumfries
Accommodation: None but plentiful in Dumfries
Licensed for Civil Ceremonies: No

An Historic Scotland property, Sweetheart Abbey was founded in 1273 by Lady Devorgilla of Galloway in memory of her husband John Balliol. On her death, she was laid to rest next to her husband's embalmed heart and the Cistercian monks named their abbey in memory of her. The red sandstone remains of Sweetheart Abbey are situated at the bottom of a fertile valley, close to the point where the River Nith flows into the Solway Firth. This is a most tranquil and appealing spot even today.

Contact details: Historic Scotland, Longmore House, Salisbury Place, Edinburgh, EH9 1SH; tel 0131-668 8973 or 8916; hs.weddings@scotland.gsi.gov.uk; www.historic-scotland.gov.uk

Country Houses

This category includes stately homes which are open to the public, and privately-owned large houses in their own, often extensive, grounds. Most of them are in rural surroundings although there are a few in the centres of Edinburgh and Glasgow.

Many of the stately homes are owned by the National Trust for Scotland (NTS) and run as tourist attractions by them. Generally these do not have any accommodation, although a handful have limited accommodation in other buildings in the grounds. There is a useful search facility on the 'Hospitality' page of the NTS website which allows you to search for venues by region, room style, party size and price range.

In most cases, the private houses are let for single parties, and are either self-catering or have the option for cooking and cleaning staff to be provided. This can give you and your guests the benefit of a country-house hotel atmosphere with the added privacy and intimacy of having the place to yourselves. They tend to be smaller than most country house hotels so are generally more suitable for medium-sized weddings. They often have overflow accommodation in cottages or other buildings in the grounds.

Ardverikie House

Location: Highland: 15 miles (24km) south west of Newtonmore
Accommodation: Five self-catering cottages sleeping 48 in total
Licensed for Civil Weddings: Yes
Capacity: 50

Built in the Scottish baronial style in 1870, Ardverikie is one of the finest private houses in the Scottish Highlands. Having starred as Glenbogle in the long-running BBC drama *Monarch of the Glen* for many years, the house has reverted to its former role as a splendid family residence and is the perfect setting to begin life together. The splendid bay-windowed and wood-panelled dining room seats up to 40 and also has magnificent views across the loch to the mountains beyond.
Contact details: Ardverikie Estate Office, Kinlochlaggan, Newtonmore, Invernesshire PH20 1BX ; tel 01528-544300; ardverikie@ardverikie.com; www.ardverikie.com

Bighouse Lodge & Estate

Location: Highland: 16 miles (25km) west of Thurso
Accommodation: 12 en suite double or twin bedrooms
Licensed for Civil Weddings: Yes
Capacity: 24

Built in 1765 and a former home of the Chief of the Clan Mackay, the lodge offers all the warmth, comfort and charm expected of a traditional Scottish Highland house that has been recently refurbished and tastefully decorated. The reception floor is spacious yet comfortable. The drawing room, study and dining room all feature open fires. Facilities also include a large ballroom, television lounge, and games room. The walled garden with its unique pavilion extends to over an acre and provides fresh herbs for the kitchen. Menus take advantage of the fine local produce.
Contact details: Bighouse Lodge, by Melvich, Sutherland, KW14 7JY; tel 01641-531207; info@bighouseestate.com; www.bighouseestate.com

Cortes House

Location: Grampian: Aberdeenshire, 10 miles (16km) north of Peterhead
Accommodation: Sleeps 30 in 10 bedrooms and two family suites
Licensed for Civil Weddings: Yes
Capacity: 30

First and foremost a family home, Cortes has recently been refurbished to the highest standard. It has four large reception rooms, a cinema and table tennis room, and it retains many of its original features including stunning cornices, marble fireplaces and 14 foot high ceilings giving a sense of elegance and space. The vast kitchen and bathrooms have the latest in modern facilities. The house is peacefully located in its own grounds of five acres. These include a children's playground and woodlands which brim with wild flowers in the springtime. It is not unusual to spot deer, badgers and foxes.
Contact details: Cortes House, Lonmay, Aberdeenshire, AB43 8UU; tel 0845-057 4211; cortes@perfect-manors.com; www.corteshouse.co.uk

Culross Palace

Location: Fife: on the north side of the River Forth, 8 miles (12km) west of Dunfermline
Accommodation: None, but accommodation available in Dunfermline
Licensed for Civil Weddings: Yes
Capacity: 40

Culross Palace is a merchant's house, a compound of buildings built for George Bruce (later Sir George Bruce of Carnock) between 1597 and 1611. Known also as the Great Lodgings, many of the building materials were obtained by Baltic barter, returning as ballast in coal and salt ships. Red pantiles from the Low Countries, Baltic pine and Dutch floor tiles and Dutch glass all feature in this splendid merchant's house. There is a model 17th century garden with raised beds, covered walkway and crushed shell paths.

Contact details: Culross Palace, Culross, Fife, KY12 8JH; tel 0844-4932189 or 0131-243 9405; functions@nts.org.uk; www.nts.org.uk/Property/22

Falkland Palace

Location: Fife: 11 miles (17km) west of Cupar
Accommodation: None, but some accommodation in Falkland, more at Glenrothes (10 miles)
Licensed for Civil Weddings: Yes
Capacity: 100

A National Trust property, the magnificent Royal Palace of Falkland was built by James IV and James V between 1450 and 1541 as their country residence. The Stuarts used Falkland as a lodge when hunting deer and wild boar in the forests of Fife. Portraits of the Stuart kings and queens hang in the palace and you can get a flavour of palace life when you enter the King's Bedchamber and the Queen's Room, both restored by the Trust. The Chapel Royal and the Keeper's Apartments in the Gatehouse are also on view. The gardens, as with most Trust properties, are magnificent.

Contact details: Falkland Palace, Falkland, Cupar, Fife KY15 7BU; tel 0844-4932186 or 01337-957397; functions@nts.org.uk; www.nts.org.uk/Property/93

Gean House

Location: Forth Valley: on the outskirts of Alloa, close to Stirling.
Accommodation: 18 double bedrooms
Licensed for Civil Weddings: Yes
Capacity: 100

Set amidst peaceful parkland and extensive private gardens, Gean House provides an elegant and tranquil setting for weddings. Gean is rich in fascinating architectural features and period charm. Log fires and tasteful furnishings make for a welcoming & relaxing atmosphere. The house and gardens provide the perfect backdrop for wedding photographs, ensuring that whatever the weather, the photographs will be splendid. Weddings can be on an exclusive basis, where the wedding party and guests enjoy sole occupancy of the house, the reception areas and the bedrooms.

Contact details: Gean House, Tullibody Road, Alloa, Clackmannanshire, FK10 2EL; tel 01259-226400; info@geanhouse.co.uk; www.geanhouse.co.uk

Georgian House

Location: Lothian: Edinburgh
Accommodation: None but ample accommodation in Edinburgh
Licensed for Civil Weddings: Yes
Capacity: 50

The Georgian House has been magnificently restored to show a typical Edinburgh New Town House of the late 18th-early 19th century. The house's exquisite collections of china, silver, paintings and furniture all reflect the domestic life and social and economic context of the times. The Drawing Room, with its paintings and furniture and magnificent views over Charlotte Square, provides an elegant yet relaxing setting for drinks receptions. The remainder of the House can, by prior arrangement, be left open for guests to wander through at their leisure.
Contact details: Georgian House, 7 Charlotte Square, Edinburgh, EH2 4DR; tel 0844-4932118 or 0131-243 9405; thegeorgianhouse@nts.org.uk; www.nts.org.uk

Haddo House

Location: Grampian: near to Ellon, 19 miles (30km) north of Aberdeen
Accommodation: Two bedroom Stables Flat sleeping 4
Licensed for Civil Weddings: Yes
Capacity: House 120; Hall 150; Marquee 1000

Haddo is a wonderful combination of crisp Georgian architecture with sumptuous Victorian interiors, and is surrounded by a terrace garden leading to the country park, with breathtaking views down its magnificent avenue of lime trees. The Library, with its cedar and ebony bookcases, is a stunning room to hold either a drinks reception or a dinner and the Victorian Hall adjacent to the house can accommodate ceilidhs and larger dinners. Haddo also has a beautiful ecumenical chapel seating up to 100.
Contact details: Haddo House, Ellon, Aberdeenshire AB41 7EQ; tel 0844-4932179 or 0131-243 9405; functions@nts.org.uk; www.nts.org.uk/Functions/Venue/13

Harburn House

Location: Lothian: 10 miles (16km) west of Edinburgh
Accommodation: 17 bedrooms
Licensed for Civil Weddings: Yes
Capacity: House 120; Marquee 250

This Georgian mansion surrounded by its own 3,000 acre sporting and leisure estate lies within half an hour of both Edinburgh and Glasgow. There are beautiful churches in the near vicinity but for those who wish to marry at Harburn there are many favourite spots. There are several reception rooms of which the drawing room is the most popular for indoor ceremonies. A marquee can be hired for larger parties. The lake, lawn and island provide a beautiful setting for outdoor ceremonies. The stunning floodlit grounds and long Scottish evenings combine perfectly for romance.
Contact details: Harburn House, West Calder, West Lothian, EH55 8RN; tel 01506-461818; information@harburnhouse.com; www.harburnhouse.com

Innes House

Location: Grampian: 6 miles (10km) north east of Elgin, by the Moray Coast
Accommodation: One single and six double bedrooms
Licensed for Civil Weddings: Yes
Capacity: House 80; Marquee 100

Innes is a beautiful seventeenth century Scottish Renaissance building with Edwardian additions, and is set in magnificent walled gardens surrounded by parkland. This splendid building, the home of the Tennant family, provides the perfect setting for weddings. The reception and dinner may be held in the East Dining Room or larger parties can be held in the marquee extension which covers a walled garden complete with a summer house for the bar and a fountain around which the tables are set.

Contact details: Innes House, Elgin, Moray, IV30 8NG; tel 01343-842410; enquiries@inneshouse.co.uk; www.inneshouse.co.uk

Pollok House

Location: Strathclyde: 3 miles (5km) south of Glasgow city centre
Accommodation: None, but plentiful throughout Glasgow
Licensed for Civil Weddings: Yes
Capacity: 60

Managed in partnership with Glasgow City Council since 1998, Pollok House is only a few miles from Glasgow's vibrant city centre. The ancestral home of the Maxwell family who lived on the site for over six centuries, the present house was begun in the mid-18th century and extended in the Victorian period. The interiors at Pollok House are fabulous and visitors will be delighted by the period furnishings, silverware and ceramics on display. A bonus for art lovers is the superb collection of paintings. Here you can see works by El Greco, Blake and Murillo, amongst others.

Contact details: Pollok House, 2060 Pollokshaws Road, Glasgow G43 1AT; tel 0844-493 2202 or 0131-243 9405; pollokhouse@nts.org.uk; www.clyde-valley.com/glasgow/pollock.htm

Threave House

Location: Dumfries & Galloway: Castle Douglas
Accommodation: Two self-catering cottages in the grounds
Licensed for Civil Weddings: Yes
Capacity: Dining Room 50; Restaurant 160

A National Trust for Scotland property, this Scottish Baronial house, built in 1872, has been fully restored to the way it was in the 1930s. Threave House was opened to the public for the first time in 2002 and its elegant Georgian interiors are used for a wide range of events such as seminars, dinners and receptions The panoramic views of the gardens from the house are a major draw for visitors. Threave is best known for its superb gardens, which attract some 60,000 visitors annually. The gardens are famed for their springtime daffodils and with each season provide a stunning backdrop to the house.

Contact details: Threave House, Castle Douglas, Dumfries & Galloway DG7 1RX; tel 0844-493 2245 or 0131-243 9405; threave@nts.org.uk; www.nts.org.uk/Functions/Venue/17

Traquair House

Location: Scottish Borders: 30 miles (48km) south of Edinburgh
Accommodation: Three double bedrooms
Licensed for Civil Weddings: Yes
Capacity: House 50; Chapel 50; Marquee larger parties

Dating back to 1107, Traquair House was originally a hunting lodge for the kings and queens of Scotland. Later a refuge for Catholic priests in times of terror, the Stuarts of Traquair supported Mary Queen of Scots and the Jacobite cause without counting the cost. Today Traquair is a unique piece of living history welcoming visitors from all over the world, providing a magical and romantic setting for weddings. Traquair has its own Catholic Chapel. The interior of the house is both fascinating and sumptuously furnished, and the bedrooms are quite stunning.

Contact details: Traquair House, Innerleithen, Peeblesshire, EH44 6PW; tel 01896-830323; enquiries@traquair.co.uk; www.traquair.co.uk

Hotels

The beauty of choosing a hotel for your wedding is that they are normally able to provide for all aspects of the event. Even if they don't have certain facilities on-site – such as a hotel hairdresser and beautician, for example – they should be able to arrange for one to visit you in your hotel room. Depending on the size of the hotel, there may be restrictions on the number of your guests who can be accommodated overnight, especially if you're having a large wedding, but the hotel staff should be able to recommend local accommodation.

Some hotels have their own wedding organisers on the staff and may offer standard wedding packages. However, even if this is the case, they should be able to provide those individual touches which will make your wedding unique and ensure that you don't feel you are being offered a 'production line' wedding.

Even if the hotel is beautiful inside, do check that they have a nice spot in the grounds for your photographs? If the information isn't readily available on the website or in the information sent to you, ask them for details and pictures of the grounds. Some nice hotels are in built-up surroundings, a fact they may try and conceal from potential guests in their advertising literature. However, all is not lost if you love the hotel but they can't offer good outside picture opportunities – in Scotland you are never far from some beautiful scenery, and the hotel or the photographer will know where you can go locally for some stunning shots.

Ask the hotel if they have a bridal suite, or alternatively which is their best room, and check whether it is available on your wedding night.

There may be a choice of the room(s) you use for your ceremony and reception, so if at all possible, it is worth visiting the hotel and having a look at the alternatives before deciding. If you live too far way for this to be feasible, ask for photographs of the actual rooms you will be using.

If you are having a large wedding, check whether you can have exclusive use of the hotel. Even if this is not possible, or the charge is too high for your budget, do ask them whether there will be any other weddings on the same day. This may be something you wish to avoid – it could make your day feel a bit less special if there are other brides being catered for.

Many hotels can provide a marquee in the grounds, which is useful to accommodate very large weddings. Or maybe you would just prefer a marquee – they can be beautifully decorated and for a summer wedding are lovely, being a good solution if you would like to spend as much of the day outdoors as possible, with the meal and dancing taking place in the marquee.

It is worth checking whether the hotel is part of a large chain, and whether they specialise in hosting business meetings and conferences. Such hotels can feel a touch too 'corporate' for a wedding. Family-run, country house style hotels usually have a more intimate, informal feel which may suit you better.

Ardanaiseig Hotel
Location: Argyll & Bute: on the western shore of the northern tip of Loch Awe.
Accommodation: 18 double bedrooms
Licensed for Civil Weddings: Yes
Capacity: 50
Ardanaiseig was built in the Scottish Baronial manner in 1834. The ceremony may be held in the hotel itself, in the grounds, in the lochside amphitheatre or on an island on Loch Awe. Alternatively, the local village church at Kilchrenan is a beautiful building located on a hillside with wonderful views and is only four miles from the hotel. Each of the 18 bedrooms has been furnished with beautiful antiques and works of art. The hotel can be hired for exclsuive use by your wedding party. Won Scottish Intimate Hotel of the year 2008.
Contact details: Ardanaiseig Hotel, Kilchrenan by Taynuilt, Argyll, PA35 1HE; tel 01866-833333; info@ardanaiseig.com; www.ardanaiseig.com

Ardoe House

Location: Grampian: 3 miles (5km) from Aberdeen city centre on the South Deeside Road B9077
Accommodation: 109 en suite bedrooms
Licensed for Civil Weddings: Yes
Capacity: 50-500

Reminiscent of a fairy tale castle, Mercure Ardoe House Hotel & Spa is the most beautiful setting for the perfect wedding, with the ceremony in the wood-panelled Drawing Room, drinks on the lawns and the reception in one of the individual suites. Ardoe House offers a selection of impressive rooms to host your wedding, ranging from the Fraser Room, ideal for the smaller reception, accommodating up to 50 guests for a formal meal, to the superb Ballroom which hosts up to 500 guests. Facilities include pool, jacuzzi, steam room, sauna, tennis courts, fully equipped gym, aerobics studio, state of the art beauty salons.
Contact details: Mercure Ardoe House, South Deeside Road, Aberdeen, AB12 5YP; tel 01224-860600; www.mercure.com/gb/hotel-6626-mercure-ardoe-house-hotel-spa-aberdeen/index.shtml

Balinakill Country House Hotel

Location: Argyll & Bute: the Kintyre peninsula near to Tarbert
Accommodation: 10 double/twin *en suite* bedrooms
Licensed for Civil Weddings: Yes
Capacity: Hotel 24; Marquee 80

Balinakill is a stately, B listed, Mansion House dating from the 1890s. The House is furnished with antiques and displays all the richness of the Victorian Age in its beautiful panelling, plasterwork, fireplaces and tiles. Cloaked in the peace and seclusion of some of Scotland's finest Highland scenery, it looks out between the hills to the Sound of Jura and Islay beyond. Balanakill Country House will ensure that extra special touch of romance all year round, with log fires in most of the bedrooms.
Contact details: Balinakill Country House, Clachan, nr. Tarbert, Argyll, PA29 6XL; tel 01880-740206; www.balinakill.com

Boath House

Location: Highland: by Nairn on the Moray Firth
Accommodation: Eight double bedrooms
Licensed for Civil Weddings: Yes
Capacity: 26

Once described as the most beautiful Regency House in Scotland, Boath House is set in 20 acres of land, including a beautiful lake and tranquil, traditional walled garden where kitchen herbs, salad leaves, fruit and vegetables are grown. It has been restored to its original splendour by a meticulous refurbishment. Original art, opulent furnishings, a spa, beauty salon, sumptuous bedrooms and outstanding cuisine make Boath House an ideal location for a romantic Highland wedding. With lake view or woodland view, each bedroom has been described as an individual work of art.
Contact details: Boath House Hotel, Auldearn, Nairn, IV12 5TE; tel 01667-454896; info@boath-house.com; www.boath-house.com

Corsewall Lighthouse Hotel
Location: Dumfries & Galloway: the north tip of the Stranraer peninsula.
Accommodation: Ten suites/rooms
Licensed for Civil Weddings: Yes
Capacity: 28
Corsewall Lighthouse Hotel has the charm and romance of an 1815 functioning lighthouse with the comforts of a small but unique luxury hotel and restaurant. The Lighthouse is an A listed building of major national importance. Its light still beams a warning for ships approaching the mouth of Loch Ryan. Some of Scotland's most spectacular coastline is found within and nearby the 20 acre grounds of the hotel. The lighthouse has fine views of the Kintyre Peninsula, Arran, the Firth of Clyde, Ailsa Craig and even the coast of Ireland.
Contact details: Corsewall Lighthouse Hotel, Corsewall Point, Kirkcolm, Stranraer DG9 0QG; tel 01776-853220; info@lighthousehotel.co.uk; www.lighthousehotel.co.uk

Cringletie House
Location: Scottish Borders: Peebles, 18 miles from Edinburgh
Accommodation: 12 bedrooms, 1 suite, sleeping up to 26 adults, 4 children
Licensed for Civil Weddings: Yes
Capacity: 50
Cringletie House is a luxurious, romantic and comfortable small country house hotel and restaurant, an AA Top 200 hotel. The Victorian baronial mansion is set in the tranquil and rural countryside where sheep outnumber humans! The House dates back to 1861 and the Walled Garden goes back as far as 1661, when the first Cringletie House was built. It sits in 28 acres of lush grounds, providing perfect opportunities for the very best memorable pictures of your Day of Dreams. The Celebration Dinner in the ornate Sutherland Room will be a truly memorable experience.
Contact details: Cringletie House, Edinburgh Road, Peebles, EH45 8PL; tel 01721 725750; enquiries@cringletie.com; www.cringletie.com

Culloden House
Location: Highland: just east of Inverness
Accommodation: 28 bedrooms
Licensed for Civil Weddings: Yes
Capacity: 60
At the time of the Jacobite rising in 1745-46, Culloden House was requisitioned by Bonnie Prince Charlie and used as his lodging and battle headquarters prior to the final battle on Culloden Moor in 1746. Today, this handsome Palladian country house stands in nearly 40 acres where guests are free to wander about the elegant lawns and parkland to enjoy the exceptional peace and majesty of the grounds. The interior is simply stunning with sumptuous décor and furnishings. Culloden House is rated Scottish Tourist Board and AA four stars, and two Rosettes for food.
Contact details: Culloden House Hotel, Culloden, Inverness, IV2 7BZ; tel 01463-790461; info@cullodenhouse.co.uk; www.cullodenhouse.co.uk

Drumkilbo House

Location: Tayside: Perthshire, 12 miles (19km) north west of Dundee
Accommodation: Four suites and four bedrooms sleeping a total of 31 guests
Licensed for Civil Weddings: Yes
Capacity: Dining 28; Buffet 50; Marquee 150

Drumkilbo is an historic manor house available only on an exclusive basis for wedding parties. It is easily accessible from Edinburgh airport. It is a venue overflowing with history and offering luxury comparable to a five-star hotel but with complete exclusivity. Ceremonies can be held on the front lawn or in a marquee or in the beautifully furnished and decorated house interior. The suites are simply gorgeous with views of the gardens and the Sidlaw hills.

Contact details: Drumkilbo House, Meigle, Blairgowrie, Perthshire, PH12 8QS; tel 01828-640445; www.drumkilbo.co.uk

Hotel Eilean Iarmain

Location: Highland: Isle of Skye, overlooking the Sound of Sleat
Accommodation: 16 bedrooms, of which four are suites; 2 holiday cottages in grounds sleeping 6 each
Licensed for Civil Weddings: Yes
Capacity: Hotel 20; Talla Dearg 50; Talla Dhuisdeil 80

Hotel Eilean Iarmain, also known as Isle Ornsay Hotel, is small and privately owned, situated on a sheltered bay in the south of Skye, with expansive views over the Sound of Sleat to the hills of Knoydart on the mainland. The hotel forms part of Fearann Eilean Iarmain, a traditional Estate covering 23,000 acres. There are log fires in the reception rooms, and a wood-panelled dining room where candlelit dinners can be enjoyed overlooking the bay and the island of Ornsay. Receptions can also be held at Talla Dearg (The Red Hall) beside the hotel, and Talla Dhuisdeil, a converted church about ¼ mile away.

Contact details: Hotel Eilean Iarmain, Sleat, Isle of Skye, IV43 8QR; tel 01471-833332; hotel@eileaniarmain.co.uk; www.eilean-iarmain.co.uk

Enterkine Country House

Location: Strathclyde: 13 miles (29km) east of Ayr
Accommodation: Six bedrooms and two self-catering properties nearby
Licensed for Civil Weddings: Yes
Capacity: Hotel 70; Marquee 200

An elegant house, built originally as a private residence in the late 1930s, and now enjoying a new role as a beautifully appointed country house hotel. The House may be hired for exclusive use for weddings of over 40 guests. Small Civil Marriage Ceremonies can take place in the Garden Room. The six luxury bedrooms are spacious with high ceilings and large windows. Each has been furnished and decorated in its own unique manner to provide quality accommodation. There are two self-contained properties in the grounds: Woodland Lodge is a romantic hideaway for 2; Kirk House sleeps up to 12.

Contact details: Enterkine House, Annbank, Ayrshire, KA6 5AL; tel 01292-520580; mail@enterkine.com; www.enterkine.com

Flodigarry Hotel

Location: Highland: the eastern edge of the northernmost tip of the Isle of Skye
Accommodation: 18 bedrooms in total of which 7 are in Flora MacDonald's cottage next to the hotel
Licensed for Civil Weddings: Yes
Capacity: 50
Award-winning Flodigarry Hotel looks out from Skye across the Inner Sound to the Torridon Mountains on mainland Scotland. In an ancient woodland setting sheltered by the Quiraing Mountains, Flodigarry is a traditional, non-trendy hotel, friendly with genuine Highland hospitality, easy atmosphere, beauty and Jacobite past blending to create a very special place that people return to year after year. Famous Scottish heroine Flora MacDonald lived in the cottage in the hotel grounds, raising five of her children there.
Contact details: Flodigarry Hotel, Staffin, Isle of Skye, IV51 9HZ;
tel 01470-552203; info@flodigarry.co.uk; www.flodigarry.co.uk

Forest Hills Hotel

Location: Forth Valley: Aberfoyle, 30 miles (48km) north of Glasgow in the Trossachs
Accommodation: 50 bedrooms and 65 luxury lodges
Licensed for Civil Weddings: Yes
Capacity: Hotel 20-120; Marquee 300
Forest Hills Hotel stands on the shores of Loch Ard, near Aberfoyle, amid 25 acres of private land where pathways wind through woodland and alongside tumbling burns. Forest Hills even has a leisure centre with jacuzzi, sauna, steam room, indoor pool, gym and two snooker tables. There are suites of various sizes licensed for holding civil marriage ceremonies, or a marquee can be erected in the grounds.
Contact details: Macdonald Forest Hills Hotel, Kinlochard, Aberfoyle, FK8 3TL;
tel 0844-879 9057; www.macdonaldhotels.co.uk/foresthills/index.asp

Gleneagles Hotel

Location: Tayside: Perthshire, one hour north east of Glasgow, just off the A9
Accommodation: 232 bedrooms, including 26 exclusive suites
Licensed for Civil Weddings: Yes
Capacity: Approx 460 (as many as can be accommodated in the hotel)
Gleneagles is set in 850 acres of stunning scenery in Perthshire which are home to three of the top Scottish Championship Golf Course. It celebrated its 80th anniversary in June 2004. The Gleneagles Hotel is a member of The Leading Hotels of the World, Great Golf Resrts of the World and Connoisseurs Scotland, and provides an authentic flavour of Scotland to discerning guests. Gleneagles is a byword for grace and luxury and is a premier wedding venue where romance is part of the scenery. Gleneagles staff can handle every aspect of your wedding plans. Weddings and receptions can only be hosted where all guests are resident in the hotel.
Contact details: The Gleneagles Hotel, Auchterarder, Perthshire, PH3 1NF;
tel 0800 389 3737 or 01764-662231; resort.sales@gleneagles.com;
www.gleneagles.com

Houstoun House

Location: Lothian: 10 miles (16km) west of Edinburgh
Accommodation: 71 bedrooms
Licensed for Civil Weddings: Yes
Capacity: 400

Set within 20 acres of mature woodlands, the hotel comprises a 16th Century tower house and steading. While retaining its original character and offering exclusivity and seclusion, both Glasgow and Edinburgh are within easy reach. There are a number of suites including the Houstoun Suite, which has a large dance floor and bar. It has an attractive courtyard area for drinks receptions. There are other suites, too, and the gardens are also licensed for Civil Ceremonies and Civil Partnerships. The bedrooms are luxuriously furnished and have splendid views.

Contact details: Houstoun House, Nr Edinburgh, West Lothian, EH52 6JS; tel 0844-879 9043; www.macdonaldhotels.co.uk/houstounhouse

Loch Torridon Hotel

Location: Highland: at the head of Upper Loch Torridon, Ross-shire
Accommodation: 17 bedrooms, 1 suite
Licensed for Civil Weddings: Yes
Capacity: 42

Once a grand shooting lodge, built for the first Earl of Lovelace in 1887, the hotel enjoys one of the most impressive coastal positions in the Scottish Highlands. It is set in 58 acres of mature trees and parkland at the foot of Ben Damph on the shores of Upper Loch Torridon. The hotel is one of the most idyllic and romantic locations in the Highlands of Scotland, and an ideal venue for an intimate wedding celebration. The ceremony itself can take place either in the Library or the Drawing Room, with photographs afterwards in the grounds with the imposing Torridon Mountains as backdrop.

Contact details: Loch Torridon Hotel, Torridon, Ross-shire, IV22 2EY; tel 01445-791242; info@thetorridon.com; www.lochtorridonhotel.com

Marcliffe Hotel

Location: Grampian: just west of Aberdeen
Accommodation: 7 suites and 35 bedrooms
Licensed for Civil Ceremonies: Yes
Capacity: 400

A luxurious, relaxed and elegant 5-Star country hotel set in the picturesque north east of Scotland on the outskirts of the historic city of Aberdeen. Their wedding team will tailor the special occasion precisely to your needs and budget. The gardens and grounds are ideal for outdoor weddings, for both the ceremony and reception, in addition to barbecues, garden parties and musical events. The Marcliffe Hotel and Spa offers a choice of 6 private banqueting and conference rooms. The hotel offers superb facilities including a spa, which has earned it membership of the coveted Small Luxury Hotels of the World.

Contact details: The Marcliffe Hotel & Spa, North Deeside Road, Pitfodels, Aberdeen, AB15 9YA; tel 01224-861000; www.marcliffe.com

Mar Hall Hotel
Location: Strathclyde: south bank of the Clyde and 10 miles (16km) west of Glasgow city centre
Accommodation: 53 suites
Licensed for Civil Weddings: Yes
Capacity: 450
The magnificent Mar Hall is a fine example of Gothic Architecture. Steeped in history, the Earl of Mar Estate holds many fascinating stories, involving the likes of Mary Queen of Scot and Robert the Bruce. Built in 1828, the present Mar Hall was constructed 100 years after the famous Earl's death and, after a massive restoration, its owners proudly present the city with a precious gem. Undoubtedly one of Scotland's premier luxury hotels, Mar Hall delights the most discerning guest. This large, luxury hotel is even available for exclusive hire. 10 minutes from Glasgow airport.
Contact details: Mar Hall Hotel, Mar Hall Drive, Bishopton, Nr. Glasgow, PA7 5NW; tel 0141-812 9999; sales@marhall.com; www.marhall.com

Monaltrie House
Location: Grampian: Ballater, Royal Deeside
Accommodation: Two suites with two bedrooms each; two additional bedrooms
Licensed for Civil Weddings: Yes
Capacity: House 18; Marquee 250
Built in 1782, Monaltrie House is set in six acres of private grounds and offers guests relaxation and privacy. Situated in the heart of Royal Deeside it is an hour from the city of Aberdeen and airport, and also has its own helicopter landing area. The standard of accommodation is outstanding. Individually decorated and distinctively Scottish, all rooms and apartments have private bathrooms. Double rooms have 6ft wide four poster beds. Twin rooms have zip and link beds to create additional double beds if required. Receptions can take place in the beautiful dining room. Alternatively there is a permanent site in the grounds that will accommodate a marquee.
Contact details: Monaltrie House, Ballater, Aberdeenshire, AB35 5NX; tel 01339-753101; info@monaltriehouse.com; www.monaltriehouse.com

The Moorings Hotel
Location: Highland: Fort William at the head of Loch Linnhe
Accommodation: 27 bedrooms
Licensed for Civil Weddings: Yes
Capacity: 120 dining; 200 evening reception
The Moorings Hotel lies alongside the Caledonian Canal at the famous Neptune's Staircase, series of locks on the Caledonian Canal. With splendid panoramic views of Ben Nevis and Aonach Mor, The Moorings offers comfort and style coupled with the convenience of a modern hotel. It has beautiful gardens and the spectacular backdrop of Ben Nevis and the Caledonian Canal. The Caledonian Lounge can cater for sit down meals and evening receptions.
Contact details: The Moorings Hotel, Fort William, PH33 7LX; tel 01397-772797; reservations@moorings-fortwilliam.co.uk; www.moorings-fortwilliam.co.uk

Park Lodge Hotel
*Location:*Forth Valley: Stirling
Accommodation: 10 double bedrooms
Licensed for Civil Weddings:
Capacity: 120-180
This lovely Georgian House, built in 1825, has been beautifully restored and is now a Country House Hotel situated near to the town centre of Stirling. The Hotel overlooks Kings Park and Stirling Golf Course with splendid views of Stirling Castle. The interior of the hotel has been furnished in keeping with the character of the building, with the help of local craftsmen. The Garden Room can hold 120 people comfortably for your main reception. An additional 60 people can be accommodated for the evening reception. There are French doors leading to the patio and enchanting garden.
Contact details: Park Lodge Hotel, 32 Park Terrace, Stirling FK8 2JS; tel 01786-474862; info@parklodge.net; www.parklodge.net

Pittodrie House
Location: Grampian: 18 miles (28km) north west of Aberdeen
Accommodation: 27 bedrooms
Licensed for Civil Weddings: Yes
Capacity: Hotel 1260; Marquee 800
Set on the edge of the Grampians within its own ancient estate that extends as far as the eye can see, Pittodrie House is a tranquil retreat. With its turrets, spiral staircases, period furniture and ancestral portraits, it will appeal to the romantic couple seeking easily-accessible tranquillity. The Orangery, Drawing Room, Ballroom and the Georgian walled garden are all licensed for civil marriage ceremonies. The Orangery and adjoining patio are ideal for the smaller wedding with up to 40 guests. The Ballroom and Bennachie Room can cater for up to 160 guests for an evening reception.
Contact Details: Pittodrie House, Chapel of Garioch, Aberdeenshire, AB51 5HS; tel 0844-879 9066; www.macdonaldhotels.co.uk/pittodrie

Raemoir House Hotel
Location: Grampian: 10 miles (16km) west of Aberdeen, just north of Banchory
Accommodation: 20 bedrooms sleeping 36
Licensed for Civil Weddings: Yes
Capacity: 60; Marquee for larger weddings
Situated in Royal Deeside, the original House of Raemoir, known as 'Ha' Hoose' is of great historical importance. The main mansion was built in 1750, and became a hotel in 1941. It sits in an idyllic 3,500 acre estate sheltered by the Hills of Fare which rise to 1,500 feet to the rear of the house. The Oval Ballroom is ideal for weddings. It really is oval, and it has tapestried walls and a huge fireplace. The 20 principal bedrooms are of unique design, featuring antique features and sumptuous furnishings. They combine the traditional with the luxuries now expected in top class modern accommodation.
Contact details: Raemoir House Hotel, Banchory, Kincardineshire, AB31 4ED; tel 01330-824884; hotel@raemoir.com. www.raemoir.com

Roxburghe House

Location: Scottish Borders: 2 miles (3km) south of Kelso
Accommodation: 22 bedrooms
Licensed for Civil Weddings: Yes
Capacity: Main house 120; Marquee 150

Owned by the Duke of Roxburghe, the hotel nestles privately amongst woodlands on the banks of the River Teviot. Many of the 22 bedrooms have been individually designed by the Duchess herself. Some of them have four poster beds and log fires. Weddings can be 'houseparty style' with exclusive use. The hotel has a health and beauty suite and its own golf course in the grounds.
Contact details: The Roxburghe Hotel & Golf Course, Kelso, Roxburghshire, TD5 8JZ; tel 01573-450331; reservations@roxburghe.net; www.roxburghe.net

Shieldaig Lodge Hotel

Location: Highland: the southern edge of Gairloch, Ross-shire
Accommodation: 13 bedrooms and two self-catering cottages
Licensed for Civil Weddings: Yes
Capacity: 34

Shieldaig Lodge, the shooting lodge for Shieldaig Forest, still offers the hospitality and comfort reminiscent of Victorian times, when it could take a week by train and steamer to reach the estates. The ambience of the Victorian lodge has been retained but with subtle and sympathetic improvements. The bedrooms all have more than a touch of olde worlde charm, and most enjoy a superb outlook over Loch Gairloch and the surrounding hills. Most have en suite facilities. The gardens lead down to the shore's edge and provide the perfect setting for those treasured wedding photographs.
Contact details: Sheildaig Lodge, Badachro, Gairloch, Ross-shire, IV21 2AN; tel 01445-741250; enquiries@shieldaiglodge.com; www.shieldaiglodge.com

Skeabost Hotel

Location: Highland: Isle of Skye, 6 miles (10km) north of Portree
Accommodation: 14 rooms
Licensed for Civil Weddings: Yes
Capacity: 100

The Skeabost Country House Hotel is set in its own estate of landscaped grounds and woodland on the Isle of Skye in the west Highlands of Scotland. This stylish but traditional Victorian hunting lodge nestles comfortably on the coastal shores of Loch Snizort. Every aspect of the Skeabost is unique, from each lavish guest room, to the fine dining, and individual service. It is the perfect relaxing retreat. The Conservatory, which overlooks the loch, is licensed for civil weddings.
Contact details: Skeabost Hotel, Skeabost Bridge, Isle of Skye, IV51 9NP; tel 01470-532202; reservations@ohiml.com; www.oxfordhotelsandinns.com/OurHotels/SkeabostCountryHouse

Stonefield Castle Hotel

Location: Argyll & Bute: overlooking Loch Fyne, 2 miles (3km) north of Tarbert on the east side of the Mull of Kintyre

Accommodation: 32 en-suite bedrooms

Licensed for Civil Weddings: Yes

Capacity: 130

Stonefield Castle occupies a commanding position overlooking Loch Fyne just off the main Inverary to Campbeltown road. Its grounds have some of the finest redwoods and rhododendrons decorating the hill above Castle Bay where cruising yachts tie up for shelter. The wedding ceremony can be held inside the castle or at the pretty church nearby, with reception back at the hotel.

Contact details: Stonefield Castle Hotel, Tarbert, Loch Fyne, Argyll, PA29 6YJ; tel 01880-820836; www.oxfordhotelsandinns.com/OurHotels/StonefieldCastleHotel

Tulloch Castle Hotel

Location: Highland: Dingwall, the small county town of Ross-shire

Accommodation: 19 bedrooms

Licensed for Civil Weddings: Yes

Capacity: 50

In an imposing position, with highland views spread out like an open atlas, the castle is on the edge of the bustling market town of Dingwall, with its characterful shops and museum, just 15 miles north of Inverness. Swift new roads make Tulloch Castle the perfect base to explore the enchanting Black Isle to the east, and the stunning contrasts of the west highlands with its deep glens and rugged coastlines, all just a day-trip away. Tulloch Castle dates from the 12th century, when first the Bains and later the Clan Davidson laid claim to its lands. Each of the nineteen bedrooms is sumptuous, with elegant furnishings.

Contact details: Tulloch Castle Hotel, Tulloch Castle Drive, Dingwall, IV15 9ND; tel 01349- 861325; www.tullochcastle.co.uk

Miscellaneous

This section includes just a small selection of more unusual wedding venues which do not fit into the other categories. Here there are swish and historic city centre venues, a boat, a mountain top and some other stunning locations set in beautiful gardens or parkland. Most, but not all, of these venues include reception catering in their wedding packages. Where they do not, they may be able to advise on you on suitable places nearby. Although none of these have accommodation on site, all are close to a wide choice of accommodation.

The venues selected here are all 'approved places' for civil ceremonies. If you check the latest list of places approved by the General Register Office for Scotland you will find other unusual venues, including sports grounds and even a former jail! With couples increasingly looking for more quirky venues, the choice is sure to grow.

28 Charlotte Square
Location: Lothian: Edinburgh
Accommodation: None, but plentiful in the area
Licensed for Civil Weddings: Yes
Capacity: 60

Charlotte Square was conceived by Robert Adam as a paradigm of the Georgian ideal in the centre of Edinburgh. The townhouse at No 28 has been beautifully restored and is now the head office of The National Trust for Scotland. The Drawing Room Gallery, with its paintings and furniture and magnificent views over Charlotte Square, provides an elegant yet relaxing setting for drinks receptions. The award winning restaurant, available also for exclusive use, features contemporary Scottish cuisine which uses local produce and fine wines served in a crisp yet classical interior.

Contact details: The National Trust for Scotland, Wemyss House, 28 Charlotte Square, Edinburgh, EH2 4ET; tel 0844-4932102 or 0131-243 9405; charlottesquare@nts.org.uk; www.nts.org.uk/Property/4

CairnGorm Mountain
Location: Highland: 9 miles (14km) east of Aviemore
Accommodatiuon: None, but plentiful in Aviemore
Licensed for Civil Weddings: Yes
Capacity: 100
Every bride is on cloud nine on her wedding day, but at CairnGorm Mountain that is almost literally the case! The Ptarmigan Restaurant is a spectacular reception venue and can accommodate up to 100 guests for a full seated reception. Nowhere will you find a better backdrop for those special wedding photographs. CairnGorm Mountain is located at the heart of the Cairngorms National Park, in some of the most spectacular scenery in the UK. Home to some of the country's rarest habitats and most elusive wildlife, this area is one of Scotland's natural playgrounds.
Contact details: CairnGorm Mountain Ltd, Aviemore, Inverness-shire, PH22 1RB; tel 01479-861336; hwink@cairngormmountain.org; www.cairngormmountain.com

Corinthian
Location: Strathclyde: Glasgow city centre
Accommodation: None, but plentiful nearby
Licensed for Civil Weddings: Yes
Capacity: Private dining 50; Lite bar 450
Corinthian has what is widely regarded as the finest Victorian interior in the UK and boasts five levels of bars, restaurant and celebration spaces within stunning surroundings. These include several bars, a traditional Scottish Restaurant, private Dining Rooms, and a variety of contemporary meeting and celebration rooms. This extraordinary city centre establishment provides an ultra-stylish, alternative venue for a sophisticated wedding celebration.
Contact details: Corinthian, 191 Ingram Street, Glasgow,G1 1DA; Tel 0845-166 6030; info@corinthian.uk.com; www.socialanimal.co.uk/GlasgowCityCentre/Corinthian

The Dome
Location: Lothian: Edinburgh
Accommodation: None, but plentiful in the area
Licensed for Civil Weddings: Yes
Capacity: Georgian Suite 120; Green Room 20
Set in the heart of Edinburgh's New Town, The Dome opened its doors in 1996 and has become established as a first choice venue for weddings. Twin staircases, trailing gilt palm leaves, pillars soaring upwards past the jewel-lights of stained glass and a waterfall of crystal chandelier set the scene of the luxury to be found in the Georgian Suite with its muted yellow walls, chandeliers, golden drapes, potted palms and high windows. The Green Room, luxuriously decorated in hues of green and gold, lit by magnificent chandeliers and wall-lights, can accommodate the smaller party of 10 to 20 guests.
Contact details: The Dome, 14 George Street, Edinburgh, EH2 2PF; tel 0131-624 8624; sales@thedomeedinburgh.com; www.thedomeedinburgh.com

Greenbank Garden

Location: Strathclyde: 6 miles (10km) south of Gasgow city centre
Accommodation: None, but plentiful in the area
Licensed for Civil Weddings: Yes
Capacity: Coach House 30; Dining Room 16; Marquee 200

Greenbank Garden, which surrounds the elegant Georgian home of a Glasgow merchant, is composed of a series of beautiful ornamental gardens, each with their own character. Within easy access of the centre of Glasgow, yet bordered by fields (complete with Highland cattle!) Greenbank offers a peaceful alternative for wedding ceremonies It is the perfect setting for a summer wedding.
Contact details Greenbank Garden, Flenders Road, Glasgw G76 8RB; tel 0844-493 2111 or 0131-243 9405; functions@nts.org.uk; www.nts.org.uk/Property/28

House For An Art Lover

Location: Strathclyde: Glasgow
Accommodation: None, but plentiful in the area
Licensed for Civil Weddings: Yes
Capacity: Dinner 110; Evening reception 130

Situated in Parkland and adjacent to magnificent Victorian Walled Gardens, the House for an Art Lover is a truly unique venue. It represents one of the most exciting pieces of recent research on Charles Rennie Mackintosh and makes for a unique and fascinating contemporary weddings venue. It was designed in 1901 by Glasgow's most celebrated architect, Charles Rennie Mackintosh. The various rooms have been realised by contemporary artists and crafts people from the designs in the original portfolio, turning Mackintosh's vision into reality. *Contact details:* House for An Art Lover, Bellahouston Park, 10 Dumbreck Road, Glasgow, G41 5BW; tel 0141-353 4770; info@houseforanartlover.co.uk; www.houseforanartlover.co.uk

Jacobite Cruises

Location: Highland: Inverness and Loch Ness
Accommodation: None, but plentiful in Inverness and Drumnadrochit
Licensed for Civil Weddings: Yes
Capacity: 40

Just imagine… You could declare your vows to each other while sailing across Scotland's most romantic waters… Enjoy a sparkling evening reception amidst a glorious Highland sunset… Take a champagne trip before your reception, pausing for wedding photographs against the dramatic background of Urquhart Castle… You could marry in the Castle and sail to your reception… Or treat all your guests to an iconic trip the evening before. Whatever you decide, you'll make your own history together on Scotland's legendary Loch. The Jacobite Legend and the Jacobite Spirit are both licensed wedding venues and offer a unique place to host your entire wedding.
Contact details: Jacobite Cruises, Tomnahurich Bridge, Glenurquhart Road, Inverness, IV3 5TD; tel 01463-233999; e-mail info@jacobite.co.uk; www.jacobite.co.uk

Oran Mor

Location: Strathclyde: Glasgow West End
Accommodation: None, but plentiful nearby
Licensed for Civil Weddings: Yes
Capacity: Auditorium 100-250; Private Dining Room 15-32

Òran Mór, meaning the 'great melody of life' or 'big song', is a cultural centre and meeting place in the heart of Glasgow's West End. Inside are two bars, two restaurants, a nightclub and stunning private event space available for hire in this converted church, formerly Kelvinside Parish Church. Wedding ceremonies may be held in The Auditorium or the Private Dining Room. There is a most magnificently painted ceiling above The Auditorium which would make any wedding a special, magical occasion.

Contact details: Oran Mor, Top of Byres Road, Glasgow, G12 8QX; tel 0141-357 6200; info@oran-mor.co.uk; www.oran-mor.co.uk

People's Palace & Winter Gardens

Location: Strathclyde: Glasgow city centre
Accommodation: None, but plentiful in the area
Licensed for Civil Weddings: Yes
Capacity: 200

Attached to the People's Palace is the elegant Victorian glasshouse, the Winter Gardens, which is a magnificent, unique structure combining indoor tropical gardens, dining area and venue for weddings and wedding receptions. It is a popular location for Glaswegian weddings, the ceremony often taking place at the nearby St Andrew's Church and the festivities being held in the Winter Gardens The whole Glasgow Green area has been the subject of recent regeneration with landscaping and the relocation of a Victorian terracotta fountain outside the front entrance to the Palace.

Contact details: People's Palace & Winter Gardens, Glasgow Green, Glasgow, G40 1AT; tel 0141-353 9148 / 9108; www.encorecatering.co.uk

Royal College of Physicians of Edinburgh

Location: Lothian: Edinburgh
Accommodation: None, but plentiful in the area
Licensed for Civil Weddings: Yes
Capacity: New Library 150; Great Hall 200

The centrally located Royal College of Physicians in Edinburgh is available for both wedding ceremonies and receptions. The beautiful Georgian and Victorian rooms offer a truly romantic setting. The Victorian New Library, accommodating up to 80 guests, is licensed for civil weddings. Parties from 20 up to 250 people can be catered for in the New Library, Great Hall or Cullen Suite, with ample space for music and entertainment. The magnificent entrance hallway leads up to the historic rooms where the wedding or reception can be held. The Great Hall has a purpose built dance floor.

Contact details: Royal College of Physicians, 9 Queen Street, Edinburgh, EH2 1JQ; tel 0131-225 7324; events@rcpe.ac.uk; www.rcpe.ac.uk

Wallace Monument
Location: Forth Valley: Bridge of Allan, just outside Stirling
Accommodation: None, but plentiful in Stirling and Bridge of Allan
Licensed for Civil Weddings: Yes
Capacity: 20

When England and Scotland faced each other at the Battle of Stirling Bridge in 1297, Scotland was led to victory by a figure destined to become a national hero: William Wallace, perhaps better known as *Braveheart*. The National Wallace Monument stands proudly in his name on the Abbey Craig, overlooking the city of Stirling. The topmost platform of the tower is one of the most spectacular locations you could choose for a wedding ceremony. But, be warned: it is not for the faint-hearted!

Contact details: The National Wallace Monument, Hillfoots Road, Causewayhead, Stirling, FK9 5LF; tel 01786 472140; e-mail info@nationalwallacemonument.com. www.nationalwallacemonument.com

Register Offices

If you choose to have a civil ceremony at a register office, you will need to arrange your reception and accommodation nearby. The ceremony will take place in the Marriage Room at the register office. These are always pleasant rooms, although sometimes a little lacking in any 'wow' factor. Some of them, however, are rather splendid: if you go to the General Register Office for Scotland website at www.gro-scotland.gov.uk you will find pictures of some of the marriage rooms.

Depending on the size of the room, there may be a restriction on the number of guests who can attend the ceremony. Enquire beforehand if this might be a problem.

If you are marrying in the register office itself, you need only attend the office at the time arranged for your ceremony. The registrar will have all the paperwork there and make sure that all the information needed has been supplied. If you are having a civil ceremony at an approved place other than the register office, you will first need to visit the register office so the registrar can check everything is in order. The registrar will then bring the Marriage Schedule to the venue.

The national Directory of Registrars can be found at www.gro-scotland.gov.uk/regscot/groslocate/index.html

Other Venues

It has only been possible to list a small selection of the hundreds of lovely wedding venues in Scotland. There are many more, each one offering its own special atmosphere to your special day. Most wedding venues now have their details on the internet, so it is far easier to find these than once was the case. The following sites have details of and/or links to many more venues.

If you want further guidance on venues, or do not wish to do the sourcing yourself, an independent wedding agency will be happy to help. They may advise you on specific venues which will suit your requirements and give you their contact details. If you do not wish them to organise the rest of the wedding for you, they may charge you a 'finder's fee' for the information.

Of course, there is no reason to tie yourself to a specific building: in Scotland it is possible to marry in the great outdoors, surrounded by spectacular scenery, if you have a religious or non-religious ceremony. If you wish to find a natural location suitable for your wedding, or already have the perfect spot in mind, you will need to check that the landowner agrees. You will need to ascertain the map co-ordinates of the spot you have chosen, as this will be entered in the official documentation. To find suitable places, try contacting the local council in the area you choose, and they should be able to put you in touch with their Countryside Ranger Service. Alternatively, contact Scottish Natural Heritage, who look after many beautiful areas of Scotland.

Useful Websites
Approved Places for Civil Ceremonies: These are listed both by council area and by place name and are regularly updated as new ones are added.
www.gro-scotland.gov.uk/regscot/getting-married-in-scotland/civil-marriages-in-approved-places.html
Directory of Registrars in Scotland:
www.gro-scotland.gov.uk/regscot/groslocate/index.html
VisitScotland (Scottish Tourist Board): Details of tourist attractions and all types of accommodation, quality graded and listed by area. www.visitscotland.com.
VisitScotland Romantic Breaks: http://scottishwedding.visitscotland.com
Historic Scotland: www.historic-scotland.gov.uk/weddings
National Trust for Scotland: www.nts.org.uk
Scottish Castles: www.celticcastles.com/find_scottish.asp
A-Z of Scottish Castles on the Web: www.castles.org/Chatelaine/list.htm
Weddings & Honeymoons in Scotland:
www.scotland-inverness.co.uk/weddings.htm
Wedding Venues by Scottish region: www.hitched.co.uk/venues/scotland.asp
Historic Churches in Scotland:
www.britainexpress.com/scotland/cathedrals/index.htm
Scotland's Heritage Hotels: www.scotlandsheritagehotels.co.uk
Scotland's Hotels of Distinction: www.hotels-of-distinction.com
Hotels of Excellence: www.britainsfinest.co.uk/hotels
Large Holiday Houses in Scotland: www.lhhscotland.com
Castles & Large Houses: www.scotland-holiday-homes.co.uk
Restaurants in Scotland:
http://dining-out-uk.com/entrylist.php?county=Scotland
Edinburgh Restaurateurs Association: www.edinburghrestaurants.co.uk
Glasgow Restaurateurs Association: www.bestglasgowrestaurants.com
Scottish Tourist Attractions: www.british-towns.net/scottish/attractions.asp
Scottish Natural Heritage: www.snh.org.uk
Scottish Local Councils: www.oultwood.com/localgov/countries/scotland.php

PERSONAL WEDDING STORIES

Joanne & Craig Dickson

When and where did you get married?
July 18, 2005, Edinburgh Castle.

Where were you and your partner living at that time?
Pleasant Valley, New York, USA.

How old were you and your partner at the time?
Joanne 45, Craig 53.

Why did you decide to get married in Scotland?
Scottish heritage first, but also we had both been married before, and weddings are usually for everyone else: a huge celebration that most brides and grooms never really get to enjoy. This one was for us; we wanted to make it very special. I asked Joanne what in her wildest dreams could she envision for a special wedding if she could dream anything. She said to be married in a castle. Knowing that, and knowing the beauty and vast number of castles in Scotland, we began to inquire about the possibilities.

Did you consider any other country for your wedding?
Yes, various venues in the US in case Scotland was not feasible.

Why did you choose to use a wedding planner rather than organise it yourself?
Both Joanne and I made separate inquiries to castles and other venues in Scotland, and also to wedding planners specialising in Scottish Weddings. We realised that legal requirements, and also the logistics of organising all the details from the US, might be better handled by someone who knew the venue and various services available. While we could research much of that online, it seemed better to let someone with experience and local contacts to advise us and suggest possibilities based on our needs and budget. What I discovered was that it did not cost us more than doing it ourselves. In fact they made all the planning more efficient and cost-effective, having contacts and relationships with various services we could not have from the States.

How did you decide which wedding planner to use?
Both Joanne and I made separate searches and inquiries, then compared notes, and discussed what we found. It was interesting that in some cases we had both written to the same planners and got quotes for the same exact thing but with different prices, and the differences were significant. We asked for a detailed break down of that total package price; none of the planners we contacted initially were willing to break it down. With that type of mistrust, we almost gave up on the idea completely, but I found Highland Country Weddings and tried for one more contact. What I found, and instantly sensed, was not only their honesty, but also a passion for what they do. They instantly made a number of suggestions

198

based on what information I provided to them, and they continued to ask about us too, so they could suggest exactly what we dreamed of, and also consider our budget. They provided detailed requirements for the legal issues, links to the Consulate and Registrar, regarding visas etc. long before getting any deposit or commitment from us. I commented on this type of honesty – the suggestions were so detailed, with links, names of castles, photographers, e-mail addresses, hotel websites, pipers, ministers, kilt rental shops, florists, car hire etc. Far more than anyone else bothered to provide. We had an instant sense that these people cared more about making it special, than the bottom line.

Did you leave all the arrangements to them, or were there things you had to do, or chose to do, yourself?
With their guidance and detailed instruction, we contacted the British Consulate here in New York, filed the papers here, then also at the Registrar's Office in Edinburgh. Other than that, they made all other arrangements from the castle, to the minister, piper, bridal suite, dinner etc. The only additional arrangements we handled were travel, and reservations for an apartment for family members, since I have much experience with travel. If I did not, I would have trusted them to do it all with no hesitation at all.

Was it clearly explained to you what procedures you had to go through, and which documents you had to produce?
Yes, they left nothing to chance. They gave us clear instructions, and kept in constant contact to make sure we did everything in a timely fashion, and they were excellent.

Did you find the legislative procedure straightforward?
Yes. It was a bit time consuming collecting all the papers for the wedding visa, but once that was done, all moved very smoothly.

How did you decide on the venue?
It had all the elements we wanted, and having a major international airport eight miles from the city was a plus, which meant there was not a lot of land travel requirements and more time to sightsee, dine, explore and enjoy time with family.

Did you have a religious or civil wedding?
Religious.

Where did the wedding ceremony and reception take place? Where did you and your partner stay before and after the wedding?
The wedding ceremony was in St Margaret's Chapel, Edinburgh Castle. We stayed in a beautiful suite at the Witchery right outside the Castle Gates.

How many guests did you have at your wedding? Did you arrange their accommodation?
We had three additional guests, family members, and I made the arrangements for their transportation and accommodation.

199

Please describe your wedding.

Once upon a time, in a land far far away, two people touched by each other's love dreamt of being wed in a castle. Well, dreams can come true. This is our special day.

Two black cars slowly wind up the cobblestone streets, past many security check points, through the tunnels to the top of Castle Hill, the highest point of the castle, and finally arrive at the chapel. As the main car pulls away we realise the wedding rings and papers are still in the back seat, but the very fast-acting security team intercepts the car before it exits the castle, and retrieves the rings in short time. All is set.

The chapel rests high atop an extinct volcano in the city of Edinburgh. St Margaret's Chapel, circa 1120AD, is the oldest building in Edinburgh and sits at the highest point of the Castle. We were blessed to have Rev. Norman Faulds, a minister from the Church of Scotland, to perform the ceremony in St Margaret's Chapel. Norman, as he prefers to be called, was not just a minister, but instantly a friend. There are things in life that you cannot choose, they are just meant to be.

We were ready to begin. At one o'clock there was a sudden and loud report, thus signalling the commencement of the ceremony. The one o'clock gun was fired by Staff Sergeant Tom Mackay, MBE, the longest serving District Gunner of all time. Known affectionately as 'Tam the Gun', he has been firing the gun since 1978. Piper John MacKintosh was already in place. He began to play, and led the celebrants up a windy path to the tiny tenth century chapel, which was until just recently reserved for royal and military weddings, and thus begins a union based in Love, and built on Honour, Trust, Loyalty and Respect.

In attendance: as Maid of Honor, Jacqueline De Luca; Best Man, Thom Dunlap and Adam Montgomery as Jacqueline's escort. Reverend Norman Faulds officiated and we can't thank him enough for such a beautiful ceremony. It was a wonderful beginning to a lifetime promise. The tourists all wanted a picture with the bride. In many cultures it is good luck to be photographed with the bride. We accommodated them, it was fun. It was a traditional Scottish wedding, and everything turned out perfect, including the weather. If you believe in things that were meant to be, this was one of them. We were blessed on this special day.

Did your wedding day meet with your expectations or were there any disappointments?

Some briefly tense moments immediately before, due to a complete traffic jam at the castle gates, and heavy rain. But all turned out fine at the time we needed it to. The skies cleared, the sun came out, traffic vanished and all went as planned. Well, almost. It just added to the adventure. I managed to 'forget' our passports, wedding notice and the wedding rings in the rear seat of the car that had just delivered us to the chapel. This small hitch, which I put down to nerves, was handled quite professionally and quickly by the castle security team.

They were all wonderful, providing a private guided tour the day before, making suggestions on photography locations in case of rain, and scheduling the procession and ceremony. It all ran like a Broadway play that had many rehearsals, which we did not. But the staff, planners and everyone involved worked so well together because they had all done this before. They took away all the stress, with reassurances and such a wonderful attitude.

Did Scotland live up to your expectations?

Scotland exceeded my expectations, I think everyone had the same opinion. You have to experience it to believe it. I put together a slide show presentation to music for a gathering of family and friends back in the states. We brought them all to a favourite restaurant a few months later, and the presentation was not just of the wedding, but of our travels before the wedding throughout the countryside and Highlands. Not only did everyone comment that they had no idea how beautiful Scotland really was, but many now wanted to make it their next trip. The restaurant owners also were overwhelmed with the beauty. They were from Europe but admitted they had never been to Scotland, and would love to go there now. Even one of the waitresses asked for a copy of the presentation we showed there.

Any advice for other couples arranging their own wedding?

Go for your dreams: if you can dream it, you can make it come true. Highland Country Weddings helped make all our dreams come true. While I could have planned and booked much of this, being a former travel agent, convention planner, entertainer, and frequent traveller, I have learned that someone with the contacts and relationships in this type of planning can deliver so much more detail and quality.

The last thing you need is problems on that special day. They were there through the entire event to worry for us, and ensure all went well, make sure we met our deadlines, and made sure all the plans were in place. They made it all so much more enjoyable.

What we came away with was a dream come true, and so much more. We have new friends, very special ones, who truly cared about making our dreams come true. We now are planning a return to a land we fell in love with, one where some of our dreams began.

Emma & Mark Goodjohn

When and where did you get married?
Broadford, Isle of Skye, 27/05/2002.

Where were you and your partner living at that time?
St Neots, Cambridgeshire, England.

How old were you and your partner at the time?
Emma 28, Mark 26.

Why did you decide to get married in Scotland?
We did not like the idea of the local English registry office – talk about grey and dreary! We wanted a beautiful magical place with lots of nature, peace and space. We've always wanted to visit Scotland and thought this was the ideal opportunity.

Did you consider any other country for your wedding?
England briefly, purely because of the convenience for family and friends.

Why did you choose to organise it yourself rather than use a wedding planner?
Lack of money and time were the main reasons. We also didn't want to get caught up in the usual wedding paraphernalia, throwing lots of money at what can turn out to be a very fake day. We were interested in declaring our love for each other in a peaceful, beautiful and romantic place.

How easy was it to find out what procedures you had to go through, and which documents you had to produce?
The internet had all the information we needed. The very helpful Scottish sites were easily accessed using Yahoo search engine for all areas from accommodation to downloading the forms themselves online.

Did you find the legislative procedure straightforward?
Yes, very.

Were there any problems with the pre-wedding arrangements?
Just getting everything delivered in time for the wedding e.g: rings and dress, as we arranged everything in two months. It was hard to judge how far hotels were from the Register Office because we had not visited Skye before. We could not arrange flowers because of lack of knowledge of local businesses without websites.

How much do you reckon you saved by doing it yourself rather than employing a wedding planner?
Hard to judge, but we reckon thousands of pounds.

What was the biggest problem you came across in planning it yourself?
Not knowing the area or having local contacts, it took a lot of time and effort to get it right, but it was worth it.

Would you recommend to others to do it themselves or to use a wedding planner?
Money depending, if you've got loads of cash use a wedding planner, just make sure they organise what you want and not just some carbon copy of everyone else's wedding. Alternatively, do it yourself and save the money. Have your own wedding, don't just copy everyone else's.

How did you decide on the venue?
Because of our budget, time and lack of local knowledge we used Broadford Register Office as all the information we needed was listed on the internet. The hotel we used afterwards also had a very comprehensive website and were very helpful with arrangements over the phone.

Did you have a religious or civil wedding?
Civil.

How easy was it to find a registrar to perform the ceremony?
Very easy. All information is listed on the internet. The queen was in Portree on the day we were married so the registrar's deputy married us. They were very helpful before and during the wedding.

Where did the wedding ceremony and reception take place? Where did you and your partner stay before and after the wedding?
The ceremony was in Broadford Register Office, we stopped for photographs, coffee and cake at Armadale Castle and had the reception at The Duisdale Lodge towards the south of Skye. The night before the wedding we were booked to stay north of Portree but we did not realise how far away from Broadford it was, down small back roads, so we stayed at The Hebridean in Broadford in the end.

How many guests did you have at your wedding? Did you arrange their accommodation?
Just three guests. We arranged their accommodation online at local b&bs.

Please describe your wedding.
It was our wedding and nobody else's: small, relaxed and informal but fun and very classy.

Did your wedding day meet with your expectations or were there any disappointments?
We had a fantastic day. Everything was just perfect, although we all got a bit peckish before dinner. We would have arranged more than coffee and cake after the wedding had we known.

Did Scotland live up to your expectations?
The whole experience was amazing, the people warm and friendly, the scenery is inspirational with plenty of space for us. Scotland and the people who live there made it as good as it could be. In fact, we loved it so much that we have now moved to the Highlands permanently.

Any advice for other couples arranging their own weddings?
Be well organised and stick to your budget. Remember that the fact that you are getting married is the most important thing and not whether you arrive at the ceremony in a Bentley or a Ford Escort!

Kerry & Steve Pantony

We were married on 16 September 2005 at Dunnottar Castle near Aberdeen. We had been living together for a couple of years. I was 45 and Steve was 34.

We decided that if we were going to get married we wanted everyone to be there or no-one. We live in England and Steve's family is all there but my family and a lot of my friends are in Australia. To get everyone together seemed like a logistic and financial impossibility so we opted for no-one (that we knew).

We considered a variety of holiday destinations for the wedding. Unfortunately, many of the more tropical locations appear to marry people off at a rate of knots that made it all seem a little like a mass production factory. We didn't want to get married in England nor in Australia as we thought more people would be more upset at not having been invited. Scotland seemed like a good choice both because it is quick and easy to get to from England and because we figured that the paperwork required would be very similar (if not the same) as it would be in England. But because it was just the two of us we also wanted the location to be very picturesque. We like the Highlands of Scotland and we liked the idea of being married in a castle (or another ancient building). But we had no specific area of Scotland in mind and no particular castle.

We chose to go with a wedding planner because we wanted the memory of our wedding to be dominated by pleasure rather than the hassle of organisation. Also because we were a bit vague about what we wanted and what was required by law. We looked up 'weddings in Scotland' on the internet – the number of hits that that phrase brings up is very scary. But we eventually went for more specific locations in Scotland. We ended up making enquiries with two wedding planners: one was Highland Country Weddings and the other was a firm more oriented towards the west of Scotland.

The decision re which wedding planner to use was easy and was entirely due to the quality of response that we got. We're both quite realistic and we accept that in the scheme of things it is probably far more profitable for a wedding planner to do a big wedding and that we were really small potatoes. But it's your wedding – you don't want to feel that you're not very important. We told both wedding planners that it would be just the two of us (and that we'd need witnesses). Highland Country Weddings grasped this immediately. The other wedding planner said that they did but then immediately e-mailed us a standard form, two thirds of which seemed to be about the size of the wedding party and the number of guests. So we re-informed them that there would only be the two of us. We then asked them specific questions about the number of photographs – the answer included information about how the photographer would come to the bride's home and get all those shots with the bride's family. We informed them that there would only be the two of us. We asked for more information re accommodation – we were told it depended on the size of the party. At this point we stopped giving them the benefit of the doubt and gave up.

We did get an enormous amount of assistance from Highland Country Weddings. They suggested a few places for the wedding itself and we chose Dunnottar. We wanted accommodation not too far away and we were happy to be guided by their suggestions (Banchory Lodge Hotel – we stayed two nights, one before, one after the wedding). We wanted flowers – I had a vague idea of what I wanted but again it was their input that helped me decide, and the result was gorgeous. They arranged the celebrant (humanist) and we were able to have vows that suited us. They told us what documents they thought we would need and gave us contact details of the relevant registrar, but they were very clear that we needed to send those documents directly to the registrar (which we did). What we had to do was very clear and very easy and the registrar was great.

On the day of our wedding we got dressed up in our room at Banchory Lodge. A car came to the front and drove us to Dunnottar Castle. We met the wedding planner, photographer and celebrant in the car park. We then walked into Dunnottar Castle itself. (Luckily I had already been advised by the wedding planner that a different pair of shoes other than the high heels I planned to get married in would be a good idea. This proved to be absolutely essential and my enjoyment of the day would have been considerably impaired if I hadn't had this information.)

I changed back into my heels and the photographer checked out locations for photographs while Steve and I decided on where exactly we'd like the ceremony to be held. We decided on the green in the centre. We had the ceremony, which was more emotional than we expected. We then all signed the marriage schedule. The rest of the time we wandered about from attractive spot to attractive spot while the photographer took about 200 photographs. This was quite fun as it was rather windy and made it easier for us to have a laugh as we tried not to be blown over, hence making the smiles in shot a lot more natural. Eventually we made it back to the car and were driven back to Banchory Lodge Hotel where we had a belated luncheon of champagne and smoked salmon.

We had a lovely wedding day and we genuinely feel that it was unlike anyone else's (certainly unlike anyone's that we've known). We were doing it just for us and it was what we wanted. The photographs are fantastic reminders of the day, but the memory of it is even better. Scotland was not an unknown quantity. We expected the scenery and the people and the customer service to be of a high standard and we were not disappointed.

For anyone else arranging their own wedding I'd certainly recommend Highland Country Weddings. I don't think we could have arranged it on our own – we relied quite heavily on their advice. It may be different if you live in the area. However, I do feel that we were incredibly lucky in our choice of wedding planner as there was a certain amount of randomness involved.

Peter Mok & Graham Smith

When and where was your Civil Partnership ceremony?
12th June, 2006, Dornoch, Sutherland.

Where were you and your partner living at that time?
China.

How old were you and your partner at the time?
Graham 40, Peter 39.

Why did you decide to have your ceremony in Scotland?
We wanted our guests to go to a place they normally do not get a chance to see.

Why did you choose to use a wedding planner rather than organise it yourself?
We chose a wedding planner because civil partnership is relatively new to the UK and we do not live in the UK.

How did you decide which wedding planner to use?
We researched on the internet and found several planners. We ruled out the biggies (i.e. serving the entire UK.) and settled for Highland Country Weddings because we liked them being local (Scotland only). In addition, our initial e-mail exchanges gave us a very professional impression and their fees are very reasonable.

Did you leave all the arrangements to them, or were there things you had to do, or chose to do, yourself?
We pretty much left everything to them. Of course, we had to do our bits to get the guest list (food options) ready ourselves. Otherwise, we answered their questionnaire and just let them take charge.

Was it clearly explained to you what procedures you had to go through, and which documents you had to produce?
Our wedding planner was superb at explaining things and going between us and the Civil Partnership registrar in Dornoch. And she was always one step ahead of us to make sure nothing would fall through the cracks.

Did you find the legislative procedure straightforward?
Yes, mostly. Peter, being a non-UK citizen (Hong Kong), had to go to the Hong Kong British Consulate to get a special civil partnership visa. This was a bit unexpected because Hong Kong Special Administrative Region passport holders usually are not required to have a visa to visit the UK..

How did you decide on the venue?
Our wedding planner gave us several suggestions and after many rounds of discussion she came to understand what we had in mind (a fun and homey type of place) and recommended the Dornoch Castle Hotel.

Where did the ceremony and reception take place? Where did you and your partner stay before and after the ceremony?

The ceremony took place at the local library which is a five minute walk from the hotel, where we spent two nights (one night before and one night after).

How many guests did you have at your ceremony? Did you arrange their accommodation?

We had about 40 guests. Our wedding planner worked with the Dornoch Castle Hotel to set aside rooms for our guests to call and reserve themselves before the end of November 2005. They also managed to negotiate a 10% discount for our guests, for which we are very grateful.

Please describe your special day.

We rose early on the day of the ceremony to meet with the Registrar, Angie, to go through the details. She was extremely efficient, fun and obviously as happy as we were about our civil partnership. After about 45 minutes with her, we came back to the hotel to change into our formal attire. Then we took a 30 minute walk to the beach nearby.

By the time we got back from the beach, our guests were already waiting in the lobby of the hotel before the ceremony. Then, led by a Scottish piper, Will, we all walked five minutes to the library where the ceremony was held. The weather was a bit cloudy but not too cold. And the kids loved the sound of the Scottish pipes. There was a Canadian photojournalist who happened to be in Dornoch. He said he would like to take our pictures, and we gave him our permission. Angie presided over the short and simple ceremony – we just followed the script the Dornoch Registrar came up with. Then we all got piped back to the hotel garden (which is wonderful).

By the time we left the library, the clouds began to clear and the sun came through. It was just a lovely day and the Pimms at the reception in the hotel garden was FABULOUS! The lunch was superb and staff service was very professional and yet homey. Again we were piped into the dining hall, which is like a solarium with a full view of the green garden.

After lunch, everybody just hung around chatting, either in the dining hall, garden or the lounge (the nooks and crannies of the hotel were ideal for conversation). Our guests had travelled from Hong Kong, the United States, England and Wales – some of them we had not seen for years. Our wedding planner stayed with us the entire day, making sure everything was in order, for which we are extremely grateful.

Did the day meet with your expectations or were there any disappointments?

It was an amazing day, on which everything went just perfectly, thanks to Highland Country Wedding and Dornoch Castle Hotel. Both helped make our wedding exactly how we would like to have it.

Did Scotland live up to your expectations?

Yes, much more than what we expected.

Any advice for other couples arranging their own Civil Partnership ceremony?

Definitely have a wedding planner to make sure the documents are properly processed in a timely manner, and to provide advice on venues. This would be of particular importance for someone coming from outside of the UK. We also found the wedding planner's presence on the big day to help manage and smooth things out was absolutely essential.

Ellie & David Thomson

Ellie & David (not their real names) married in July, 2003, at Eilean Donan Castle in the Scottish Highlands.

It was simply wonderful, although I have to say it was a tremendous amount of work for both me and David and was very stressful.

I started thinking about getting married in Scotland just before we got engaged in 2002 and we decided we wanted something special, something different. We didn't want the usual English-type wedding in a church and then a hotel, and because we both have Scottish ancestors, the Highlands seemed the natural thing to go for. I'm a Robertson on my mother's side and David's a MacIntyre on his mother's side too, although they have both lived in the south east of England for many years, which is where we live now.

We spent hours and days looking at magazines and searching the internet and we decided on Eilean Donan castle because it appears as the image of the Highlands in so many places and has been used in a few movies, I believe. Anyway, we just knew it would be beautiful so we drove up there one weekend to look the place over and fell in love with it when we saw it for real. The trip was a bit of a last minute thing and a bit of a dash so we didn't get the chance to speak with anybody at the castle but the woman who ran the b&b in the little village nearby was very helpful with the names of the people we should contact. It seems everybody in the area knew all about weddings at Eilean Donan. A pity they didn't warn us about the midges!

The biggest problem we had in organising the wedding wasn't with the castle or the minister, it was with our guests because they kept changing their minds about who was coming, who wasn't, where they were going to stay, how they were going to travel, and so on. They nearly drove us insane, but the wedding itself would have been no problem if we could have sorted the guests out early on.

We ended up having 35 guests altogether and arranging accommodation for them all was a nightmare. Some stayed in local b&bs, some in local hotels and some even ended up staying in Kyle of Lochalsh and in Plockton which was a very pretty village about 10 miles away. We decided to escape from it all after the reception and we drove off up the west coast the same night to spend our honeymoon touring the Highlands. We left them to it and that was probably the wisest decision we made.

The people at the castle were great. They helped us no end and contacting the people they usually use for weddings, the minister and so on, was simple. Everybody was so helpful, even with regard to the legalities, which were a bit confusing at first but became fairly straightforward once we had researched the requirements on the internet. But, as I said, the difficulty was that the number of guests kept changing and they all wanted different things and pestered us for information before we had it all ourselves.

But I'm not sorry we arranged it ourselves except that we could have done with someone 'orchestrating' the whole thing on the day. David and I were too busy, of course, so we ended up relying on Mark, the Best Man, and my dad to do much of the last minute chasing around. A wedding planner would have come in very handy then, but we saved money by doing it ourselves and I'm a bit of a control freak anyway so wouldn't have been happy handing it over to anybody else. But, like I say, to have somebody in overall control on the day would have been handy. In hindsight, I suppose I could have spoken with a planner and asked them to take on that limited role. That might have been money well spent, plus I could have liaised with them during the planning process. But it gave me a buzz to pull the whole thing off successfully from a distance. I don't know how we would have coped without the internet though.

My biggest disappointment was with the flowers, to be honest. They weren't quite what we ordered and they seemed a bit tired because they had been brought over from Inverness the day before, as had the traditional Highland dress for David and the other men in the main wedding party. They all wore the Flower of Scotland tartan because it would have cost too much to get the family tartans specially ordered. The stock tartans were Black Watch and Flower of Scotland so they decided to all have the same. They looked very smart too but all had to be returned the next day so, once again, the Best Man did that, something the wedding planner would have done if we had used one.

I wore a simple ivory silk dress with a tartan sash in the Robertson clan tartan. My father gave me away and my younger sister was my only bridesmaid and she wore a beautiful deep red dress that I had bought for her specially for the wedding. Everybody else wore what they liked. We didn't want to impose on them too much because we'd already 'made' them travel hundreds of miles to get there.

On the morning of the wedding, a local girl came to the hotel in Dornie where we stayed the night before to do my hair. She had a lovely local accent as she chattered away, telling us about all the weddings there had been at the castle.

The piper was great. He was a short, jolly, stocky highlander who liked a dram of whisky or two and the sound of the pipes as we crossed the causeway to the castle is one of my best memories. He played for us afterwards too on the battlements while we had photographs taken – which seemed to go on for hours – and also while we had the champagne reception in the room underneath the grand, main hall where the ceremony took place. We could have had the ceremony outside but it was such a nice, still day that the midges were out and they would have eaten us alive out there, so I'm glad we decide to hold it in the great hall. It's such a beautiful place.

The wedding presents weren't a problem. They were simply left at home and had been given to us off a list I had prepared weeks earlier. We thought it would have been pointless to bring them all the way to the Highlands to take them back home again. We wanted to make things as simple as possible for everybody and, by and large, we succeeded.

Me and my dad were taken to the church from the hotel in Dornie in a wedding car hired from Inverness. It could have driven us to the castle itself but we decided to walk across the causeway behind the piper who played us across. All the other guests, plus David of course, had gathered in the Great Hall and, as tradition demands, we were about 10 minutes late so I know that David was a bit worried. But that walk gave the photographer lots of opportunities for some really nice photographs.

We then went into the castle and I have to say I'm glad I wore something simple because I had to climb some narrow winding steps to get to the Great Hall where everybody was waiting. The piper played as we entered the Hall and walked around the room, then back to stand in from of the main window where David and the Minister were waiting. It was a beautiful setting and I would recommend it to anyone.

The ceremony was a simple one, again just as we wanted, and it lasted only about 15 minutes. There was no singing, but afterwards the harpist played some Gaelic tunes at the reception and she was much quieter than the piper and very sweet.

There was a bit of confusion after the ceremony as to what we were all supposed to do and where we were supposed to go and, as I said, that's where a wedding planner would have come in handy, I think.

But, all in all, I think it was a great success. I enjoyed arranging it all even if it was a bit stressful at times and, with hindsight, might do thing slightly differently. But I would recommend the venue to anybody thinking of a romantic wedding in Scotland. We have some wonderful memories of the day.

Fiona & Graham McGirr

When and where did you get married?
Saturday 7th October, 2006, in Gean House, Alloa.

Where do you and your partner live?
Clackmannan, Scotland.

How old were you and your partner?
Fiona 24, Graham 25.

Why did you choose to organise it yourself rather than use a wedding planner?
Principally for reasons of cost, but we didn't want an extravagant wedding anyway.

How easy was it to find out what procedures you had to go through, and which documents you had to produce?
Very easy, the staff at the registry office were very helpful. They had an information pack and someone was always available to speak to in person. They were also happy to be phoned or e-mailed.

Did you find the legislative procedure straightforward?
Yes, again the registrar explained everything.

What was the biggest problem you came across in planning it?
Trying to make sure I had remembered to do everything! It was helpful having a sister who'd just organised her own wedding (see Julie White's story in *Our Wedding*). I was concentrating on the wedding so much I forgot to get things sorted for the honeymoon – Julie reminded me to book vegetarian meals for the flight!

How did you decide on the venue?
Being local we knew places anyway, but we looked on the internet and phoned places to arrange to view them. We discounted some places because they were too big or too small. However, when we saw Gean House we loved it and knew that was where we wanted to have the wedding.

Did you have a religious or civil wedding?
Civil.

How easy was it to find a registrar to perform the ceremony?
I booked the registrar at relatively short notice (about three months) and perhaps we were lucky that the date was available, but it was very straightforward.

Where did the wedding ceremony and reception take place? Where did you and your partner stay before and after the wedding?

The ceremony and reception were both in Gean House. We hired the entire place which has 11 bedrooms. We stayed there on the wedding night and so did our families. The night before the wedding I stayed at my parents' house and Graham stayed at home.

How many guests did you have at your wedding?

There were 41 at the meal and 90 in total in the evening.

Please describe your wedding.

It was quite a laid back occasion. Everybody joined in at the reception – there was a great party atmosphere. Overall, it was the best day ever and exceeded my expectations!

Any advice for other couples arranging their own weddings?

Don't get hung up on details!!! I saw a magazine article that said, 'It took me *just* 6 months to arrange my wedding flowers!' I saw it six days before the wedding and mine weren't sorted then, but despite that they were ready on the day. It doesn't matter if you have a big or small wedding, lavish or on a budget, at the end of the day it's all about enjoying it!

Lightning Source UK Ltd.
Milton Keynes UK
22 January 2010

148960UK00001B/8/P